Thinking on Paper

Thinking on Paper

A Writing Process Workbook with Readings

Fourth Edition

Judy Markline
Allan Hancock College

Rose Hawkins
Community College of Southern Nevada

Bob Isaacson
Allan Hancock College

Harcourt Brace College Publishers

Fort Worth   Philadelphia   San Diego   New York   Orlando   Austin
San Antonio   Toronto   Montreal   London   Sydney   Tokyo

Publisher	Earl McPeek
Acquisitions Editor	Steve Dalphin
Product Manager	Laura Brennan
Developmental Editor	Camille Adkins
Project Editor	Claudia Gravier
Art Director	Garry Harman
Production Manager	Serena Barnett

ISBN: 0-15-505223-3
Library of Congress Catalog Card Number: 98–070008

Address for Orders
Harcourt Brace College Publishers, 6277 Sea Harbor Drive, Orlando, FL 32887-6777
1-800-782-4479

Address for Editorial Correspondence
Harcourt Brace College Publishers, 301 Commerce Street, Suite 3700, Fort Worth, TX 76102

Web site Address
http://www.hbcollege.com

Harcourt Brace College Publishers will provide complimentary supplements or supplement packages to those adopters qualified under our adoption policy. Please contact your sales representative to learn how you qualify. If as an adopter or potential user you receive supplements you do not need, please return them to your sales representative or send them to: Attn: Returns Department, Troy Warehouse, 465 South Lincoln Drive, Troy, MO 63379. [Include this paragraph only when ancillaries accompany the text.]

Printed in the United States of America

8 9 0 1 2 3 4 5 6 7   0 6 6   9 8 7 6 5 4 3 2 1

Harcourt Brace College Publishers

> There is no reasonable separation between the acts of reading and writing. Each activity is twin to the other, providing us with a disciplined way of finding meaning in that information, with the special bonus of being able to share that meaning with others. . . . write to learn [sic] to read and read to learn how to write.
>
> Don Murray

Thinking on Paper: A Reading-Writing Process Workbook, Fourth Edition, puts Don Murray's basic theory into practice. Our book is designed to help developmental students negotiate the complex interaction between reading and writing and establish essential connections between the two activities. Our book is based on the premise that developmental students must intensely and repeatedly practice writing as a means of exploring, defining, and evaluating what they read and that these two interrelated activities must be thoroughly integrated in order for students to explore meaning fully in both their reading and their writing.

THE INTEGRATION OF READING AND WRITING

Each of our ten writing assignments, whether it focuses on a poem, a short story, or an essay, emphasizes the active process of integrating reading and writing skills. Our students need to see reading and writing as a single process. Our experimentation in the classroom and our studies in reader-response theory have led us to believe that developmental students can grow into more confident and capable readers. However, they must be allowed to discover that they are capable of making vital connections between what they read and what they already know through the authority of their own personal experience. This discovery of the new undiscovered territory that is created when the self is permitted to interact with the text liberates the developmental reader, freeing him or her to bring meaning to the text as well as to receive meaning from the text.

Louise Rosenblatt's transactional model allows this vital interaction between reader and text: meaning lies in the transaction between the reader and the text. Thus, the reading and writing process that our students practice repeatedly attempts to highlight the interrelationship between the world of the self and the world of the text. Our developmental students are allowed to bring themselves and their experiences to the text and, through reading and writing activities, to explore the text and its range of meaning-making features.

Reading, like writing, is a process that our students need to practice and, ultimately, to internalize in their own way for their own use. We believe not only that our students should be able to write in many situations ranging from personal narratives to formal arguments, but also that they should be allowed to read and experience the full range of a variety of texts, from the intense, personal world of a short poem to the larger, more abstract, impersonal world of an essay on a broad social issue.

In this textbook we have included a variety of challenging reading and writing assignments. The reading texts were selected with the developmental student in mind. We have aimed to include clearly written material at appropriate reading levels which nonetheless offers complex and suggestive ideas and themes. We have included poems, short stories, and essays by professional writers whose backgrounds and experiences reflect the rich and diverse ethnic and cultural realities of today's world.

The Fourth Edition contains some of the readings used successfully in the former edition as well several new ones, and each of the writing assignments is now accompanied by a student model to help guide students through the writing process. Of course, the fourth edition continues to place a strong emphasis on the integration of reading and writing activities.

Each reading and writing assignment includes an interconnected mosaic of activities:

1. Prereading questions designed to engage the reader.
2. A double-entry question journal to encourage critical thinking by interrogating the text through student-based questioning and answering.
3. A summarization exercise.
4. "Closer Look" questions intended to focus the student on specific issues.
5. Practice in writing topic or thesis sentences to encourage concise, focused thinking on the purpose or meaning of the text.
6. A paragraph or essay writing assignment, the topic of which grows out of a theme or topic connected to the reading material.

The writing process involved in each paragraph or essay assignment includes responding to a writing task or prompt, prewriting, developing a topic or thesis sentence, exploring the range of rhetorical modes, writing a rough draft, revising, editing, and producing the final copy.

THEMES

We have included four chapters of thematically linked reading and writing assignments. These four chapters have been carefully organized and sequenced to help our students explore a full spectrum of reading and writing experiences, ranging from those focused on the immediacy of personal experience to those dealing with larger, more abstract issues that concern us all. Thus, our integration of the reading and writing assignments reflects and encourages our students' general movement from the small, intimate world of the self to the larger world we live in. Our integration of reading and writing attempts to create a framework in which our students can feel comfortable in the world of ideas that college, in the final analysis, offers them. Our rich variety of readings, like the writing assignments, reflects the road from the inner world to the outer world and from the self to society that all students must travel to succeed in college and in life.

SEQUENCING OF READINGS AND ASSIGNMENTS

Each chapter contains three readings: a story, a poem, and a personal essay. In Chapter 1, The Self: Personal Reflections, the writing assignments focus on exploring personal topics and material close to the students' immediate world and also introduces them to paragraph-level narrative and descriptive writing. The assignments in Chapter 2, The Family: Our Own Little World, require students to move the focus of attention away from the self to the familiar world immediately outside themselves, while at the same time teaching the more demanding essential essay-level strategies of cause/effect, contrast, and argument. The writing assignments in Chapter 2 are a transition to writing the essay. Here students are introduced to the thesis statement and the larger patterns required in multi-paragraph writing. Chapter 3, Society: Our Values, provides reading and writing assignments that continue the process of exploring larger and larger worlds. The writing assignments in this chapter offer students a choice of strategies and permit them to make important rhetorical decisions depending on what their purpose and topic dictate. Finally, Chapter 4, The World Around Us: Issues and Choices, deals with yet larger, more complex, social and moral situations while introducing students to research-based essay writing.

ADDITIONAL READINGS

We have included additional selections for those who wish to add more reading to the course. The four stories, four poems, and four essays in this section may be assigned as needed.

REVIEWING THE BASICS

Exercises on topic sentences, concluding sentences, transitions, and being specific are included here along with a review of sentence-level grammar and punctuation.

The Instructor's Manual to the fourth edition offers a variety of instructional resources: a sample course outline, assignment schedules, a student attendance calendar, sample tests, sample in-class writing, prompts, sample final exams, and suggested teaching techniques for collaboration in class and lab settings. Also included are notes on key topics such as the integration of reading and writing, reader-response activities, portfolio assessment, journal writing, peer-editing workshops, classroom-based research, holistic grading, and commentary on different modes of instruction.

ACKNOWLEDGMENTS

For their sound advice, we thank the following reviewers of the fourth edition :

Karen Blaske, Arapahoe Community College;
Dottie Burkhart, Davidson County Community College;
William Lawlor, University of Wisconsin, Steven's Point;
Linda Patterson, State Technical Institute, Memphis;
Sara Lee Sanderson, Miami-Dade Community College; and
Lois Silverstein, Contra Costa College.

We also thank the following employees of Harcourt Brace for their guidance: Stephen Dalphin, Senior Acquisitions Editor; Camille Adkins, Senior Developmental Editor; Claudia Gravier, Project Editor; Serena Barnett, Senior Production Manager; and Garry Harman, Senior Art Director.

Thinking on Paper: A Reading-Writing Process Workbook is designed to help you see that reading and writing are exciting acts of discovery about yourself and the world around you.

The first four chapters contain poems, short stories, and essays that allow you to practice the reading process with prereading, journal, close reading, and reader-response activities. They will also introduce you to some important themes (the self, the family, society, and the world around you) that will serve as springboards for thought and discussion.

In Chapter 1, The Self: Personal Reflections, you will focus on personal topics and material close to your immediate world. Here you will be introduced to narrative and descriptive paragraphs. The assignments in Chapter 2, The Family: Our Own Little World, require you to move the focus of attention away from yourself to the familiar world immediately outside yourself. At the same time you will explore multi-paragraph essay writing. The writing assignments in Chapter 2 will help you make a transition to the essay; Chapter 2 introduces you to the thesis statement and more complex organizational patterns, such as cause/effect, contrast, and argument, which are required in essay writing. Chapter 3, Society: Our Values, will provide you with reading and writing assignments that continue the process of exploring larger and larger worlds. The writing assignments in this chapter will offer you a choice of strategies and allow you to make important decisions as a writer. Finally, Chapter 4, The World Around Us: Issues and Choices, deals with yet larger, more complex, social and moral situations, while introducing you to research-based essay writing.

Reviewing the Basics includes exercises on topic sentences, concluding sentences, and transitions as well as the basic patterns of English sentences and punctuation. Your instructor may choose to assign all or part of these exercises or to use this section as a handbook, showing you how to find answers to specific questions.

So whether you are a student who is unsure about your reading and writing or a student who needs a refresher course, you will enjoy discovering the fascinating world of ideas that already exists in your heart and your head. Most of all, as you gain confidence in your reading and writing ability, you will know the satisfaction of being able to communicate your ideas.

CONTENTS

CHAPTER 1   THE SELF: PERSONAL REFLECTIONS   1

Reading Assignment 1: "The Jacket" by Gary Soto   2
    Prereading   **2**
    "The Jacket"   **2**
        Double-Entry Question Journal   **5**
        A Closer Look   **6**

Writing Assignment 1: Narrating a Story   8
    A Student Model: "The Wu-fone River" by Shui Jane Yeh   **8**
    Prewriting   **9**
        Clustering   **9**
        Listing   **11**
        Freewriting   **12**
        Asking Journalistic Questions   **12**
    The Writing Process   **14**
        Purpose   **14**
        Audience   **14**
        Tone   **14**
    Finding a Topic   **15**
    Prewriting   **15**
    The Topic Sentence   **16**
    Writing a Topic Sentence   **16**
    Transitional Words   **17**
        Time Order Transitions   **17**
        Linking Transitions   **19**
    Writing a Rough Draft   **19**
    Being Specific   **20**
    The Concluding Sentence   **20**
    Revising   **21**
    Peer Editing   **21**
    Submitting the Final Copy   **23**

Reading Assignment 2: "Lying in a Hammock" by James Wright   24
    Prereading   **24**
    "Lying in a Hammock"   **24**

Double-Entry Question Journal **25**
A Closer Look **26**

Writing Assignment 2: Describing A Place **27**
A Student Model: "My Silent Moment" by Niele S. Janzantti **27**
Sample Peer Editing Sheet **29**
Sample of the Final Revised Copy: "From the Shadow of a Tree"
by Niele S. Janzantti **31**
Finding a Topic **32**
Prewriting **33**
Writing the Topic Sentence **33**
Transitional Words **34**
Space Order Transitions **34**
Writing a Rough Draft **35**
Being Specific **35**
Revising **35**
Peer Editing **35**
Submitting the Final Copy **37**

Reading Assignment 3: "Uncle Willie" by Maya Angelou **39**
Prereading **39**
"Uncle Willie" **39**
Double-Entry Question Journal **42**
A Closer Look **43**

Writing Assignment 3: Describing a Person **44**
A Student Model: "Age, Sun, and Shadows" by Korrene Edwards **44**
Finding a Topic **45**
Prewriting **45**
Writing the Topic Sentence **45**
Transitional Words **46**
Importance Order Transitions **46**
Writing a Rough Draft **46**
Being Specific **46**
Revising **47**
Peer Editing **47**
Submitting the Final Copy **49**

CHAPTER 2   THE FAMILY: OUR OWN LITTLE WORLD   **50**

Reading Assignment 4: "Battling Illegitimacy: Some Words against the Darkness"
by Greg Sarris **51**
Prereading **51**

"Battling Illegitimacy: Some Words against the Darkness" **51**
    Double-Entry Question Journal **57**
    A Closer Look **58**

Writing Assignment 4: Cause/Effect Essay *59*
    The Essay **59**
    A Cause/Effect Model **60**
    A Student Model: "Daddy's Little Girl" by Justine Boyer **61**
    An Optional Cause/Effect Model **62**
    Finding a Topic **63**
    Prewriting **63**
    The Thesis Statement **64**
    Writing the Thesis Statement **64**
    Transitional Words **65**
        Cause/Effect Transitions **65**
    Writing a Rough Draft **65**
    Being Specific **65**
    The Concluding Paragraph **66**
    Revising **66**
    Peer Editing **66**
    Submitting the Final Copy **69**

Reading Assignment 5: "Migratory Birds" by Odilia Galván Rodríguez *70*
    Prereading **70**
    "Migratory Birds" **70**
        Double-Entry Question Journal **72**
        A Closer Look **73**

Writing Assignment 5: Comparison/Contrast Essay *74*
    A Student Model: "Two Cultures" by Cuc Thi Nguyen **74**
    Finding a Topic **76**
    Prewriting **76**
    The Thesis Statement **77**
    Writing the Thesis Statement **77**
    Transitional Words **78**
        Comparison/Contrast Transitions **78**
    Comparison/Contrast Outline **79**
    Writing a Rough Draft **81**
    Being Specific **81**
    The Concluding Paragraph **81**
    Revising **82**

Peer Editing   **82**
Submitting the Final Copy   **85**

Reading Assignment 6: "Reparation Candy" by Maxine Hong Kingston   *86*
Prereading   **86**
"Reparation Candy"   **86**
Double-Entry Question Journal   **90**
A Closer Look   **91**

Writing Assignment 6: Argument Essay   *92*
A Student Model: "The Older Generation" by Erika Valdez   **92**
Finding a Topic   **94**
Prewriting   **94**
The Thesis Statement   **95**
Writing the Thesis Statement   **95**
Transitional Words   **96**
Argument Transitions   **96**
Writing a Rough Draft   **97**
Being Specific   **97**
The Concluding Paragraph   **97**
Revising   **98**
Peer Editing   **98**
Submitting the Final Copy   **101**

CHAPTER 3   SOCIETY: OUR VALUES   *102*

Reading Assignment 7: "The Storm" by Kate Chopin   *103*
Prereading   **103**
"The Storm"   **103**
Double-Entry Question Journal   **108**
A Closer Look   **109**

Writing Assignment 7: An Essay   *110*
A Student Model: "Love and Marriage" by Theresa White   **110**
Prewriting   **112**
Writing the Thesis Statement   **112**
Writing a Rough Draft   **113**
Being Specific   **113**
The Concluding Paragraph   **113**
Revising   **113**
Peer Editing   **113**
Submitting the Final Copy   **117**

Reading Assignment 8: "To a Child Trapped in a Barber Shop" by Philip Levine **118**
    Prereading **118**
    "To a Child Trapped in a Barber Shop" **118**
        Double-Entry Question Journal **120**
        A Closer Look **121**

Writing Assignment 8: An Essay **122**
    A Student Model: "Fitting In" by Linda Bonilla **122**
    Prewriting **124**
    Writing the Thesis Statement **124**
    Writing a Rough Draft **125**
    Being Specific **125**
    The Concluding Paragraph **125**
    Revising **125**
    Peer Editing **125**
    Submitting the Final Copy **128**

Reading Assignment 9: "The Lottery" by Shirley Jackson **129**
    Prereading **129**
    "The Lottery" **129**
        Double-Entry Question Journal **137**
        A Closer Look **138**

Writing Assignment 9: An Essay **139**
    A Student Model: "The Ritual of the Tree" by Heather Gaertner **139**
    Prewriting **141**
    Writing the Thesis Statement **141**
    Writing a Rough Draft **142**
    Being Specific **142**
    The Concluding Paragraph **142**
    Revising **142**
    Peer Editing **142**
    Submitting the Final Copy **145**

CHAPTER 4 *THE WORLD AROUND US: ISSUES AND CHOICES* **146**

Reading Assignment 10: "The Secret" by Alberto Moravia **147**
    Prereading **147**
    "The Secret" **147**
        Double-Entry Question Journal **153**
        A Closer Look **154**

Writing Assignment 10: Information Essay, Part I   155
    A Student Model: "Flashing Lights" by Kevin K. Green   **155**
    Searching for Information   **158**
    Exploring a Topic   **158**
    Finding a Topic   **159**
    The Thesis Statement   **160**

Reading Assignment 11: "Footbinding" by John King Fairbank   161
    Prereading   **161**
    "Footbinding"   **161**
        Double-Entry Question Journal   **166**
        A Closer Look   **167**

Writing Assignment 10, Information Essay, Part II   168
    Direct and Indirect Quotations   **168**
    The Works Cited Page   **170**
    Searching for Information   **174**
    Paraphrasing and Summarizing   **174**
    Interviewing   **176**

Reading Assignment 12: "Rites of Passage" by Sharon Olds   177
    Prereading   **177**
    "Rites of Passage"   **177**
        Double-Entry Question Journal   **178**
        A Closer Look   **179**

Writing Assignment 10, Information Essay, Part III   181
    Prewriting   **181**
    Revising Your Thesis Statement   **181**
    Writing a Rough Draft   **182**
    Being Specific   **182**
    Revising   **182**
    Peer Editing   **182**
    Submitting the Final Copy   **185**

Additional Readings   186
    Fiction
        "Can Can" by Arturo Vivante   **187**
        "Blue Day" by Joel Antonio Villalon   **189**
        "I See You Never" by Ray Bradbury   **192**
        "El Hoyo" by Mario Suarez   **195**
    Poetry
        "Sindhi Woman" by Jon Stallworthy   **197**

"Homage to My Hips" by Lucille Clifton **197**

"Marks" by Linda Pastan **198**

"Hazel Tells LaVern" by Katharyn Howd Machan **198**

Essays

"Shame" by Dick Gregory **199**

"Mother Tongue" by Amy Tan **203**

"Home is a Freeway" by Neil Morgan **208**

"The Jeaning of America" by Carin Quinn **211**

Reviewing the Basics **213**

Topic Sentences and Directing Words **214**

Directing Words **214**

Concluding Sentences **216**

Transitional Words that Signal Order **219**

Transitional Words: Time Order **220**

Transitional Words: Space Order **222**

Transitional Words: Importance Order **223**

Transitional Words That Link Sentences and Ideas **225**

Giving Additional Information **226**

Showing Results **226**

Transitional Words That Link Sentences and Ideas: Giving Examples **227**

Transitional Words That Link Sentences and Ideas: Contrasting Ideas **227**

Transitional Words That Link Sentences and Ideas: Giving Additional Information **228**

Transitional Words That Link Sentences and Ideas: Showing Results **228**

Transitional Words That Link Sentences and Ideas **229**

Being Specific **230**

Consistency of Tense, Number, and Person **232**

Consistency of Tense **232**

Past Tense **234**

Present Tense **235**

Consistency of Tense **236**

Consistency of Number **237**

Consistency of Person **242**

Basic Sentence Patterns **245**

Basic Sentence Patterns: Subjects **246**

Basic Sentence Patterns: Verbs **247**

Basic Sentence Patterns: Completers **252**

Sentence Types: The Simple Sentence **254**

Sentence Types: The Compound Sentence **265**

S/V; S/V Pattern **268**

Sentence Types: The Complex Sentence **272**

Relative Pronouns: Who, Which, and That   **275**
Sentence Types: The Compound-Complex Sentence   **280**
A Word About Fragments   **285**
Commas   **288**
Other Punctuation Marks: The Apostrophe, Colon, and Semicolon   **292**

Appendix   *295*
Guideline for Final Drafts   **296**
A List of Irregular Verbs   **297**
Writing a Summary   **299**

Index   *301*

1

The Self: Personal Reflections

This first chapter offers you three readings that focus on personal reflections. These readings will help you discover how others have used writing to reflect on who they are and to express their thoughts about personal experiences they have had. The ideas you get by reading and responding to these selections through "Double-Entry Question Journals" and "A Closer Look" will help you to examine significant experiences in your own life and serve as springboards for your own writing.

If you are a beginning writer, you may mistakenly think you are a poor writer simply because you are unable to produce a final copy on your first try. The truth is that experienced writers view writing as a process with the following basic stages: prewriting, writing, and revising. Good writers constantly revise because they are continually reseeing and rethinking their ideas, just to make sure that they are communicating exactly what they mean to their readers.

In this chapter you will be introduced to several invention strategies—journal keeping, close observation, and prewriting (clustering, listing, and freewriting, and asking journalistic questions)—to help you get started in writing. You will also learn about topic sentences, transitions that indicate order in your writing, and revision strategies, such as being specific.

Starting with the inner world of the self, the sequence of assignments in *Thinking on Paper* is designed to lead you to the outer world of society and, eventually, to the world at large, where you will begin to see that the more informed you are, the better equipped you will be to make wise, conscious choices about the important issues in life. Throughout this first chapter, your thinking and writing will in some way be connected to the theme of "The Self: Personal Reflections." Also, this theme of the self is echoed in the readings to help prepare you for writing assignments based on your own personal experiences.

Reading Assignment 1: "The Jacket" by Gary Soto

Writing Assignment 1: Narrating a Story

Reading Assignment 2: "Lying in a Hammock . . ." by James Wright

Writing Assignment 2: Describing a Place

Reading Assignment 3: "Uncle Willie" by Maya Angelou

Writing Assignment 3: Describing a Person

Holt, Rinehart and Winston

Reading Assignment 1: "The Jacket"

Prereading

"The Jacket" by Gary Soto, like all of the reading assignments in this chapter, focuses on the theme of the self. Its primary purpose is to help you think critically about issues related to your personal experiences and to help you discover who you are. Thus, the story is not intended to be a model for your writing assignment, but rather, a source of ideas.

The Jacket
Gary Soto

My clothes have failed me. I remember the green coat that I wore in the fifth and sixth grades when you either danced like a champ or pressed yourself against a greasy wall, bitter as a penny toward the happy couples.

When I needed a new jacket and my mother asked what kind I wanted, I described something like bikers wear: black leather and silver studs with enough belts to hold down a small town. We were in the kitchen, steam on the windows from her cooking. She listened so long while stirring dinner that I thought she understood for sure the kind I wanted. The next day when I got home from school, I discovered draped on my bedpost a jacket the color of day-old guacamole. I threw my books on the bed and approached the jacket slowly, as if it were a stranger whose hand I had to shake. I touched the vinyl sleeve, the collar, and peeked at the mustard-color lining.

From the kitchen mother yelled that my jacket was in the closet. I closed the door to her voice and pulled at the rack of clothes in the closet, hoping the jacket on the bedpost wasn't for me but my mean brother. No luck. I gave up. From my bed, I stared at the jacket. I wanted to cry because it was so ugly and so big that I knew I'd have to wear it a long time. I was a small kid, thin as a young tree, and it would be years before I'd have a new one. I stared at the jacket, like an enemy, thinking bad things before I took off my old jacket whose sleeves climbed halfway to my elbow.

I put the big jacket on. I zipped it up and down several times, and rolled the cuffs up so they didn't cover my hands. I put my hands in the pockets and flapped the jacket like a bird's wings. I stood in front of the mirror, full face, then profile, and then looked over my shoulder as if someone had called me. I sat on the bed, stood against the bed, and combed my hair to see what I would look like doing something natural. I looked ugly. I threw it on my brother's bed and looked at it for a long time before I slipped it on and went out to the backyard, smiling a "thank you" to my mom as I passed her in the kitchen. With my hands in my pockets I kicked a ball against the fence, and then climbed it to sit looking into the alley. I hurled orange peels at the mouth of an open garbage can and when the peels were gone I watched the white puffs of my breath thin to nothing.

I jumped down, hands in my pockets, and in the backyard on my knees I teased my dog, Brownie, by swooping my arms while making bird calls. He jumped at me and missed. He jumped again and again, until a tooth sunk deep, ripping an L-shaped tear on my left sleeve. I pushed Brownie away to study the tear as I would a cut on my arm. There was no blood, only a few loose pieces of fuzz. Damn dog, I thought, and pushed him away hard when he tried to bite again. I got up from my knees and went to my bedroom to sit with my jacket on my lap, with the lights out.

That was the first afternoon with my new jacket. The next day I wore it to sixth grade and got a D on a math quiz. During the morning recess Frankie T., the playground terrorist, pushed me to the ground and told me to stay there until recess was over. My best friend, Steve Negrete, ate an apple while looking at me, and the girls turned away to whisper on the monkey bars. The teachers were no help: they looked my way and talked about how foolish I looked in my new jacket. I saw their heads bob with laughter, their hands half-covering their mouths.

Even though it was cold, I took off the jacket during lunch and played kickball in a thin shirt, my arms feeling like braille from goose bumps. But when I returned to class I slipped the jacket on and shivered until I was warm. I sat on my hands, heating them up, while my teeth chattered like a cup of crooked dice. Finally warm, I slid out of the jacket but a few minutes later put it back on when the fire bell rang. We paraded out into the yard where we, the sixth graders, walked past all the other grades to stand against the back fence. Everybody saw me. Although they didn't say out loud, "Man, that's ugly," I heard the buzz-buzz of gossip and even laughter that I knew was meant for me.

And so I went, in my guacamole jacket. So embarrassed, so hurt, I couldn't even do my homework. I received C's on quizzes, and forgot the state capitals and the rivers of South America, our friendly neighbor. Even the girls who had been friendly blew away like loose flowers to follow the boys in neat jackets.

I wore that thing for three years until the sleeves grew short and my forearms stuck out like the necks of turtles. All during that time no love came to me—no little dark girl in a Sunday dress she wore on Monday. At lunchtime I stayed with the ugly boys who leaned against the chainlink fence and looked around with propellers of grass spinning in our mouths. We saw girls walk by alone, saw couples, hand in hand, their heads like bookends pressing air together. We saw them and spun our propellers so fast our faces were blurs.

I blame that jacket for those bad years. I blame my mother for her bad taste and her cheap ways. It was a sad time for the heart. With a friend I spent my sixth-grade year in a tree in the alley waiting for something good to happen to me in that jacket, which had become the ugly brother who tagged along wherever I went. And it was about that time that I began to grow. My chest puffed up with muscle, and strangely, a few more ribs. Even my hands, those fleshy hammers, showed bravely through the cuffs, the fingers already hardening for the coming fights. But that L-shaped rip on the left sleeve got bigger; bits of stuffing coughed out from its wound after a hard day of play. I finally Scotch-taped it closed, but in the rain and cold weather the tape peeled off like a scab and more stuffing fell out until that sleeve shriveled into a palsied arm.

Holt, Rinehart and Winston

That winter the elbows began to crack and whole chunks of green began to fall off. I showed the cracks to my mother, who always seemed to be at the stove with steamed-up glasses, and she said that there were children in Mexico who would love that jacket. I told her that this was America and yelled that Debbie, my sister, didn't have a jacket like mine. I ran outside, ready to cry, and climbed the tree by the alley to think bad thoughts and watch my breath puff white and disappear.

But whole pieces still casually flew off my jacket when I played hard, read quietly, or took vicious spelling tests at school. When it became so spotted that my brother began to call me "camouflage," I flung it over the fence into the alley. Later, however, I swiped the jacket off the ground and went inside to drape it across my lap and mope.

I was called to dinner: steam silvered my mother's glasses as she said grace; my brother and sister with their heads bowed made ugly faces at their glasses of pow-dered milk. I gagged too, but eagerly ate big rips of buttered tortilla that held scooped up beans. Finished, I went outside with my jacket across my arm. It was a cold sky. The faces of clouds were piled up, hurting. I climbed the fence, jumping down with a grunt. I started up the alley and soon slipped into my jacket, that green ugly brother who breathed over my shoulder that day and ever since.

INVENTION STRATEGIES: DISCOVERING IDEAS

Invention strategies are an important part of the writing process because they can help you discover what you want to say about a topic. Some basic techniques are as follows:

- Journal writing
- Reading, observing, researching
- Prewriting (clustering, listing, freewriting)
- Asking journalistic questions

Journal Writing

One way to discover ideas is to keep a journal. There are many journal styles, but one that encour-ages you to think both critically and independently is the Double-Entry Question Journal.

If you are writing a paper in response to literature, asking genuine questions will help you unlock the meaning of the story. Thus, in a journal response to "The Jacket" by Gary Soto, you might ask, "Why didn't he leave the jacket somewhere and say he lost it?" Then you would jot down some pos-sible answers. You are encouraged to explore different options, even far-fetched ones, to see what discoveries come up. To complete the journal process, you would write a sentence that states the cen-tral idea of the story. Later on, your journal notes could help you to write either a literary analysis or a paper based on your own personal experiences.

Holt, Rinehart and Winston

Reading Assignment 1: "The Jacket"

Double-Entry Question Journal

Note: Some students find it easier to do the double-entry journal as they are reading. Others find the process more effective after they have finished reading the entire piece. You should experiment to discover the method that works best for you.

In the left column, jot down at least five "What?" "Why?" or "How?" questions. Then in the right column, jot down some possible answers and responses. If further questions come up, jot them down also. One purpose of this exercise is to learn how to think critically, so you might end up with several answers or possibilities. Go ahead, take a risk! The first one is done for you as an example.

1. *What is the significance of the color of the jacket that the narrator's mother bought him?*

   1. *The "day-old guacamole" color even sounds ugly. The "mustard-colored lining" reminds me of a dirty diaper. Is guacamole a Spanish word? I wonder if he feels it labels him as a Hispanic. Was he ashamed of his heritage?*

2.

   2.

3.

   3.

4.

   4.

5.

   5.

Brief Summary (Example): This story is about a sensitive young boy who hated his jacket. He imagined that his classmates and teachers were looking at him and laughing whenever he wore it. Since the story takes place at a time when his self-esteem is low, he blames all of his social problems on the is jacket; however, in the end he slips back into his jacket, thereby accepting everything that it represents.

Note: Please refer to the Appendix if you need further help in writing a summary.

Reading Assignment 1: "The Jacket"

Reading and Observing

Another way to discover ideas for writing about is through close reading and observation of other people's writing. Of course, your best resource for your writing is often yourself, but interpretation keeps your mind open to new ideas. You may also find it useful to discuss ideas from your reading with friends or family. You may even want to do additional research in the library or on the Internet. Finally, feel free to explore nonprint sources like television, film, interviews, and audio- or videocassettes.

In your textbook you will notice that the prereading section prior to the reading selections contains a number of questions that might trigger the reading-thinking-writing process. This will help you make connections between the story and your personal experiences. Soto's story, for example, should help you recover something significant in your own past. If a professional writer, like Soto, can take something so seemingly trivial (the jacket he hated in elementary school) and turn it into a memorable piece of writing, then almost anything from your past, no matter how ordinary it seems on the surface, can be turned into a serious (or humorous) exploration of your past.

Following each reading assignment, the exercises titled "A Closer Look" will allow you to examine the readings through specific questions. Coming up with a "Central Idea" at the end of each of the exercises titled "A Closer Look" will help you to take responsibility for being a thoughtful reader and ultimately to come to terms with what you feel is the central message of the piece.

A Closer Look

1. When the narrator's mother asks him what kind of jacket he wants, why do you think he describes a black leather biker's jacket?

_____

_____

_____

_____

2. In spite of his negative feelings about his new jacket, he gives his mom a smile of thanks as he passes her in the kitchen. What is the significance of that smile?

_____

_____

_____

Holt, Rinehart and Winston

3. How would you characterize or describe those three years that he wears his jacket?

_____

_____

_____

4. At the end of the story he describes his jacket as "that green ugly brother who breathed over my shoulder that day and ever since." What do you think he means?

_____

_____

_____

CENTRAL IDEA (THEME)

What do you think the narrator is trying to tell us about his jacket and how it affected his fifth- and sixth-grade years? What is the purpose of the story? In your own words, state the central idea (theme) in a single sentence.

Examples

Even though the young boy in the story hates to wear his jacket, he realizes that it stands for everything that he is.

The young boy in the story uses his jacket as a scapegoat for all of the problems he faces in his adolescent life.

_____

_____

_____

Holt, Rinehart and Winston

Writing Assignment 1: Narrating a Story

A *narrative* is a story about an incident or a series of incidents. The details in narrative are often arranged in chronological (time) order, exactly the way the incident occurred. However, sometimes a narrative begins in the middle of a story or even at the end of a story, then moves back to the beginning to fill in the details. Narratives rely on the use of transitional words like *first, next, before that,* and *finally* to keep the timeline clear.

A Student Model

The following paragraph was written by a student in a college English class. Read it to see how another student, like yourself, responded to this writing assignment. Although it may be tempting to write a close imitation of this paragraph, try to explore ways to develop your own thinking and individual style of writing.

Shui-Jane Yeh
English 501: Ms. Allegre
Assignment 1: Narrating a Story
September 28, 1997

The Wu-Fone River

Swimming in a river for the first time taught me an important lesson in life. Early one sunny morning, my family got ready for our trip to the Wu-Fone River. I put on my new swimsuit that I had tried on a dozen times that week. It was bright blue and made of a shiny, stretchy material. It smelled like rubber. We jumped into the van which was already full of folding chairs and straw mats. Also, the foam plastic cooler was full of orange soda pop and ripe, sweet melons and meat threaded onto bamboo sticks. About ten o'clock, my family and I reached the river. Near the bank of the river there were two rows of dense trees. Three gigantic rocks stood upriver, making a natural platform. Next to the rocks was an old wooden sign that read, "No Swimming." The water was so clear. I could see fish swimming in it. While my parents barbecued, I climbed up on the rocks. "Shui," my mother warned, "be careful!" The bright sun heated the rocks and warmed my body. Then, without my parents' permission, I darted into the icy water. It seemed like the right thing to do. That is, I felt like a fish returning to water. I was fascinated by the colorful, tiny stones spread across the bottom of the river. Hundreds of tiny fish and shrimp swam between the rocks. The smaller rocks looked like fists and were coated with slimy green and brown weeds. Suddenly, I slid into a swirling hole. At that moment, I was so scared. I could not remember how to swim. I closed my eyes. I tried flapping my arms like a duck. I struggled to float up to get air. Of course, there was no lifeguard since swimming was not allowed there. The people on the bank yelled and pointed at me, but they were in shock. As a result, they stared at me with no idea what to do. I stared back, unable to cry out. I was sinking and floating away in the current. The more I struggled, the deeper I went. Finally, I was rescued by a tourist who was just playing with his lifeboat down the river. I remember feeling weak for a long, long time. I did not drown that day, but I learned a big lesson: nothing in life has guarantees.

Holt, Rinehart and Winston

PREWRITING

Prewriting will help you discover ideas for writing. It is an important stage of the writing process because it can help you get beyond that "blank page," a place where beginning writers often get stuck. The most common types of prewriting are clustering, listing, freewriting, and asking journalistic questions.

Clustering

One prewriting method, clustering, is a quick and easy way to record ideas as you think of them. Clustering works through sheer instinct and free association. Thus, it is the ultimate right-brain activity for a writer. To begin clustering, write your topic in the middle of a piece of paper. Circle your topic and simply start to form clusters of ideas, thinking and writing at the same time. It's like brainstorming, where one idea leads to another. An advantage of this method is that you are visually starting to organize your ideas at the same time they pop out of your head and get recorded on paper. Some students find clustering too frustrating because it is so open-ended. Still, you should give it a chance to work because it is a powerful technique. Keep clustering until you have jotted down all the details you can remember about your incident. After about six minutes of clustering, you should have made a mental breakthrough. If not, switch topics.

When you are finished with clustering, think of where your prewriting has led you. In the final analysis, all of the ideas you have jotted down must be reckoned with or your subsequent paragraph will have no direction or purpose. Writing the topic sentence (for a paragraph) or a thesis statement (for an essay) will help you make an important generalization about your topic. Sometimes, in a narrative, you might simply tell a story without a significant point. However, coming up with a good topic sentence will help give your narrative a sharper focus.

Keep in mind that most of your writing in college classes will require a thesis statement or at least a main idea. If you are having difficulty coming up with a topic sentence or a thesis statement, ask yourself the following question: "So what?" The answer to that question should lead you to your central point. College writing requires not just a story, but a story that reveals the truth of a generalization.

Holt, Rinehart and Winston

Writing Assignment 1: Narrating a Story

Example of Clustering for Shui-Jane Yeh's Narrative

Topic: <u>The Wu-Fone River</u>

Topic Sentence (Central Idea): <u>Swimming in a river for the first time taught me an important lesson in life.</u>

Holt, Rinehart and Winston

Writing Assignment 1: Narrating a Story

Listing

Another prewriting method, besides clustering, is listing. Listing is similar to clustering in that you record your ideas as they come to mind. However, in listing you jot down words or phrases in rows or columns. This method allows you to prewrite freely without too much initial worrying about organization.

Example of Listing for Shui-Jane Yeh's Narrative

Topic: <u>The Wu-Fone River</u>

getting ready   swirling hole
folding chairs   swift current
straw mats   flapping arms
ice chest   going under
melons   people watching
steak   getting saved
soda   the lesson
new swimsuit
riverbank
dense trees
clear water
huge rocks
tiny stones
fish/shrimp
slimy weeds
old sign

Topic Sentence (Central Idea): <u>Swimming in a river for the first time taught me an important lesson in life.</u>

Holt, Rinehart and Winston

Writing Assignment 1: Narrating a Story

Freewriting

Yet another prewriting method, besides clustering and listing, is freewriting. It is similar to both of the other prewriting methods in capturing ideas in free association. In freewriting, though, you write longer phrases without worrying about correct spelling, punctuation, organization, or grammar rules. If you are unable to focus on a writing topic, you simply write what is on your mind at that given moment, for example, "I'm tired" or "I'm hungry." You are encouraged to keep repeating yourself until the act of repetition triggers a new discovery. Ideally, one thought will lead to another until you discover a topic and a direction.

Example of Freewriting for Shui-Jane Yeh's Narrative

Topic: The Wu-Fone River

I want to write about the river—almost drowning. I was so scared. The water was like ice. How did it happen? I was so excited,—I could hardly wait to go to the river. My mom bought me my first real swimsuit—it was blue, or was it green? I still remember the smell—like rubber. Our van was jam-packed for the bar-b-q. We had everything—meat, soda, fruit, chairs, straw mats. The river was beautiful but Mom was worried. Trees, water, huge rocks—everything so perfect! Let's see—I can't think of anything else.—so long ago. I was so little. Why did I jump in? Too hot—too stupid? Thought I could swim—I was drowning—the current so strong—pulling me down. I was saved—a man grabbed me. pulled me out. What else? Mom so mad—I was covered with mud and slimy weeds—smelled like a sewer. Never thought about danger before—how could it happen? Did I learn anything? Now I am scared to take chances—no more swimming for me.

Topic Sentence (Central Idea): Swimming in a river for the first time taught me an important lesson in life.

Asking Journalistic Questions

A final invention strategy you could use to discover new ideas for writing is to ask journalistic questions: *Who? What? Why? Where? When? How?*

This is a structured way to examine your topic and to make sure that you have covered all angles. If you use this method, keep in mind that you will have to ask certain questions for certain types of writing. Not every question is appropriate for a particular type of writing.

Writing a narrative, for example, will probably require you to ask the following questions: *Who did it? What happened? When did it happen? Where did it happen?*

Holt, Rinehart and Winston

Writing a description, however, might require a different set of questions that point to sensory details: *What does it look like? What does it feel like? What does it sound like? What does it taste like? What does it smell like?* Other questions that lend themselves to descriptive writing are as follows: *What are its characteristics? What impressions does it make?* Thus, each of the various modes or types of writing will require you to ask a slightly different set of questions. In reality, though, the different modes of writing often overlap.

In her narrative about the Wu-Fone River, Shui-Jane uses the questions for a narrative as well as for a description because she wants her readers to visualize both the scene and the incident.

Example of Journalistic Questions for Shui-Jane Yeh's Narrative

Topic: <u>The Wu-Fone River</u>

Narrative Questions

Who?	Me, my parents, some tourists.
What happened?	I almost drowned.
Why?	I ignored the "No Swimming" sign.
Where?	At the Wu-Fone River
When?	I was about eleven years old.
How?	The current was too swift.

Descriptive Questions

What does it look like?	The van is packed with straw mats and chairs, the ice chest full of meat, orange soda, ripe melons. The river is beautiful—trees, huge rocks, clear water, fish, shrimp, colored stones. My swimsuit is blue. People with round, scared eyes, water like a whirlpool.
Feel like?	Hot rocks, icy water, sharp stones, slimy weeds. Sound like? Parents talking, water rippling and swirling, people crying out, underwater tunnel, echoing sounds.
Taste like?	Spring water at first, later: rotting weeds, sewers, mud.
Smell like?	Swimsuit like rubber, mats like dry straw, smoky barbecue, rocks a little moldy, like a hot stove, seaweed

Topic Sentence (Central Idea): <u>Swimming in a river for the first time taught me an important</u> <u>lesson in life.</u>

Holt, Rinehart and Winston

Writing Assignment 1: Narrating a Story

THE WRITING PROCESS

Before you begin your own paragraph for Writing Assignment 1, think about writing as a constant meaning-making process of discovery. You want to make sure that your writing will convey exactly what you want to say. Thus, at every stage of the process, writing requires you to think critically and to make certain choices, such as what to add and what to omit. Also, a key part of planning your paper is to think about purpose, audience, and tone.

Purpose

For college writing, you will usually write to inform or to explain. However, you will also write for a variety of other purposes: to persuade, to entertain, to analyze, to criticize, to speculate, to identify problems and offer solutions, or to show cause and effect. Define your purpose by asking yourself what you are writing. Then ask why you are writing it.

Audience

Audience refers to your readers. To determine audience, you might ask yourself the following questions: Are you writing for an English class or a class in another discipline? Are you addressing an individual or a group? Are you writing to a political organization or a special-interest group? Are you expecting your audience to have a certain expertise with your topic?

Who are you addressing in your writing? Much of the writing you will do for a college English class is addressed to an academic audience, namely your instructor, who will assign you a grade based on standardized rules of grammar and usage. Even if your audience is made up of other students in the classroom (your peers), their responses are usually geared to helping you achieve a good grade on your paper. Regardless of who your audience is, it will determine the arrangement of your material as well as the language and tone you use.

Tone

Tone refers to the attitude and feelings you portray in your writing. Do you intend to convey a playful, cynical, intimate, respectful, or serious tone? The tone you choose should be consistent with your message. It should also be appropriate for your topic.

Holt, Rinehart and Winston

Writing Assignment 1: Narrating a Story

Writing Task: When you are young, acting like your friends and wearing the same clothing styles that most of them wear seem very important. It is not until you are older and wiser that you realize that other things are far more significant in your life. Write a narrative paragraph about an incident from your early years that had a powerful and lasting effect on you.

Finding a Topic

Think about the experiences from your early years that taught you some type of lesson about life. List one or two incidents that might make good topics. Having a backup topic is a good idea in case your first choice does not work out.

Possible Topics:

_____

_____

Prewriting

Use any one of the invention strategies (clustering, listing, freewriting, or asking journalistic questions) to discover ideas about the topic that is most interesting to you. Jot down whatever comes to mind until you come up with enough ideas to write your narrative.

Your Topic: _____

Holt, Rinehart and Winston

Writing Assignment 1: Narrating a Story

The Topic Sentence

A topic sentence consists of two main parts:

1. Your topic (what your paragraph is about)
2. Directing words (the point you want to make about your topic)

Swimming in a river for the first time <u>taught me an important lesson in life.</u>

Adding a different set of directing words to the same topic can guide the paragraph in other directions:

Swimming in a river for the first time <u>gave me a wonderful appreciation of nature.</u>
Swimming in a river for the first time <u>was a lesson in ecology.</u>
Swimming in a river for the first time <u>taught me never to take life for granted.</u>
Swimming in a river for the first time <u>was the most embarrassing experience of my life.</u>

Do you see how the same topic can go in different directions? As a writer, you can control the direction and content of your paragraphs. Your directing words should forecast the point you want to make.

Writing a Topic Sentence

Look back at your prewriting and ask yourself, "So what?" What did your experience teach you? Your response should help you write a tentative topic sentence.

Tentative Topic Sentence (Central Idea):

_____

_____

Does your topic sentence state what happened and what you learned from the experience?

If not, revise it to make your purpose clear.

Note: Please refer to Reviewing the Basics if you need further help in writing a topic sentence.

Holt, Rinehart and Winston

Writing Assignment 1: Narrating a Story

TRANSITIONAL WORDS

An important lesson to consider before you begin to write your rough draft is the use of transitional words and phrases. The purpose of transitional expressions is to signal the various types of order found in different kinds of paragraphs.

Narrative paragraphs require the use of "time order" transitions to show the passage of time. Using transitional expressions that signal order and provide links between sentences is one way to achieve coherence in your writing. *Coherence* means keeping ideas logically connected within paragraphs. A piece of writing is held together when its sentences are arranged in logical order and when each idea is linked to previous ones.

"Time Order" Transitions

Order is the logical arrangement of sentences within a paragraph. Items should be grouped or ordered in a particular sequence to avoid chaos. Paragraphs in which you might use a "time" or "chronological" order include the following types:

1. Narratives (telling stories)
2. Process paragraphs (explaining a process)
3. Historical pieces (describing a sequence of events)

Examples of "Time Order" Transitions

first	to begin with	in the past	in the morning
second	next	now	at noon
third	then	soon	in the afternoon
last	finally	in the future	at night
at breakfast	in 1920	in the fall	before
at lunch	in 1930	in the winter	then
at dinner	in 1940	in the spring	during
	in 1950	in the summer	finally

EXERCISE

Look back at the student model, "The Wu-Fone River" by Shui-Jane Yeh. Notice that the transitions she uses tell us that she is using "time" order and "space" order because she is telling us a story as well as describing the physical scene. Focusing only on "time" order for now, circle any transitional words or phrases that indicate time or sequence. List a few of her "time" transitions in the space below:

_____   _____

_____   _____

Note: Please refer to Reviewing the Basics if you need further help in using transitions that signal time order.

Holt, Rinehart and Winston

Writing Assignment 1: Narrating a Story

Linking Transitions

Another function of transitions (in addition to showing a paper's order) is to link the sentences within a paragraph. Using "linking" transitions to connect sentences helps to clarify the relationship of one sentence to another.

Examples of "Linking" Transitions

Giving Examples	Giving Additional Information	Contrasting Ideas	Showing Results
in other words	in addition	however	as a result
for example	furthermore	in contrast	consequently
for instance	also	on the other hand	therefore
as an illustration	likewise	on the contrary	thus
that is	of course	otherwise	
	moreover	nevertheless	

EXERCISE

Again, look back at the student narrative by Shui-Jane Yeh. As you read, underline any transitional words or phrases that link sentences or indicate the relationship of one idea to another. List a few of her "linking" transitions in the space below:

_____   _____

_____   _____

Note: Please refer to Reviewing the Basics if you need further help in using linking transitions.

Writing a Rough Draft

Now take your prewriting one step further by creating a rough draft. A rough draft is usually written after you have completed the prewriting stage and most of the ideas concerning the topic are jotted down so you will not forget them. Analyze your prewriting for Assignment 1 and organize your ideas in a chronological order to indicate the sequence of events in your story.

Begin with your topic sentence. Always feel free to revise your topic sentence if your writing starts to go in a different direction. Select the best ideas from your prewriting, and write until you have thoroughly described the incident so that your readers can experience it. Add "time order" transitions (first, next, then, after that, finally) to make sure your reader is clear about the sequence of your story. Also, use "linking" transitions to add details and explanations.

Holt, Rinehart and Winston

Being Specific

A piece of writing is not really finished until it contains specific examples and vivid details that make it complete and whole. Your first draft may initially satisfy you, but you may not be taking into account the needs of your audience, who require specific examples and descriptive details to experience fully what you are trying to communicate.

For example, in Shui-Jane Yeh's narrative, "The Wu-Fone River," she does not simply mention her swimsuit. Instead, she provides her readers (who obviously were not there at the river) with enough sensory details so that they, too, can actually see and smell the new suit: *"I put on my new swimsuit that I had tried on a dozen times that week. It was bright blue and made of stretchy material. It smelled like rubber."*

Likewise, she does not simply mention the cooler as a minor detail. She shows her readers what kind of cooler it is and even what it contains: *"Also, the foam plastic cooler was full of orange soda pop and ripe, sweet melons and meat threaded onto bamboo sticks."*

Being specific, that is, adding enough details, is the mark of a mature writer. Notice that Shui-Jane uses rich sensory details that include the senses of sight, smell, touch, sound, and taste. Reread your rough draft, watching out for words, phrases, and sentences that are too general. Underline the parts of your writing that might benefit from being more specific. Write a new draft, changing the passages you have underlined into more interesting, exact, detailed writing. Use names, numbers, colors, and examples wherever you can.

Note: Please refer to Reviewing the Basics if you need further help in being specific.

The Concluding Sentence

A conclusion is a final sentence or sentences that bring closure to your paragraph. Many options are available for concluding a piece of writing. In her narrative paragraph, "The Wu-Fone River," Shui-Jane Yeh ends with a personal reflection about the incident she is describing: *"I did not drown that day, but I learned a big lesson: nothing in life has guarantees."* Her brush with death causes her to realize her own vulnerability and the uncertainties with which we must all live.

To write a conclusion for your paragraph, you might consider the following possibilities:

- Restate the idea in your topic sentence:

  I learned that nothing in life has its guarantees.

- Make a final, overall impression on your reader:

  I did not drown that day, but I remember feeling weak and powerless for a long time.

- End with a prediction:

  I realized that the experience was just one of many that I would have to face in my life.

Holt, Rinehart and Winston

- Use a quotation followed by a comment:

  "Mother knows best," I have often heard my mother say. That day I did not listen to my mother, and I almost lost my life.

- Suggest a possible course of action:

  We should listen to our parents when they tell us to be careful.

Above all, your conclusion should provide a smooth exit for your reader as well as a sense of completion. Avoid endings that are too obvious, like "In conclusion . . ." or "In closing . . ."

Note: Please refer to Reviewing the Basics if you need further help with concluding sentences.

Revising

Revision is an ongoing process in which you delete words, add phrases, and rearrange sentences to make your meaning clear to your reader. Thus, revision may occur at any point in the writing process. After you have written your rough draft, reread it carefully, being as objective as possible. Underline all words, phrases, or sentences that could benefit from more specifics, details, and examples.

Peer Editing

Using your revised copy, read your paper out loud to a peer editor. Likewise, listen as your peer editor reads his or her paper back to you. When both papers have been read aloud, exchange papers, using the Editing Sheets provided for this assignment to write helpful comments to each other. In some cases it might be more appropriate to exchange papers at the start and have each peer editor read silently before completing the editing sheet. Another option would be to use the Editing Sheet as a checklist for oral feedback. A final option would be for your instructor to create peer editing groups of three or four members for collaborative learning.

Whatever option you use, the Editing Sheet that follows will provide useful guidelines for this assignment. Only one set of Editing Sheets is provided, which is sufficient if you are using collaborative groups. However, if you are using two individual editors, you will need to obtain a photocopy of the Editing Sheet. Please check with your instructor.

Holt, Rinehart and Winston

Writing Assignment 1: Narrating a Story

Editing Sheet (to be completed by peer editors)

Directions: Either pair up and exchange papers with another student in class, or form editing groups of three or four members. Papers may be read silently or aloud. Every paper requires at least two peer editors who will work collaboratively to complete an Editing Sheet. The completed Editing Sheet should then be attached to the rough draft and returned to the writer for reference during the revision process.

Some peer editors may prefer to write comments directly on a student's rough draft, using the Editing Sheet as more of a checklist. Check with your instructor to see which method works best for your situation.

1. Has the writer selected a topic that is interesting, sufficiently narrowed, and appropriate for a narrative paragraph? If the topic is weak, suggest prewriting strategies (clustering, listing, freewriting, or asking journalistic questions) to generate enough ideas for a new topic.

_____

_____

2. Draw a circle around the directing words in the topic sentence. If the directing words are missing, ask the writer, "So what? What did you learn from this experience? What point are you trying to make in this paper?" Suggest ways to make the topic sentence more effective, if necessary.

_____

_____

3. Draw a wavy line under words or phrases that would benefit from detailed examples. Has the writer included enough examples and specific sensory details (sight, sound, smell, touch, taste) for a fully developed paragraph?

_____

_____

4. Is dialogue used? If not, would the use of dialogue (direct quotations) make this paper more realistic and interesting? If dialogue is used, does it express a particular emotion? If necessary, make suggestions for improvement.

_____

_____

Holt, Rinehart and Winston

5. Underline the transitional expressions that signal "time" order. Is the sequence of the narrative clearly signaled by the use of transitions that show the passage of time? Offer suggestions.

_____

_____

6. Does the writer also use "linking" transitions that show the relationship between ideas in a sentence? Where would you add more? Where would you omit some?

_____

_____

7. Does the concluding sentence wrap up the paragraph effectively or leave a lasting impression on you? What ideas do you have about writing a more effective conclusion?

_____

_____

8. Does the title intrigue you and really catch your attention as a reader? Think of recent movie titles. What suggestions do you have for a more interesting, creative title?

_____

9. What is the most powerful part of this paper? Be as specific as possible.

_____

_____

Peer Editors' Initials: ____   ____   ____   ____   (This verifies the paper is ready for a Revised Copy.)

Submitting the Final Copy

Once you have had your paper edited, you should revise your paper once again. Remember that experienced writers constantly revise their work to make sure it communicates exactly what they meant to say. Before you write the final copy of your paper, your instructor or tutor may want to skim over your revised draft. Then write your final copy in ink on notebook paper or type it on a typewriter or a computer. Make sure you follow the rules of manuscript form located in the Appendix.

After writing the final copy of your paper, exchange it with other members of your editing group to proofread for spelling, punctuation, and grammar errors. Ask your peer editors to initial your final copy to indicate that it has been through the final editing process. When your edited paper is returned to you, make the final corrections and submit your final copy along with your rough draft and completed Editing Sheet. Stapling the whole packet together will allow your instructor to check your progress during each stage of the writing process.

Holt, Rinehart and Winston

Reading Assignment 2: "Lying in a Hammock . . ."

Prereading

In his poem, "Lying in a Hammock at William Duffy's Farm in Pine Island, Minnesota," James Wright describes what he observes around him, using exact, vivid details. As he allows the beautiful images from the surrounding natural world to sink into his mind, what do you feel he is thinking about? In what ways do his thoughts and the images from nature surprise you? What questions would you like to ask him about the meaning of this poem? As you read the selection, reflect on your own memory of a special place that has real meaning for you. Can you recall all the details that would help you describe this place? What effect does the place have on you? What is its significance for you?

Lying in a Hammock at William Duffy's Farm in Pine Island, Minnesota
James Wright

Over my head, I see the bronze butterfly,
Asleep on the black trunk,
Blowing like a leaf in green shadow.
Down the ravine behind the empty house,
The cowbells follow one another
Into the distances of the afternoon.
To my right,
In a field of sunlight between two pines,
The droppings of last year's horses
Blaze up into golden stones.
I lean back, as the evening darkens and comes on.
A chicken hawk floats over, looking for home.
I have wasted my life.

Holt, Rinehart and Winston

Reading Assignment 2: "Lying in a Hammock at William Duffy's Farm in Pine Island, Minnesota"

Double-Entry Question Journal

Note: Some students find it easier to do the double-entry journal as they are reading. Others find the process more effective after they have finished reading the entire piece. You should experiment to discover the method that works best for you.

In the left column, jot down at least five "What?" "Why?" or "How?" questions. Then in the right column, jot down some possible answers and responses. If further questions come up, jot them down also. One purpose of this exercise is to learn how to think critically, so you might end up with several answers. Go ahead, take a risk!

1.   1.

2.   2.

3.   3.

4.   4.

5.   5.

Brief Summary: _____

_____

_____

_____

_____

Note: Please refer to the Appendix if you need help in writing a summary.

Reading Assignment 2:
"Lying in a Hammock at William Duffy's Farm in Pine Island, Minnesota"

A Closer Look

1. Draw a rough but detailed sketch of the scene described in the poem. Include the poet lying in his hammock. (Stick figures will do if you are not an artist.)

2. Reread lines 1 through 12. Make a thorough list below of all of the physical details the author uses to create a detailed description of the scene.

_____   _____

_____   _____

_____   _____

_____   _____

3. How does the last line, "I have wasted my life," fit into the poem? How did the narrator arrive at this conclusion?

_____

_____

CENTRAL IDEA (THEME)

What do you feel James Wright is trying to teach us in his poem? What is his main point?

_____

_____

Holt, Rinehart and Winston

Writing Assignment 2: Describing a Place

Description tells what something looks like. A descriptive paragraph often reflects the way you look at a scene. Thus, you would use "space order" transitions (on the left, in the center, to the right) to signal the arrangement of details in spatial order (left to right, near to far, top to bottom). Unlike other paragraphs, descriptive place paragraphs do not always begin with a topic sentence. However, they are almost always held together by a dominant impression, which can take the place of a topic sentence. Description also relies heavily on the senses (sight, sound, smell, taste, touch).

Note: If you decide to include inner feelings about the place as well as some important incidents that happened over time, you may need to add "time order" transitions or even "importance order" transitions for clarity.

A Student Model (with Peer Editor's Comments)

The following rough draft was written by a student in a college English class. Read it to see how a student, like yourself, responded to this writing assignment. Also look over the written comments and sample Editing Sheet that follows to get an idea of typical comments made by an effective peer editor. Make sure you read the final revised copy to see what changes the writer made to ensure that her paper would say exactly what she wanted to say.

Niele S. Janzantti
English 501: Zipperian
Assignment 2: Description of a Place (Rough Draft)
June 24, 1997

So what? What impression are you trying to convey?

My Silent Moment

Work on title! (Solitude?)

When I was nine years old, my family and I went to the beach called Porto Seguro, Bahia State, in Brazil./Early in the morning, I cooked a wonderful breakfast for everyone. I prepared eggs, breads, juice, cereal, milk, and some fruit./ At about *focus more on the scene* 8 o'clock, we went to the beach, and I was excited to see the ocean. I put on my striped brown and silver swimming suit, I packed a picnic basket, and after 10 minutes of walking, we were there. The view was so beautiful, and I could see the ocean

Holt, Rinehart and Winston

through the wooden bridge. I left my things and ran by myself to the water. It was *add specific detail*

warm, and I saw my feet through (limpid) and quiet water. On my left side, between the *what?*

hills, I could see many gorgeous and marvelous large homes. On the right side, I saw *be more specific*

the gold and hot sun. At the moment, I saw my parents were leaving and I was finally

alone. It was great, I kept walking and I was attracted by the color (yellow, blue, *what were these objects?*

what kind of tree? fawn, mauve, and turquoise). I stopped in the shadow of a tree. From there, *Somehow I really like this part*

I can't picture this scene I was able to view a hot dog cart and other tourists. Then I could hear the sounds of

the wind, which stirred up the sand, causing it to stick to the sunblock on my face, so I

tasted what? tasted it. I did not smell or see any pollution. The whole area was clean. There were

circular blue trash cans situated every half mile. All too soon, my quiet time was over.

Mom called me to lunch, and (I could no longer stay alone.)

↑
Do you mean your solitude was over?

Holt, Rinehart and Winston

SAMPLE PEER EDITING SHEET

1. Has the writer selected a topic that is interesting, sufficiently narrowed, and appropriate for a descriptive paragraph? If the topic is weak, suggest prewriting strategies (clustering, listing, freewriting, or asking journalistic questions) to generate enough ideas for a new topic.

Yes, I think the writer chose a good topic. She seems to have strong memories about the place.

2. Draw a circle around the topic sentence or the dominant impression. If one or the other is missing, ask the writer, "So what? What is the personal significance of the place, or what is the overall impression of the place that you want to communicate?" Suggest ways to make the topic sentence more effective, if necessary.

Well, she doesn't come right out and state her point, but it's there somewhere. She's trying to say something about being alone, but it could be made clearer.

3. Draw a wavy line under words or phrases that would benefit from detailed examples. Has the writer included enough examples and specific sensory details (sight, sound, smell, touch, taste) for a fully developed paragraph?

She is very specific in some places, like the blue trash cans, but she needs to use more details about the bridge and the homes. It's hard to picture what they look like.

4. Does the writer mistakenly focus more on the physical description of the place rather than on the activities or events that occurred there? (Remember, this assignment asks for a description, not another narrative or story.) Offer suggestions if the focus seems fuzzy.

At times she gets away from what the place looked like. For example, maybe she can get rid of the breakfast part because it just tells what she was doing.

5. Underline the transitional expressions that signal either "space" order or "time" order, whichever seems more appropriate. Is the physical arrangement of the scene clearly signaled by the use of transitions that show where things are located? Offer suggestions about spatial relationships.

She uses mostly "space" transitions, but she also uses "time" order. It's a little confusing. Maybe she should avoid writing about activity.

Holt, Rinehart and Winston

6. Does the writer also use "linking" transitions that clearly show the relationship between ideas in a sentence? Where would you add more? Where would you omit some?

I don't think she uses many linking transitions—but I can't tell where she could add them. Somehow they do not really seem necessary.

7. Does the concluding sentence wrap up the paragraph effectively or leave a lasting impression on you? What ideas do you have about writing a more effective conclusion?

Her idea is good (being "alone"), but she needs to communicate it more clearly. Maybe she can get the idea across without really stating it.

8. Does the title intrigue you and really catch your attention as a reader? Think of recent movie titles. What suggestions do you have for a more interesting, creative title?

I kind of like it, but I don't think it's really about one moment. Maybe she should use the word "shadow" in her title because it sounds poetic.

9. What do you think is the most powerful part of this paper? Try to be as specific as possible.

I really like the part where she stops "in the shadow of a tree." It symbolizes how she likes being alone. She conveys the special feeling she has.

Peer Editor's Initials: _pn_ (This verifies that the paper is ready for a Revised Copy.)

Holt, Rinehart and Winston

Sample of the Final Revised Copy

Niele S. Janzantti
English 501: Zipperian
Assignment 2: Description of a Place
June 24, 1997

From the Shadow of a Tree

When I was nine years old, my family and I went to a beach called Porto Seguro in the Bahia State of Brazil. It was the first time I understood the meaning of solitude. I was so excited to see the ocean. I put on my striped brown and silver swimming suit, and after ten minutes of walking, we were finally there. The view was so beautiful. I could see the turquoise ocean sparkling through the wooden bridge. I left my family and ran by myself to the water. It was warm, and I could see my feet through the quiet water. On my left, between the hills, were many large homes with red tile roof tops. On my right the golden hot sun was climbing high in the sky. In the distance I could see my parents, but at that moment I was really alone. I felt great. I kept walking, attracted by all the colors around me: yellow, blue, fawn, and mauve, just like in a painting. In silence I stood in the shadow of a tree. From there, I was able to view a red and white hot dog cart and other tourists. I could hear the sound of the wind. It stirred up the sand, causing it to stick to my face. It tasted like the fresh salty sea. I did not smell or see any pollution, only the circular blue trash cans situated every half mile. From far away, I could hear my mom calling me to lunch. All too soon, my quiet time was over.

Writing Assignment 2: Describing a Place

Writing Task: James Wright wrote "Lying in a Hammock at William Duffy's Farm in Pine Island, Minnesota" because he remembers it as an important place in his life, a place where he learned something significant about himself and how he had been living his life. As a response to the poem, write a descriptive paragraph about a place from your own past. Select a place that you can describe in vivid, exact details, as James Wright does in his poem. Above all, reflect on its significance to you and your life.

Finding a Topic

Think about a place from your past that had personal significance to you. List one or two places that might make good topics. Remember, having a backup topic is a good idea in case your first choice does not work out.

Possible Topics:

_____

_____

Sketching a Scene

Before prewriting, it often helps to draw a brief sketch of the scene you will be describing. Include as many physical details as you can.

Holt, Rinehart and Winston

Writing Assignment 2: Describing a Place

Prewriting

Use any one of the invention strategies (clustering, listing, freewriting, or asking journalistic questions) to discover ideas about the topic that is most interesting to you. Jot down whatever comes to mind until you come up with enough ideas to write your narrative.

Your Topic: _____

Writing the Topic Sentence

Tentative Topic Sentence (Central Idea) or Dominant Impression: _____

_____

Does your topic sentence name the place and state the personal significance of that place, or does it convey a dominant impression? If not, revise it to make your purpose clear.

Holt, Rinehart and Winston

Writing Assignment 2: Describing a Place

TRANSITIONAL WORDS

Place descriptions often require the use of "space order" transitions. Before you begin writing your rough draft, you will need to be familiar with the use of transitions that signal spatial relationships.

"Space Order" Transitions

In James Wright's poem, "Lying in a Hammock at William Duffy's Farm in Pine Island, Minnesota," the author is observing the natural world around him as he lies in a hammock. Notice how he signals space order by using several key phrases to show the reader exactly where those things are situated around him:

> Over my head
> Down the ravine
> To my right

Examples of "Space Order" Transitions

at the top	in front of	outside	here	on the left	on the doorstep
below the top	next to . . .	inside	farther out	in the center	across the lawn
next	beyond the	. . . there	on the right	around the corner	
at the bottom	in the distance	down the street			

EXERCISE

Look back at the student description by Niele Janzantti. As you read, underline any transitional words or phrases that signal spatial order. List a few of her "space order" transitions in the space below:

_____   _____

_____   _____

Note: Please refer to Reviewing the Basics if you need further help in using transitions that signal order.

Holt, Rinehart and Winston

Writing a Rough Draft

Now take your prewriting one step further by creating a rough draft. Selecting the best details, experiences, and reflections from your prewriting, write the draft of your paragraph. Begin with your topic sentence (or dominant impression) and write until you have described the place in detail so that your readers can see it as clearly as you can. Include important personal experiences you associate with the place as long as you do not get off focus. In your concluding sentence try to convey a mood or impression associated with the place.

Being Specific

In Wright's poem, specific visual details like "A chicken hawk floats over" help to create a reflective mood of longing and regret. Notice his use of descriptive words such as "black trunk" and "green shadow." He also describes the larger scene as "a field of sunlight between two pines" to help the reader visualize the place.

Reread your rough draft of Writing Assignment 2, watching out for general words, phrases, and sentences. Underline the parts of your writing that might benefit from being more specific. Write a new draft, changing the passages you have underlined into more interesting, exact, and detailed writing. Use names, numbers, colors, and examples wherever you can.

Revising

Go through your rough draft and revise it, applying what you have learned about space order. When appropriate, add "space order" transitions and linking transitions to help you describe your place more precisely so your reader can actually visualize it.

Peer Editing

Using your revised copy, read your paper out loud to a peer editor. Likewise, listen as your peer editor reads his or her paper back to you. When both papers have been read aloud, exchange papers, using the Editing Sheets provided for this assignment to write helpful comments to each other. In some cases it might be more appropriate to exchange papers at the start and have each peer editor read silently before completing the Editing Sheet. Another option would be to use the Editing Sheet as a checklist for oral feedback. A final option would be for your instructor to create peer editing groups of three or four members for collaborative learning.

Whatever option you use, the Editing Sheet that follows will provide useful guidelines for this assignment. Only one set of Editing Sheets is provided, which is sufficient if you are using collaborative groups. However, if you are using two individual editors, you will need to obtain a photocopy of the Editing Sheet. Please check with your instructor.

Holt, Rinehart and Winston

Writing Assignment 2: Describing a Place

Editing Sheet (to be completed by peer editors)

Directions: Either pair up and exchange papers with another student in class, or form editing groups of three or four members. Papers may be read silently or aloud. Every paper requires at least two peer editors who will work collaboratively to complete an Editing Sheet. The completed Editing Sheet should be attached to the rough draft and returned to the writer for reference during the revision process.

Some peer editors may prefer to write comments directly on a student's rough draft, using the editing sheet as more of a checklist. Check with your instructor to see which method works best for your situation.

1. Has the writer selected a topic that is interesting, sufficiently narrowed, and appropriate for a descriptive paragraph? If the topic is weak, suggest prewriting strategies (clustering, listing, freewriting, or asking journalistic questions) to generate enough ideas for a new topic.

_____

_____

2. Draw a circle around the directing words in the topic sentence. If the directing words are missing, ask the writer, "So what? What is the personal significance of the place, or what is the overall impression of the place that you want to communicate?" Suggest ways to make the topic sentence more effective, if necessary.

_____

_____

3. Draw a wavy line under words or phrases that would benefit from detailed examples. Has the writer included enough examples and specific sensory details (sight, sound, smell, touch, taste) for a fully developed paragraph?

_____

_____

4. Does the writer mistakenly focus more on the physical description of the place rather than on the activities or events that occurred there? (Remember, this assignment asks for a description, not another narrative or story.) Offer suggestions if the focus seems fuzzy.

_____

_____

Holt, Rinehart and Winston

5. Underline the transitional expressions that signal either "space" order or "time" order, whichever the writer used. Is the physical arrangement of the scene clearly signaled by the use of transitions that show where things are located? Offer suggestions about spatial relationships.

_____

_____

6. Does the writer also use "linking" transitions that clearly show the relationship between ideas in a sentence? Where would you add more? Where would you omit some?

_____

_____

7. Does the concluding sentence wrap up the paragraph effectively or leave a lasting impression on you? What ideas do you have about writing a more effective conclusion?

_____

_____

8. Does the title intrigue you and really catch your attention as a reader? Think of recent movie titles. What suggestions do you have for a more interesting, creative title?

_____

9. What do you think is the most powerful part of this paper? Try to be as specific as possible.

_____

_____

Peer Editors' Initials: ____ ____ ____ ____ (This verifies the paper is ready for a Revised Copy.)

Submitting the Final Copy

Once you have had your paper edited, you should revise your paper once again. Remember that experienced writers constantly revise their work to make sure it communicates exactly what they meant to say. Before you write the final copy of your paper, your instructor or tutor may want to skim over your revised draft. Then write your final copy in ink on notebook paper or type it on a typewriter or a computer. Make sure you follow the rules of manuscript form located in the Appendix.

After writing the final copy of your paper, exchange it with other members of your editing group to proofread for spelling, punctuation, and grammar errors. Ask your peer editors to initial your final

Holt, Rinehart and Winston

copy to indicate that it has been through the final editing process. When your edited paper is returned to you, make the final corrections and submit your final copy along with your rough draft and completed Editing Sheet. Stapling the whole packet together will allow your instructor to check your progress during each stage of the writing process.

Holt, Rinehart and Winston

Reading Assignment 3: "Uncle Willie"

Prereading

Friends, relatives, or other people we know well can have a profound and mysterious influence on our lives. In "Uncle Willie," Maya Angelou describes a childhood memory of a relative and explores how she gained a new insight into his character. As you read the selection, reflect on your own memory of a special relative, friend, or acquaintance. What is it about this person's background, personality, and interests that makes him or her play such a unique role in your life and in your memories?

Uncle Willie
Maya Angelou

When Bailey was six and I a year younger, we used to rattle off the times tables with the speed I was later to see Chinese children in San Francisco employ on their abacuses. Our summer-gray pot-bellied stove bloomed rosy red during winter, and became a severe disciplinarian threat if we were so foolish as to indulge in making mistakes.

Uncle Willie used to sit, like a giant black Z (he had been crippled as a child), and hear us testify to the Lafayette County Training Schools' abilities. His faced pulled down on the left side, as if a pulley had been attached to his lower teeth, and his left hand was only a mite bigger than Bailey's, but on the second mistake or on the third hesitation his big overgrown right hand would catch one of us behind the collar, and in the same moment would thrust the culprit toward the dull red heater, which throbbed like a devil's toothache. We were never burned, although once I might have been when I was so terrified I tried to jump onto the stove to remove the possibility of its remaining a threat. Like most children, I thought if I could face the worst danger voluntarily, and *triumph*, I would forever have power over it. But in my case of sacrificial effort I was thwarted. Uncle Willie held tight to my dress and I only got close enough to smell the clean dry scent of hot iron. We learned the times tables without understanding their grand principle, simply because we had the capacity and no alternative.

The tragedy of lameness seems so unfair to children that they are embarrassed in its presence. And they, most recently off nature's mold, sense that they have only narrowly missed being another of her jokes. In relief at the narrow escape, they vent their emotions in impatience and criticism for the unlucky cripple.

Momma related times without end, and without any show of emotion, how Uncle Willie had been dropped when he was three years old by a woman who was minding him. She seemed to hold no rancor against the baby-sitter, nor for her just God who allowed the accident. She felt it necessary to explain over and over again to those who knew the story by heart that he wasn't "born that way."

In our society, where two-legged, two-armed strong Black men were able at best to eke out the necessities of life, Uncle Willie, with his starched shirts, shined shoes and shelves full of food, was the whipping boy and butt of jokes of the underemployed and underpaid. Fate not only disabled him but laid a double-tiered barrier in his path. He was also proud and sensitive. Therefore he couldn't pretend that he wasn't crippled, nor could he deceive himself that people were not repelled by his defect.

Only once in all the years of trying not to watch him, I saw him pretend to himself and others that he wasn't lame.

Coming home from school one day, I saw a dark car in our front yard. I rushed in to find a strange man and woman (Uncle Willie said later that they were schoolteachers from Little Rock) drinking Dr. Pepper in the cool of the Store. I sensed a wrongness around me, like an alarm clock that had gone off without being set.

I knew it couldn't be the strangers. Not frequently, but often enough, travelers pulled off the main road to buy tobacco or soft drinks in the only Negro store in Stamps. When I looked at Uncle Willie, I knew what was pulling my mind's coattails. He was standing erect behind the counter, not leaning forward or resting on the small shelf that had been built for him. Erect. His eyes seemed to hold me with a mixture of threats and appeal.

I dutifully greeted the strangers and roamed my eyes around for his walking stick. It was nowhere to be seen. He said, "Uh . . . this this . . . this . . . uh, my niece. She's . . . uh . . . just come from school." Then to the couple—"You know . . . how, uh, children are . . . th-th-these days . . . they play all d-d-day at school and c-c-can't wait to get home and pl-play some more."

The people smiled, very friendly.

He added, "Go on out and pl-play, Sister."

The lady laughed in a soft Arkansas voice and said, "Well, you know, Mr. Johnson, they say, you're only a child once. Have you children of your own?"

Uncle Willie looked at me with an impatience I hadn't seen in his face even when he took thirty minutes to loop the laces over his high-topped shoes. "I . . . I thought I told you to go . . . go outside and play."

Before I left I saw him lean back on the shelves of Garret Snuff, Prince Albert and Spark Plug chewing tobacco.

"No, ma'am . . . no children and no wife." He tried to laugh. "I have an old m-m-mother and my brother's t-two children to l-look after."

I didn't mind his using us to make himself look good. In fact, I would have pretended to be his daughter if he wanted me to. Not only did I not feel any loyalty to my own father, I figured that if I had been Uncle Willie's child I would have received much better treatment.

The couple left after a few minutes, and from the back of the house, I watched the red car scare chickens, raise dust and disappear toward Magnolia.

Uncle Willie was making his way down the long shadowed aisle between the shelves and the counter—hand over hand, like a man climbing out of a dream. I stayed quiet and watched him lurch from one side, bumping to the other, until he reached the coal-oil tank. He put his hand behind that dark recess and took his cane in the strong fist and shifted his weight on the wooden support. He thought he had pulled it off.

I'll never know why it was important to him that the couple (he said later that he'd never seen them before) would take a picture of a whole Mr. Johnson back to Little Rock.

He must have tired of being crippled, as prisoners tire of penitentiary bars and the guilty tire of blame. The high-topped shoes and the cane, his uncontrollable muscles and thick tongue, and the looks he suffered of either contempt or pity had simply worn him out, and for one afternoon, one part of an afternoon, he wanted no part of them.

I understood and felt closer to him at that moment than ever before or since.

Holt, Rinehart and Winston

Reading Assignment 3: "Uncle Willie"

Double-Entry Question Journal

Note: Some students find it easier to do the double-entry journal as they are reading. Others find the process more effective after they have finished reading the entire piece. You should experiment to find the method that works best for you.

In the left column, jot down at least five "What?" "Why?" or "How?" questions. Then in the right column, jot down some possible answers and responses. If further questions come up, jot them down also. One purpose of this exercise is to learn how to think critically, so you might end up with several answers. Go ahead, take a risk!

1.   1.

2.   2.

3.   3.

4.   4.

5.   5.

Brief Summary: _____

_____

_____

_____

_____

_____

Note: Please refer to the Appendix if you need help in writing a summary.

Holt, Rinehart and Winston

Reading Assignment 3: "Uncle Willie"

A Closer Look

1. What are some of Uncle Willie's physical characteristics? Make a list of the key descriptive words the author uses to describe Uncle Willie's physical appearance throughout the reading.

_____

_____

_____

2. Reread paragraph 2. What is the impression you get of the author's childhood view of Uncle Willie. Is it a positive or a negative one?

_____

_____

_____

_____

3. Reread paragraphs 6 through 19. What is Uncle Willie trying to do with the customers? Why?

_____

_____

_____

4. Overall, how does the author feel about Uncle Willie? Come up with at least three reasons in the story to support your opinion.

_____

_____

_____

CENTRAL IDEA (THEME)

What do you feel Maya Angelou is trying to teach us by her vivid and detailed description of Uncle Willie?

_____

_____

Holt, Rinehart and Winston

Writing Assignment 3: Describing a Person

Description tells what someone or something looks like. A descriptive paragraph relies on the senses (sight, sound, smell, taste, touch) to convey a dominant impression. However, if you are more interested in describing the inner qualities of a person, it might be more appropriate to arrange details in order of importance.

A Student Model

The following student paper is provided for you as a model. Its main purpose is to demonstrate how another student responded to this particular assignment. Instead of trying to imitate this paper, you should explore ways to develop your own thinking and individual style of writing.

Korrene Edwards
English 300: Dr. Kappen
Assignment 3: Describing a Person
Sept. 22, 1993

Age, Sun, and Shadows

When I first met her, I thought Mrs. Green was a mean old witch, but I was so wrong. I learned later it was just age and sun and shadows. One day my friends and I were playing tag in the neighborhood. We were wild back then. When we came upon the chain-fenced backyard of Mrs. Green, her appearance scared us. We called her "the witch." There she was, working in her garden. She was wearing an old-fashioned, flowered dress and gold sandals. Mrs. Green was a small, old lady with white hair, and she wore a thin, gray hair net over her head. That day she had on her gardening gloves, and for some reason that scared us. She looked like someone from an Alfred Hitchcock movie. Her body was bent over like a witch. Besides her looks, she was acting strange. In her left hand she had a scoop of fertilizer. Her right hand clawed at the soil with a small pointed rake. Worst of all was that look on her face. She was definitely a witch. She had to be a witch. Of course, I was all wrong. When I finally got to know her, I really looked into her face. I saw a beautiful, kind face. I could see she was trying to tell me something I did not understand at the time. I couldn't understand it. I was too young. Yet, every day Mrs. Green taught me about plants. She told me about faraway places. My first impression of her was so wrong. Now that I think about it, she taught me about people and hearts. I guess she taught me about life.

Holt, Rinehart and Winston

Writing Assignment 3: Describing a Person

Writing Task: Maya Angelou wrote about her Uncle Willie because she remembers him as a complex human being who held a special, unique place in her childhood. As a response to Angelou's essay, describe a significant person from your own past or present. Select a person whom you know well and whose personality, background, and interests you can describe in detail. Above all, reflect on this person's importance in your life.

Finding a Topic

Think about a person from your past who is important to you. List one or two persons who might make good topics. Remember, having a backup topic is a good idea in case your first choice does not work out.

Possible Topics:

_____

_____

Prewriting

Use any one of the invention strategies (clustering, listing, freewriting, or asking journalistic questions) to discover ideas about the topic that is most interesting to you. Jot down whatever comes to mind until you come up with enough ideas to write your description of a person.

Your Topic: _____

Writing the Topic Sentence

Tentative Topic Sentence (Central Idea):

_____

_____

Does your topic sentence name the person and state the personal significance of knowing that person? If not, revise it to make your purpose clear.

Holt, Rinehart and Winston

Writing Assignment 3: Describing a Person

TRANSITIONAL WORDS

In writing about a person, most likely you will find the opportunity to use "importance order" (least to most importance) to arrange his or her personality traits in a particular order. This arrangement will help you reveal the significance of this person in your life.

"Importance Order" Transitions

Before you begin writing your rough draft, you will need to be familiar with the use of transitions that signal "importance order."

Examples of "Importance Order" Transitions

first of all	to begin with	most important	moreover
next	also	for one thing	furthermore
besides that	in addition	best (or worst) of all	above all

EXERCISE

Look back at the student description by Korrine Edwards. As you read, underline any transitional words or phrases that signal importance order. List a few of her "importance" order transitions in the space below:

_____   _____

_____   _____

Note: Please refer to Reviewing the Basics if you need further help in using transitions that signal "importance" order.

Writing a Rough Draft

Now take your prewriting one step further by creating a rough draft. Selecting the best details, experiences, and reflections from your prewriting, write the draft of your paragraph. Begin with your topic sentence (or dominant impression) and write until you have described the person in detail so that your readers can see him or her as clearly as you can. Include important personal experiences. In your concluding sentence try to convey a mood or impression associated with the person you are describing.

Being Specific

Reread your rough draft of Writing Assignment 3, watching out for general words, phrases, and sentences. Underline the parts of your writing that might benefit from being more specific. Write a new

Holt, Rinehart and Winston

draft, changing the passages you have underlined into more interesting, exact, and detailed writing. Use names, numbers, colors, and examples wherever you can.

Revising

Go through your rough draft and revise it, applying what you have learned about importance order. When appropriate, add "importance order" transitions and linking transitions to help you describe your person more precisely so your reader can get to know that person.

Peer Editing

Using your revised copy, read your paper out loud to a peer editor. Likewise, listen as your peer editor reads his or her paper back to you. When both papers have been read aloud, exchange papers, using the Editing Sheets provided for this assignment to write helpful comments to each other. In some cases it might be more appropriate to exchange papers at the start and have each peer editor read silently before completing the Editing Sheet. Another option would be to use the Editing Sheet as a checklist for oral feedback. A final option would be for your instructor to create three- or four-member peer editing groups for collaborative learning.

Whatever option you choose, the Editing Sheet that follows will provide useful guidelines for this assignment. Only one set of Editing Sheets is provided, which is sufficient if you are using collaborative groups. However, if you are using two individual editors, you will need to obtain a photocopy of the Editing Sheet. Please check with your instructor.

Writing Assignment 3: Describing a Person

Editing Sheet (to be completed by peer editors)

Directions: Either pair up and exchange papers with another student in class, or form editing groups of three or four members. Papers may be read silently or aloud. Every paper requires at least two peer editors who will work collaboratively to complete an Editing Sheet. The completed Editing Sheet should be attached to the rough draft and returned to the writer for reference during the revision process.

Some peer editors may prefer to write comments directly on a student's rough draft, using the Editing Sheet as more of a checklist. Check with your instructor to see which method works best for your situation.

1. Has the writer selected a person to write about who is interesting and has had a significant impact on the writer's life? If the topic is weak, suggest prewriting strategies (clustering, listing, freewriting, or asking journalistic questions) to generate enough ideas for a new topic.

_____

_____

2. Draw a circle around the directing words in the topic sentence. If the directing words are missing, ask the writer, "So what? What is the personal significance of the person being described?" Suggest ways to make the topic sentence more effective, if necessary.

_____

_____

3. Draw a wavy line under words or phrases that would benefit from detailed examples. Has the writer included enough examples and anecdotes for a fully developed paragraph?

_____

_____

4. Does the writer use dialogue to make that person seem real? Point out places where direct quotes would bring life and energy to the paragraph.

_____

_____

5. Underline the transitional expressions that signal "importance" order. Are the sentences arranged in order of importance, starting with the least significant point about the person and ending with the most significant point? Offer suggestions if the order is unclear.

_____

_____

Holt, Rinehart and Winston

6. Does the writer also use "linking" transitions that clearly show the relationship between ideas in a sentence? Where would you add more? Where would you omit some?

_____

_____

7. Does the concluding sentence wrap up the paragraph effectively or leave a lasting impression on you? What ideas do you have about writing a more effective conclusion?

_____

_____

8. Does the title intrigue you and really catch your attention as a reader? Think of recent movie titles. What suggestions do you have for a more interesting, creative title?

_____

9. What do you think is the most powerful part of this paper? Try to be as specific as possible.

_____

_____

Peer Editors' Initials: ____ ____ ____ ____ (This verifies the paper is ready for a Revised Copy.)

Submitting the Final Copy

Once you have had your paper edited, you should revise your paper once again. Remember that experienced writers constantly revise their work to make sure it communicates exactly what they meant to say. Before you write the final copy of your paper, your instructor or tutor may want to skim over your revised draft. Then write your final copy in ink on notebook paper or type it on a typewriter or a computer. Make sure you follow the rules of manuscript form located in the Appendix.

After writing the final copy of your paper, exchange it with other members of your editing group to proofread for spelling, punctuation, and grammar errors. Ask your peer editors to initial your final copy to indicate that it has been through the final editing process. When your edited paper is returned to you, make the final corrections and submit your final copy along with your rough draft and completed Editing Sheet. Stapling the whole packet together will allow your instructor to check your progress during each stage of the writing process.

2

The Family: Our Own Little World

Chapter 2 offers you readings that focus on the family. In these readings, you will discover how others have used writing to understand the complex issues and feelings generated by being part of a family. These readings will help you to think about your own family (or families with which you have had relationships) and the experiences you have had together. The ideas you get by reading and responding to these selections will serve as springboards for you to examine your concerns about the family as a unit and help prepare you for the writing assignments, which are based on your own experience as well as on the experience of others.

In this chapter you will continue to practice the writing process, including the various invention strategies and revision techniques covered in the previous chapter. You will also make a transition from writing paragraphs to writing essays.

Reading Assignment 4: Battling Illegitimacy: Some Words against the Darkness by Greg Sarris

Writing Assignment 4: Cause/Effect Essay

Reading Assignment 5: "Migratory Birds" by Odilia Galván Rodríguez

Writing Assignment 5: Comparison/Contrast Essay

Reading Assignment 6: "Reparation Candy" by Maxine Hong Kingston

Writing Assignment 6: Argument Essay

Holt, Rinehart and Winston

Reading Assignment 4: "Battling Illegitimacy: Some Words against the Darkness"

Prereading

In "Battling Illegitimacy: Some Words against the Darkness," Greg Sarris attempts to fill in the branches of his family tree. His notions of "family" are influenced by the fact that his unmarried mother, who was white, gave him up for adoption at birth, leaving him to grow up without knowing who his father was. When he finally discovers the name of his father, however, he finds that knowing about his mixed heritage is not enough to satisfy the deeper questions of his identity. Having "blue eyes and fair skin" only adds to his confusion because he might also be part Native American, Filipino, and Mexican.

How old were you when you first became aware that your own family heritage might be different from that of your friends or classmates? Did you have pictures in your head about what a "traditional" family should look like? Who or what shaped your attitudes about your ancestry or the ancestry of others?

Battling Illegitimacy: Some Words against the Darkness
by Greg Sarris

I have heard that someone said to American Indian writer Louise Erdrich, "You don't look Indian." It was at a reading she gave, or perhaps when she received an award of some kind for her writing. Undoubtedly, whoever said this noted Erdrich's very white skin, her green eyes and her red hair. She retorted, "Gee, you don't look rude."

You don't look Indian.

How often I too have heard that. But unlike Erdrich, I never returned the insult, or challenged my interlocutors. Not with words anyway. I arranged the facts of my life to fit others' conceptions of what it is to be Indian. I used others' words, others' definitions. That way, if I didn't look Indian, I might still be Indian.

Well, I don't know if I am Indian, I said, or if I am, how much. I was adopted. I know my mother was white Jewish, German, Irish. I was illegitimate. Father unknown. It was back in the fifties when having a baby without being married was shameful. My mother uttered something on the delivery table about the father being Spanish. Mexican maybe. Anyway, I was given up and adopted, which is how I got a name. For awhile things went well. Then they didn't. I found myself with other families, mostly on small ranches where I milked cows and worked with horses. I met a lot of Indians—Pomo Indians—and was taken in by one of the families. I learned bits and pieces of two Pomo languages. So if you ask, I call myself Pomo. But I don't know . . .

Holt, Rinehart and Winston

My mother isn't around to ask. After she had me, she needed blood. The hospital gave her the wrong type and it killed her.

The story always went something like that. It is true, all of it, but arranged so that people might see how I fit. The last lines—about my mother—awe people and cause them to forget, or to be momentarily distracted, from their original concern about my not looking Indian. And I am illegitimate. That explains any crossing of borders, anything beyond the confines of definition. That is how I fit.

Last year I found my father. Well, I found out his name—Emilio. My mother's younger brother, my uncle, whom I met recently, remembered taking notes from his sister to a "big Hawaiian type" on the football field. "I would go after school while the team was practicing," my uncle said. "The dude was big, dark. They called him Meatloaf. I think his name though was Emilio. Try Emilio."

To have a name, even a nickname, seemed unfathomable. To be thirty-six years old and for the first time to have a lead about a father somehow frightened me. You imagine all your life; you find ways to account for that which is missing, you tell stories, and now all that is leveled by a name.

In Laguna Beach I contacted the high school librarian and made arrangements to look through old yearbooks. It was just after a conference there in Southern California, where I had finished delivering a paper on American Indian education. I found my mother immediately, and while I was staring for the first time at an adult picture of my mother, a friend who was with me scanned other yearbooks for an Emilio. Already we knew by looking at the rows and rows of white faces, there wouldn't be too many Emilios. I was still gazing at the picture of my mother when my friend jumped. "Look," she said. She was tilting the book, pointing to a name. But already, even as I looked, a dark face caught my attention, and it was a face I saw myself in. Without a doubt. Darker, yes. But me nonetheless.

I interviewed several of my mother's and father's classmates. It was my mother's friends who verified what I suspected. Emilio Hilario was my father. They also told me that he had died, that I missed him by about five years.

I had to find out from others what he couldn't tell me. I wanted to know about his life. Did he have a family? What was his ethnicity? Luckily I obtained the names of several relatives, including a half-brother and a grandfather. People were quick about that, much more so than about the ethnicity question. They often circumvented the question by telling stories about my father's athletic prowess and about how popular he was. A few, however, were more candid. His father, my grandfather, is Filipino. "A short Filipino man," they said. "Your father got his height from his mother. She was fairer." Some people said my grandmother was Spanish, others said she was Mexican or Indian. Even within the family, there is discrepancy about her ethnicity. Her mother was definitely Indian, however. Coast Miwok. from Tomales Bay just north of San Francisco, and just south of Santa Rosa, where I grew up. Her name was Rienette.

Holt, Rinehart and Winston

During the time my grandmother was growing up, probably when her mother— Rienette—was growing up too, even until quite recently, when it became popular to be Indian, Indians in California sometimes claimed they were Spanish. And for good reason. The prejudice against Indians was intolerable, and often only remnants of tribes, or even families, remained to face the hatred and discrimination. My grandmother spoke Spanish. Her sister, Juanita, married a Mexican and her children's children are proud Chicanos living in East Los Angeles. Rienette's first husband, my grandmother and her sister's father, was probably part Mexican or Portugues—I'm not sure.

The story is far from complete. But how much Indian I am by blood is not the question whose answer concerns me now. Oh, I qualify for certain grants, and that is important. But knowing about my blood heritage will not change my complexion any more than it will my experience.

In school I was called the white beaner. This was not because some of my friends happened to be Mexican, but because the white population had little sense of the local Indians. Anyone with dark hair and skin was thought to be Mexican. A counselor once called me in and asked if my family knew I went around with Mexicans. "Yes," I said. "They're used to it." At the time, I was staying with an Indian family—the McKays—and Mrs. McKay was a mother to me. But I said nothing more then. I never informed the counselor that most of my friends, the people she was referring to, were Indian-Pomo Indian. Kashaya Pomo Indian. Sulfur Bank Pomo Indian. Coyote Valley Pomo Indian. Yokaya Pomo Indian. Point Arena Pomo Indian. Bodega Bay Miwok Indian. Tomales Bay Miwok Indian. And never mind that names such as Smith and Pinola are not Spanish (or Mexican) names.

As I think back, I said nothing more to the counselor not because I didn't want to cause trouble (I did plenty of that), but because, like most other kids, I never really knew a way to tamper with how the authorities—counselors, teachers, social workers, police-categorized us. We talked about our ethnicity amongst ourselves, often speculating who was more or less this or that. So many of us are mixed with other groups— white, Mexican, Spanish, Portuguese, Filipino. I know of an Indian family who is half Mexican and they identify themselves as Mexicans. In another family of the same admixture just the opposite is true. Yet for most of the larger white community, we were Mexican, or something.

And here I am with blue eyes and fair skin. If I was a white beaner, I was, more generally, a kid from the wrong side of the tracks. Hood. Greaser. Low Brow. Santa Rosa was a much smaller town then, the lines more clearly drawn between the haves and the have-nots, the non-colored and the colored. Suburban sprawl was just beginning; there was still the old downtown with its stone library and old Romancolumned courthouse. On the fringes of town lived the poorer folk. The civil rights movement had not yet engendered the ethnic pride typical of the late sixties and early seventies.

I remember the two guys who taught me to box, Manual and Robert. They said they were Portuguese, Robert part Indian. People whispered that they were black. I didn't

Holt, Rinehart and Winston

care. They picked me out, taught me to box. That was when I was fourteen. By the time I was sixteen, I beat heads everywhere and every time I could. I looked for fights and felt free somehow in the fight. I say I looked for, fights, but really, as I think about it, fights seemed to find me. People said things, they didn't like me, they invaded my space. I had reason. So I fought. And afterwards I was somebody. Manny said I had a chip on my shoulder, which is an asset for a good fighter. "Hate in your eyes, brother," he told me. "You got hate in your eyes. 91)

I heard a lot of "Indian" stories too. We used to call them old-time stories, those about Coyote and the creation. Then there were the spook stories about spook men and women and evil doings. I knew of a spook man, an old guy who would be sitting on his family's front porch one minute and then five minutes later, just as you were driving uptown, there he'd be sitting on the old courthouse steps. The woman whose son I spent so much time with was an Indian doctor. She healed the sick with songs and prayer; she sucked pains from people's bodies. These are the things my professors and colleagues wanted to hear about.

I was different here too. I read books, which had something to do with my getting into college. But when I started reading seriously—about the middle of my junior year in high school—I used what I read to explain the world; I never engaged my experience to inform what I was reading. Again, I was editing my experience, and, not so ironically, I found meaning that way. And, not so ironically, the more I read the more I became separated from the world of my friends and what I had lived. So in college when I found people interested in my Indian experience as it related to issues of ecology, personal empowerment, and other worldviews, I complied and told them what I "knew" of these things. In essence I shaped what I knew to fit the books and read the books to shape what I knew. The woman who was a mother to me came off as Castaneda's Don Juan. Think of the "separate reality" of her dream world, never mind what I remember about her—the long hours in the apple cannery, her tired face, her clothes smelling of rotten apples.

Now, as I sort through things, I am beginning to understand why I hated myself and those people at the university; how by sculpting my experience to their interests, I denied so much of my life, including the anger and self-hatred that seeps up from such denial. I wanted to strike back, beat the hell out of them; I imagined them angering me in some way I could recognize—maybe an insult, a push or shove—so that I could hurt them. Other times I just wanted them to be somewhere, perhaps outside the classroom, on a street, in a bar, where they came suddenly upon me and saw me fighting, pummelling somebody. Anger is like a cork in water. Push it down, push it down, and still it keeps coming to the surface.

Describing her life experience in a short autobiographical piece entitled "The Autobiography of a Confluence," Paula Gunn Allen says, "Fences would have been hard to place without leaving something out . . . Essentially, my life,

like my work, is a journey-in-between, a road." Poet Wendy Rose writes about how she went to the Highland Games in Fresno to search for her Scottish roots: "It may

Holt, Rinehart and Winston

have looked funny to all those Scots to see an Indian [Rose] looking for a booth with her clan's name on it." She adds: "The colonizer and the colonized meet in my blood. It is so much more complex than just white and Indian. I will pray about this, too." These American Indian writers, just as so many other ethnic minority American writers, are attempting to mediate the cultural variables that constitute their experience as Americans. They are attempting to redefine their experience based on the experience itself and not in terms of others' notions of that experience.

During the late sixties and early seventies, an odd reversal of affairs took place. Where some Indian people once denied, or at least kept quiet their Indian heritage, they suddenly began denying that part which is white, Spanish, or whatever. The point here is that in the name of ethnic pride we begin to make illegitimate so much of what we are, and have been, about. We deny aspects of our history and experience that could enrich any understanding of what it means to be an American Indian in time, in history, and not just as some relic from a prelapserian past, as the dominant culture so often likes to see us. We in fact become oppressor-like; we internalize the oppression we have felt, and, ironically, using others' definitions, or even those created by ourselves, decide who is Indian and who is not. We perpetuate illegitimacy in our ranks.

But the danger isn't just for ourselves here. Ultimately, by accepting or creating certain definitions by which we judge our own experiences, we allow others a definition by which we can be judged by them. Criteria that render certain kinds of experience illegitimate enable people to escape the broader, human issues in life as it is lived. They allow the phonies a way to dress up, showing how they are Indian, and they cheat the rest of us of a true and fully human and historical cultural identity. What we need are words—stories, poems, histories, biographies—that qualify and challenge given definitions, that allow all of us as students and teachers, Indians and non-Indians, the opportunity to examine our own framing devices in order that we might be able to see and consider the possibility of seeing beyond those frames. We need to make visible the heretofore illegitimate so that we might consider human experience in the broadest sense possible.

My father was a local hero, they say. He excelled in all sports, was voted junior class president, and served as president of the local Hi-Y. He was charming, outgoing, women loved him. But there was the other side, the black-out drinking and violence. Like a Jeckyl and Hyde, people told me. He would turn on a dime, get nasty and mean. He'd rip into people. Kick ass. You could see it coming in his eyes.

When my grandfather brought his family from East Los Angeles to Laguna Beach, there was only one other minority family in town—a black family. Grandpa worked as a cook at Victor Hugo's, a glamorous waterfront restaurant. He settled his family in a small house in "the canyon," where the black family and season migrant families lived at the time, and where Grandpa still lives today. While my father was exalted locally as an athlete, he was constantly reminded of his color and class. Behind his back, people referred to him as a "nigger." To his face, the fathers of girls he dated told him: "Go away. We aren't hiring any gardeners."

Holt, Rinehart and Winston

The Family: Our Own Little World   55

I don't need to probe far here to get the picture. Illegitimacy in any form cuts a wide swath. Those of us affected by it react in a number of ways. Our histories, if they are presented and examined honestly, tell the stories. For my father and me it was, among other things, violence. Unable to tell his story, unable to fill in those chasms between his acceptance and rejection by the world around him, my father fought, each blow a strike against the vast and imposing darkness. He became a professional boxer; in the Navy he was undefeated, and after he sparred with Floyd Patterson. He died at 52, three weeks before his fifty-third birthday, just five years before his first son would find his picture in a yearbook. He died of a massive heart attack, precipitated by years of chronic alcoholism.

Now sometimes I wonder at my being Filipino, for I am as much Filipino by one definition, that is by blood, as I am anything by that same definition. Grandpa came from a small village on the island of Panay in the South Central Philippines. He tells me I have second cousins who have never worn shoes and speak only the Bisian dialect of that island. Yet, if I am Filipino, I am a Filipino separated from my culture and to backtrack, or go back, to that culture, I must carry my life with me, as it has been lived-in Santa Rosa with Pomo Indians and all others, and in the various cities and universities where I have lived and worked.

"You have quite a legacy in that man," a friend of my father's said to me. "He was one hell of a guy."

Yes, I thought to myself, a legacy. Fitting in by not fitting in. Repression. Violence. Walls of oppressive darkness. The urge now, the struggle, the very need to talk about the spaces, to word the darkness.

Holt, Rinehart and Winston

Reading Assignment 4: "Battling Darkness: Some Words against the Darkness"

Double-Entry Question Journal

Note: Some students find it easier to do the double-entry journal as they are reading. Others find the process more effective after they have finished reading the entire piece. You should experiment to find the method that works best for you.

In the left column, jot down at least five "What?" "Why?" or "How?" questions. Then in the right column, jot down some possible answers and responses. If further questions come up, jot them down also. One purpose of this exercise is to learn how to think critically, so you might end up with several answers or possibilities. Go ahead, take a risk!

1.   1.

2.   2.

3.   3.

4.   4.

5.   5.

Brief Summary: _____

_____

_____

_____

_____

Note: Please refer to the Appendix if you need help in writing a summary.

Holt, Rinehart and Winston

Reading Assignment 4: "Battling Darkness: Some Words against the Darkness"

A Closer Look

1. How does the Sarris feel about people telling him, "You don't look Indian"?

_____

_____

_____

2. Sarris says he was "frightened" when he finally found his father (that is, the name of his father) even though he had been searching for him for years. What was it that frightened him?

_____

_____

_____

3. All through school Sarris has difficulty fitting in with one group or another. How would you explain his feelings of anger?

_____

_____

4. At the end of the essay, Sarris ponders the legacy of his mixed ancestry as well as his illegitimacy. Explain whether you think he considers his legacy to be a strength or a weakness.

_____

_____

_____

CENTRAL IDEA (THEME)

What do you think the author wants us to know about his family and his struggle for self-identity and legitimacy? What is the purpose of the essay?

_____

_____

_____

Holt, Rinehart and Winston

Writing Assignment 4: Cause/Effect Essay

A cause and effect paper examines why events occur and what happens as a result. This type of paper relies heavily on the use of transitional words like *consequently* and *as a result* because the issues are often complex. A cause and effect paper will answer questions such as, *"Why did it happen? What were the causes? What are its effects?"*

PARAGRAPH TO ESSAY

The Essay

In Writing Assignments 1 through 3, you have been asked to write paragraphs, each one with a topic sentence, supporting ideas, detailed examples, and an effective conclusion. Being able to write a fully developed paragraph is important, but most of the writing you will do for college will be longer and more fully developed than a paragraph. In fact, the essay is the most common format for the writing required in nearly all of your academic courses. Although both the paragraph and the essay are held together by one central idea, the main difference is that the essay is broader in scope.

The essay is a multiparagraph piece of writing with the following parts:

- An introductory paragraph that usually ends with the thesis statement (central idea)
- Two or more body paragraphs that support the thesis statement and usually begin with a topic sentence (main idea). The number of body paragraphs is determined by the type of essay being written. Each body paragraph contains specific details and examples that develop the central idea of the essay.
- A concluding paragraph that often restates the central idea

For Writing Assignment 4 you will be asked to write an essay—a group of paragraphs on a central idea. In writing an essay, you will follow the same writing process you used in writing a paragraph. That is, you will go through the same stages of prewriting, organizing, drafting, revising, and editing. Also, most of the paragraphs in your essay will still need a topic sentence, supporting ideas, examples, and a concluding sentence.

Holt, Rinehart and Winston

As shown in the following model, all of the paragraphs in an essay focus on the central idea, otherwise known as the thesis statement.

A Cause/Effect Model
(Several Causes Leading to an Overall Effect)

Introductory Paragraph *(hook)*
Ends with a thesis statement (central idea of the essay)

Body Paragraph *(first cause)*
Begins with a topic sentence (main idea of the paragraph)
(follows with specific details and examples)

Body Paragraph *(second cause)*
Begins with a topic sentence (main idea of the paragraph)
(follows with specific details and examples)

Body Paragraph *(third cause)*
Begins with a topic sentence (main idea of the paragraph)
(follows with specific details and examples)

Concluding Paragraph
Reiterates the overall effect and wraps up all the ideas

Holt, Rinehart and Winston

A Student Model

The following essay was written by a college English student. Its purpose is to show you how another student, like yourself, responded to this writing assignment. Remember to explore ways to develop your own thinking and individual style of writing.

Justine Boyer
English 300: Mr. Isaacson
Assignment 4: Cause/Effect Essay
March 14, 1997

Daddy's Little Girl

One of my earliest memories is being forced to play follow-the-leader with my three brothers. Most times I would find myself having to do something scary, like having to climb onto the roof of our house from a nearby tree branch. I would beg my brothers to let me go back down, but they would only laugh at me. Sometimes they would shake the branch even harder. At first I used to cry a lot, but it never helped. My brothers would imitate me: "Wah, wah, wah." Now when I think about it, I realize that being the only girl in the family turned me into the tough person that I am today.

The way my brothers treated me was one cause of how I turned out. Being the only daughter, I guess I was Daddy's little girl. All the toys were for me only, and I did not have to share them with anyone. I loved my collection of china dolls with their porcelain faces and silk dresses. My favorite doll had a red silk fan with a shiny gold tassel. I can't remember my father ever buying my brothers anything. Probably because of this, they were really jealous of me. Consequently, whenever they could, they would pick on me and hide my dolls. Of course, they never did it when my father was around. Therefore, I was forced to defend myself because if I did not fight back, I would get hurt.

Another cause of my strong personality was the way my grandmother treated me. When I was ten years old, my parents decided to set up a shoe factory, which took about a year to build. During that time I had to live with my grandmother, a woman who had raised eight children all by herself. My grandfather was never around to protect his family, so my grandmother had to do it. Instead of providing me with love andsecurity, she taught me how to run a household without a man around. I was starting to realize that I was no longer anyone's little girl.

The main cause of my toughness, however, was moving out on my own when I was only sixteen. This was very unusual for a girl, especially a Chinese girl. In fact, Chinese girls hardly ever leave home until they are married. Yet, at the time I had no other choice. I wanted to attend night school, and where we lived it was too dangerous for a girl to travel at night for such a long distance. My father tried to discourage me, but I was too stubborn. I thought I was old enough to take care of myself without my family's protection. The truth is I barely survived. I wanted so badly to go home to my family, but I would think of my brothers. I could still hear their teasing voices, "Wah, wah, wah." How could I go back and show them how weak I really was? Eventually, I learned how to handle my problems, and every day I became a stronger person.

As a result of my early experiences in life, I turned out to be the strong person that I am today. Now I sometimes think that even my brothers are proud of me. Because of their early influence, I can stand on my own instead of being "Daddy's little girl" for the rest of my life.

Holt, Rinehart and Winston

AN OPTIONAL CAUSE/EFFECT MODEL
(One Cause Resulting in Several Effects)

Introductory Paragraph *(hook)* Ends with a thesis statement (central idea of the essay)

Body Paragraph *(cause)* Begins with a topic sentence (main idea of the paragraph) (follows with specific details and examples)

Body Paragraph *(first effect)* Begins with a topic sentence (main idea of the paragraph) (follows with specific details and examples)

Body Paragraph *(second effect)* Begins with a topic sentence (main idea of the paragraph) (follows with specific details and examples)

Body Paragraph *(third effect)* Begins with a topic sentence (main idea of the paragraph) (follows with specific details and examples)

Concluding Paragraph Reiterates the thesis statement and wraps up all the ideas

Holt, Rinehart and Winston

Writing Assignment 4: Cause/Effect Essay

Writing Task: Sandra Cisneros's short story, "Mexican Movies," creates a portrait of a happy, carefree family experience, one filled with affection, fun, and security. Write an essay that examines several causes in your life (either positive or negative) and show how these causes have resulted in an overall effect on your behavior. As an option, you might prefer to examine a singular cause and show how it affected your life in several different areas.

Finding a Topic

As a response to the story, think of your own family experience or those of other families that you know well. What do you feel are the key elements that might cause a family member to be either happy or someone with real problems? Think about the influences on your life and personality. List one or two major issues that might make good topics. Having a backup topic is a good idea in case your first choice does not work out.

Possible Topics:

_____

_____

PREWRITING

Use any invention strategy (clustering, listing, freewriting, or asking journalistic questions) to discover ideas about the topic that is most interesting to you. Jot down whatever comes to mind until you come up with enough ideas to write your cause and effect essay.

Your Topic: _____

Holt, Rinehart and Winston

THE THESIS STATEMENT

The thesis statement in an essay has the same function as the topic sentence in a paragraph. A thesis statement expresses the central idea that the essay, as a whole, will explore in each of its supporting paragraphs.

Examples of Thesis Statements

Being the only girl in my family turned me into the tough person that I am today.

My mother's influence on me molded me into a shy woman who is afraid of her own shadow.

Growing up without fear of failure had a positive effect in every area of my life.

The thesis statement is the most important sentence in your essay because it is the central idea that holds all of the supporting paragraphs in the entire essay together. Thus, the ideas expressed in each of the topic sentences in the body of the essay must be closely related to the thesis statement.

Finally, like the topic sentence in a paragraph, the thesis is generally located near the beginning of your essay. It is often placed at the end of an introductory paragraph that is designed to get your reader's attention.

Writing the Thesis Statement

Make sure your thesis statement communicates the central idea of your essay and forecasts the way your paper will be developed.

Tentative Thesis Statement (Central Idea):

_____

_____

_____

Does your thesis statement hint at cause and effect (what happened and why it happened)?

Note: Please refer to Reviewing the Basics if you need further help in writing a thesis statement.

Holt, Rinehart and Winston

Writing Assignment 4: Cause/Effect

TRANSITIONAL WORDS

Before you begin writing your rough draft, you will need to be familiar with the use of transitions that signal cause/effect relationships.

Examples of "Cause/Effect" Transitions

one cause	the first cause	one effect	one of the effects
another cause	also	a second effect	another effect
furthermore	yet another cause	a third effect	besides that
the main cause	the biggest cause	the most significant effect	the worst effect
as a result	therefore	consequently	thus

EXERCISE

Look back at the student model, "Daddy's Little Girl," by Justine Boyer. Notice that the transitions she uses signal a "cause/effect" order. Circle any transitional words or phrases that indicate cause or effect. List a few of her "cause" or "effect" transitions in the space below:

_____   _____

_____   _____

Note: Please refer to Reviewing the Basics if you need further help in using transitions that signal order.

Writing a Rough Draft

Now take your prewriting one step further by creating a rough draft. Begin with an introductory paragraph that ends with a thesis statement. Then draft the body paragraphs, making sure that each one begins with a topic sentence. Select the best ideas from your prewriting, and write until you have thoroughly developed your ideas. Add "cause and effect" transitions to make sure your reader is clear about the causal order. For your conclusion, explain the result of your cause/effect analysis. (In the event that you have addressed several causes in the body of your essay, your final body paragraph might also function as your concluding paragraph, as shown in the student model.)

Being Specific

A piece of writing is not really finished until it contains specific examples and vivid details that make it complete and whole. Your first draft may seem complete to you, but often it is necessary to revise your writing to provide your readers with additional information in the form of specific examples and vivid, descriptive, exact details.

For example, in Justine Boyer's essay, "Daddy's Little Girl," she gives us a detailed description of her dolls, adding that her favorite one had a "red silk fan with a shiny gold tassel." Details like these breathe life into her writing.

Reread your rough draft of Writing Assignment 4, watching out for general words, phrases, and sentences. Underline the parts of your writing that might benefit from being more specific. Write a new draft, changing the passages you have underlined into more interesting, exact, and detailed writing. Use specific examples wherever you can.

Remember that experienced writers constantly revise their work to make sure it communicates exactly what they want it to say.

The Concluding Paragraph

A concluding paragraph should provide a graceful exit for your reader and bring closure to the essay. It should also reinforce the central idea of the essay. In her cause and effect essay, "Daddy's Little Girl," Justine Boyer concludes by reminding us of the main idea and by making a prediction. She is careful not to introduce a new topic. Instead, she stays focused and emphasizes the causal nature of the assignment. Finally, she avoids elementary phrasing such as, "In conclusion," ending with a memorable comment about her family:

> As a result of my early experiences in life, I turned out to be the strong person that I am today. Now I sometimes think that even my brothers are proud of me. Because of their early influence, I can stand on my own instead of being "Daddy's little girl" for the rest of my life.

Revising

Revision is an ongoing process in which you delete words, add phrases, and rearrange sentences to make your meaning clear to your reader. Thus, it may occur at any point in the writing process. After you have written your rough draft, reread it carefully, being as objective as possible. Underline all words, phrases, or sentences that could benefit from more specifics, details, and examples.

Peer Editing

Using your revised copy, read your paper out loud to a peer editor. Likewise, listen as your peer editor reads his or her paper back to you. When both papers have been read aloud, exchange papers, using the Editing Sheets provided for this assignment to write helpful comments to each other. In some cases it might be more appropriate to exchange papers at the start and have each peer editor read silently before completing the Editing Sheet. Another option would be to use the Editing Sheet as checklist for oral feedback. A final option would be for your instructor to create peer editing groups of three or four members for collaborative learning.

Whatever option you use, the editing sheet that follows will provide useful guidelines for this assignment. Only one set of Editing Sheets is provided, which is sufficient if you are using collaborative groups. However, if you are using two individual editors, you will need to obtain a photocopy of the Editing Sheet. Please check with your instructor.

Holt, Rinehart and Winston

Writing Assignment 4: Cause/Effect (Paragraph to Essay)

Editing Sheet (to be completed by peer editors)

Directions: Either pair up and exchange papers with another student in class, or form editing groups of three or four members. Papers can be read silently or aloud. Every paper requires at least two peer editors who will work collaboratively to complete an Editing Sheet. The completed Editing Sheets should be attached to the rough draft and returned to the writer for reference during the revision process.

Some peer editors may prefer to write comments directly on a student's rough draft, using the Editing Sheet as more of a checklist. Check with your instructor to see which method works best for your situation.

1. Has the writer selected a topic that is interesting, sufficiently narrowed, and appropriate for a cause and effect essay? If the topic is weak, suggest prewriting strategies (clustering, listing, freewriting, or asking journalistic questions) to generate enough ideas for a new topic.

_____

_____

2. Does the introductory paragraph "hook" you or seem powerful and engaging? If not, offer suggestions.

_____

_____

3. Draw a double line under the thesis statement. If it is missing, ask the writer, "So what? What is the point of this essay?" Suggest ways to make the thesis statement more effective, if necessary.

_____

_____

4. Draw a circle around the directing words in the topic sentences. Does each body paragraph have a clear topic sentence that points out the main idea of the paragraph?

_____

_____

Holt, Rinehart and Winston

5. Draw a wavy line under words or phrases that would benefit from detailed examples. Has the writer included enough examples and specific details and anecdotes (interesting little stories with a point) in each body paragraph for a fully developed essay?

_____

_____

6. Is dialogue used? If not, would the use of dialogue (direct quotations) make this essay more realistic and interesting? If dialogue is used, does it express a particular emotion? If necessary, make suggestions for improvement.

_____

_____

7. Underline the transitional expressions that signal "cause and effect" order. Does the essay seem well organized? Is the overall order of the essay clearly signaled by the use of transitions that show cause and effect? Offer suggestions.

_____

_____

8. Does the writer also use appropriate "linking" transitions that show the relationship between ideas in a sentence? Where would you add more? Where would you omit some?

_____

_____

9. Does the concluding paragraph wrap up the essay effectively or leave a lasting impression on you? What ideas do you have about writing a more effective conclusion?

_____

_____

10. Does the title intrigue you and really catch your attention as a reader? Think of recent movie titles. What suggestions do you have for a more interesting, creative title?

_____

11. What is the most powerful part of this essay? Be as specific as possible.

_____

_____

Peer Editors' Initials: ____ ____ ____ ____ (This verifies that the paper is ready for a Revised Copy.)

Holt, Rinehart and Winston

Submitting Your Final Copy

Once you have had your paper edited, you should revise your paper once again. Remember that experienced writers constantly revise their work to make sure it communicates exactly what they meant to say. Before you write the final copy of your paper, your instructor or tutor may want to skim over your revised draft. Then write your final copy in ink on notebook paper or type it on a typewriter or a computer. Make sure you follow the rules of manuscript form located in the Appendix.

After writing the final copy of your paper, exchange it with other members of your editing group to check for spelling, punctuation, and grammar errors. Ask your peer editors to initial your final copy to indicate that it has been through the final editing process. When your edited paper is returned to you, make the final corrections and submit your final copy along with your rough draft and any Editing Sheets. Stapling the whole packet together will allow your instructor to check your progress during each stage of the writing process.

Reading Assignment 5: "Migratory Birds" by Odilia Galván Rodríguez

Prereading

As we observe and learn about the lifestyles of those around us, we begin to learn how diverse our experiences and upbringings have been. In the poem, "Migratory Birds," Odilia Galván Rodríguez describes two sharply contrasting lifestyles.

As you read the poem, reflect on your own upbringing: have you and/or your family moved frequently from one place to another, or have you always lived in the same place? Which experience do you think is better? In what ways has your own experience shaped your present attitudes?

Migratory Birds
Odilia Galván Rodríguez

to Antonia

you were born
to gypsies
though you didn't
want to be
every spring
when orange blossom's
perfume
filled the air
your world was packed
into a few bundles
then your
family was off
living in tents
trailers
dirt floor shacks

you were born
to nomads
though you didn't
want to be
longed to live
with the
settled and the straight
work in the
five-and-dime
go to school

play tennis
and every time
you found a friend
it was time to go
another town
another round
in a world
that made you
dizzy

you were born
to migrants
though you didn't
want to be
from Texas to Illinois
living a blur
out a car window
roads endless
as fields of crops
to be picked by the piece
never making enough
to eat
let alone for the trip back
home
pleading for the
traveling to stop

words in the wind
wooshing by ears
of the gypsy king

you were born
to wanderers
though you didn't
want to be
when you got
the chance
you planted
yourself
deep
in concrete
and steel
to make sure
you or your
offspring
wouldn't
branch out
too far
from home
you were
settled
for
ever

I was born
to a life of never change
though I didn't
want to be
same familiar streets
same people
same stories
year after year
until one sweltering
Chicago summer night
the moon full
color of sun
reflecting off
field of green
and the sweet scent
of lilacs from
our backyard
helped me sprout wings
so I could fly away.

Reading Assignment 5: "Migratory Birds" by Odilia Galván Rodríguez

Double-Entry Question Journal

Note: Some students find it easier to do the double-entry journal as they are reading; others find the process more effective after they have finished reading the entire piece. Please experiment to find the method that works best for you.

In the left column, jot down at least five "What?" "Why?" or "How?" questions. Then in the right column, jot down some possible answers and responses. If further questions come up, jot them down also. One purpose of this exercise is to learn how to think critically, so you might end up with several answers or possibilities. Go ahead, take a risk!

1.	1.
2.	2.
3.	3.
4.	4.
5.	5.

Brief Summary: _____

_____

_____

_____

_____

Note: Please refer to the Appendix if you need help in writing a summary.

Holt, Rinehart and Winston

Reading Assignment 5: "Migratory Birds"
by Odilia Galván Rodríguez

A Closer Look

1. What are some of the characteristics of the migratory lifestyle described in the poem? Make a list below of as many characteristics of that lifestyle as you can find in the poem.

_____

_____

_____

2. Reread stanza four. What was the effect of years of the migratory lifestyle on the poet's friend (Antonia)? How did it help to form her attitudes and behavior?

_____

_____

_____

3. Reread the last stanza. In it the poet defines her own family experience and lifestyle: what were they?

_____

_____

_____

4. In the last stanza, the poet says that something "helped her sprout wings and fly away." What makes her feel this way, and why do you think she wants to "fly away"?

_____

_____

_____

CENTRAL IDEA (THEME)

What do you feel Rodríguez is trying to teach us by showing us a sharp contrast between two distinct family lifestyles in her poem, "Migratory Birds"?

_____

_____

Holt, Rinehart and Winston

Writing Assignment 5: Comparison/Contrast Essay

A *comparison and contrast* paper explores how two things are alike or different. In general, contrasts are more prevalent than comparisons. Two cars, for example, can be contrasted to find out which one is the best buy, or two musical groups can be contrasted to see which gives the best live performance. This type of paper relies heavily on the use of transitional words like "in contrast" or "on the other hand" in its paragraphs when shifting from the discussion of one item to the other. Also, in the overall order, the paragraphs in the essay are generally arranged in importance order. A comparison and contrast assignment will answer questions such as *In what basic ways do these two things differ? Which one is preferable? Why is one better than the other?*

A Student Model

The following essay was written by a college English student. Its purpose is to show you how another student, like yourself, responded to this writing assignment. Remember to try to explore ways to develop your own thinking and individual style of writing.

Cuc Thi Nguyen
English 301: Ms. Hawkins
Assignment 5: Comparison/Contrast Essay
March 15, 1997

Two Cultures

Lately my husband and I have been so troubled in our home. It is our daughter, Kim, who makes our hearts ache. She does not want to live by lessons from our old country. Which is better for Kim: the Vietnamese way or the western way? For our family the answer does not come so easily.

From a young age, a girl in our old country is trained to be a housewife. She spends most of her time at home, cooking, sewing, ironing, and cleaning. In this way she is practicing to be a good wife and mother. That is her future. For her there is no time for activities outside the home. Also, there is no need for a woman to be educated. Why does she need schooling if her natural place is in the home? In America, however, girls are different. Kim tells me, "Mother, none of my friends know how to cook and sew. Why do I have to learn?" She says, "Mother," the way her friends have taught her to say it, with her eyes rolled up to the sky. She also has a look of disgust on her face, and I wonder how she learned to show that face to her mother. In addition, I know it is true that girls in this country are busy outside the home. Kim, for instance, is on the high school swim team. She spends at least two hours every day swimming laps back and forth. Also, she has to spend hours studying to keep up her grades. Kim says she is going to college. She wants to become a lawyer. This worries us more. Who will want to marry her then?

Besides that, we worry about our daughter's personality. A Vietnamese girl is usually very shy and likes to please her elders. Growing up, I was always silent. I wanted to obey my parents and grandparents. "So quiet, so obedient," my grandmother used to brag about me. "Someday she will make a good wife." We did not approve of those who were

Holt, Rinehart and Winston

loud and outspoken. Yet, here in America, everything is so different. Kim's teachers and friends encourage her to talk and be more open. My husband is scared that she is becoming too free and independent, but he is afraid to say anything. He does not want to face that look of disgust that Kim uses on me sometimes. The disappointment on his face gets deeper each day.

One of the biggest differences between the two cultures is the attitude toward sex and marriage. In Vietnam a girl who knows everything about sex cannot marry properly. In fact, a "decent" girl is expected to know nothing at all. Her husband will teach her everything she needs to know after they are married. In contrast, American girls are taught sex education at school or they learn it from their friends. Many girls have sex before marriage. It is accepted by society as long as they use protection. Also, many couples in this country live together with no shame before they are married. Such an attitude is at war with our own cultural values.

Because of the two cultures, we do not know how Kim will turn out. All we know is that we must hold on to the values that are important to our Vietnamese culture. We must also let her make her own choices now that we live here. In the end she will find her own way.

Holt, Rinehart and Winston

Writing Assignment 5: Comparison/Contrast Essay

Writing Task: Rodríguez's poem, "Migratory Birds," contrasts two distinctive family lifestyles and shows how the attitudes and behaviors of each influenced her life. Write an essay that contrasts your own family's lifestyle or values with those of someone you know, contrasting the significant characteristics of each. In your concluding paragraph, you should end with a reflection on which lifestyle or set of values is more appropriate for you.

Finding a Topic

As a response to the story, compare or contrast your own family's lifestyle or values with those of another person or family. What are the significant characteristics of each? How do they differ? How are they similar? What can you learn from the comparison? Do you prefer one over the other? Why? List your ideas on each of the two lifestyles to discover significant points of comparison or contrast. Always keep your final purpose in mind: to show which set of values is more appropriate for you. Remember that having a backup topic is a good idea in case your first choice does not work out.

Possible Topics:

_____   versus   _____

_____   versus   _____

Prewriting

Your Topic:

_____   versus   _____

List your ideas on each of the two lifestyles to discover significant points of contrast.

One Lifestyle or Set of Values   *A Different Lifestyle or Set of Values*

_____   _____

_____   _____

_____   _____

_____   _____

_____   _____

_____   _____

_____   _____

_____   _____

Holt, Rinehart and Winston

Writing Assignment 5: Comparison/Contrast Essay

The Thesis Statement

Remember that the thesis statement in an essay has the same function as the topic sentence in a paragraph. A thesis statement expresses the central idea that the essay as a whole will explore in each of its supporting paragraphs.

Examples of Thesis Statements

> In spite of our efforts, our family is experiencing the conflicts between the ancient culture of our Vietnamese ancestors and that of the United States.

> Which is better for Kim: the Vietnamese way or the western way? For our family, the answer does not come so easily.

> Watching our daughter grow up in the United States has made our family aware of the vast differences between the American culture and the Vietnamese culture.

The thesis statement is the most important sentence in your essay because it is the central idea that holds all of the supporting paragraphs in the entire essay together. Thus, the ideas expressed in each of the topic sentences in the body of the essay should be linked to the thesis statement. Also, like the topic sentence in a paragraph, the thesis statement is generally located near the beginning of your essay for clarity. To get your reader's attention it is often placed at the end of an introductory paragraph.

Writing the Thesis Statement

Make sure your thesis statement communicates the central idea of your essay.

Tentative Thesis Statement (Central Idea):

_____

_____

_____

Does your thesis statement make it very clear what it is that you are going to compare or contrast?

Note: Please refer to Reviewing the Basics if you need further help in writing a thesis statement.

Holt, Rinehart and Winston

Writing Assignment 5: Comparison/Contrast Essay

TRANSITIONAL WORDS

Before you begin writing your rough draft, you will need to be familiar with the use of transitions that signal comparison/contrast relationships.

Comparison/Contrast Transitions

likewise	on the one hand . . . on the other hand
similarly	in contrast
in comparison	however
on the contrary	whereas

EXERCISE

Look back at the student model, "Two Cultures" by Cuc Thi Nguyen. Notice that the transitions she uses tell us that she is contrasting the two lifestyles. Circle any transitional words or phrases in her essay that indicate contrast. List a few of her contrasting transitions in the space below:

_____   _____

_____   _____

_____   _____

_____   _____

_____   _____

Holt, Rinehart and Winston

COMPARISON/CONTRAST OUTLINE

Once you have finished exploring what you have to say about your two lifestyles, sets of values, or upbringings in your prewriting, it is a good idea to outline your thoughts before you write the rough draft of your essay. This allows you to see whether or not you covered the same points in both parts. You can use either the point-by-point method or the block method.

Point-by-Point Method

I. Daughter's training for home life
   A. Vietnam
   B. United States

II. Daughter's personality
   A. Vietnam
   B. United States

III. Daughter's attitude toward sex and marriage
   A. Vietnam
   B. United States

Block Method

I. Vietnam
   A. Daughter's training for home life
   B. Daughter's personality
   C. Daughter's attitude toward sex and marriage

II. United States
   A. Daughter's training for home life
   B. Daughter's personality
   C. Daughter's attitude toward sex and marriage

Holt, Rinehart and Winston

Name_____ Date _____

Writing Assignment 5: Comparison/Contrast Essay

EXERCISE

Following either the point-by-point method or the block method, make an outline of your own using the ideas from your prewriting:

Point-by-Point Method

  I.
     A.
     B.

  II.
     A.
     B.

 III.
     A.
     B.

Block Method

  I.
     A.
     B.
     C.

  II.
     A.
     B.
     C.

Holt, Rinehart and Winston

Writing a Rough Draft

Now take your prewriting one step further by creating a rough draft on notebook paper. Begin with a thesis statement. Then draft the body paragraphs, making sure that each one begins with a topic sentence. Select the best ideas from your prewriting, and write until you have thoroughly developed your ideas. Add "compare and contrast" transitions throughout your essay to make sure your reader is clear about your ideas. For your overall order, try to organize your paragraphs in order of importance. Make your purpose clear in your conclusion. That is, make a judgment as to which lifestyle is ultimately preferable to you, and attempt to persuade your reader to see your position.

Being Specific

A piece of writing is not really finished until it contains specific examples and vivid details that make it complete and whole. Your first draft may seem complete to you, but often it is necessary to revise your writing to provide your readers with additional information in the form of specific examples and vivid, descriptive, exact details.

For example, in Cuc Thi Nguyen's essay, "Two Cultures," she gives us detailed discussion with plenty of vivid supporting examples:

> "Yet, here in America, everything is so different. Kim's teachers and friends encourage her to talk and be more open. My husband is scared that she is becoming too free and independent, but he is afraid to say anything. He does not want to face that look of disgust that Kim uses on me sometimes. The disappointment on his face gets deeper each day."

Details like these breathe life into her writing and make her experience believable.

Reread your rough draft of Writing Assignment 5, watching out for general words, phrases, and sentences. Underline the parts of your writing that might benefit from being more specific. Write a new draft, changing the passages you have underlined into more interesting, exact, and detailed writing. Use specific examples wherever you can.

Remember that experienced writers constantly revise their work to make sure it communicates exactly what they want it to say.

The Concluding Paragraph

A concluding paragraph should provide a graceful exit for your reader and bring closure to the essay. It should also reinforce the central idea of the essay. In her essay, Nguyen concludes by philosophically accepting (with numerous reservations) her daughter's freedom to "find her own way" even though as a mother she prefers the traditions of the Vietnamese culture. Her own preferences are made clear to the reader. Finally, she avoids elementary phrasing such as "In conclusion," ending instead with a thoughtful comment on her daughter's newfound independence:

> Because of the two cultures, we do not know how Kim will turn out. All we know is that we must hold on to the values that are important to our Vietnamese culture. We must also let her make her own choices now that we live here. In the end she will find her own way.

Holt, Rinehart and Winston

Revising

Revision is a continuing process in which you delete words, add phrases, and rearrange sentences to make your meaning clear to your reader. Thus, it may occur at any point in the writing process. After you have written your rough draft, reread it carefully, being as objective as possible. Underline all words, phrases, or sentences that could benefit from more specifics, details, and examples.

Peer Editing

Using your revised copy, read your paper out loud to a peer editor. Likewise, listen as your peer editor reads his or her paper back to you. When both papers have been read aloud, exchange papers, using the Editing Sheet provided for this assignment to write helpful comments to each other. In some cases it might be more appropriate to exchange papers at the start and have each peer editor read silently before completing the editing sheet. Another option would be to use the Editing Sheet as a checklist for oral feedback. A final option would be for your instructor to create peer editing groups of three or four members for collaborative learning.

Whatever option you choose, the Editing Sheet that follows will provide useful guidelines for this assignment. Only one set of Editing Sheets is provided, which is sufficient if you are using collaborative groups. However, if you are using two individual editors, you will need to obtain a photocopy of the Editing Sheet. Please check with your instructor.

Holt, Rinehart and Winston

Name_____ Date _____

Writing Assignment 5: Comparison/Contrast Essay

Editing Sheet (to be completed by peer editors)

Directions: Either pair up and exchange papers with another student in class, or form editing groups of three or four members. Papers may be read silently or aloud. Every paper requires at least two peer editors who will work collaboratively to complete an Editing Sheet. The completed Editing Sheet should be attached to the rough draft and returned to the writer for reference during the revision process.

Some peer editors may prefer to write comments directly on a student's rough draft, using the Editing Sheet as more of a checklist. Check with your instructor to see which method works best for your situation.

1. Has the writer selected a topic that is interesting, sufficiently narrowed, and appropriate for a comparison/contrast essay? If the topic is weak, suggest prewriting strategies (clustering, listing, freewriting, or asking journalistic questions) to generate enough ideas for a new topic.

_____

_____

2. Does the introductory paragraph "hook" you or seem powerful and engaging? If not, offer suggestions.

_____

_____

3. Draw a double line under the thesis statement. If it is missing, ask the writer, "So what? What is the point of this essay?" Does it suggest comparison/contrast?

_____

_____

4. Draw a circle around the directing words in each of the topic sentences. Does each body paragraph have a clear topic sentence that points out the main idea of the paragraph?

_____

_____

Holt, Rinehart and Winston

5. Draw a wavy line under words or phrases that would benefit from detailed examples. Has the writer included enough examples and specific details and anecdotes (interesting little stories with a point) in each body paragraph for a fully developed essay?

_____

_____

6. Underline the transitional expressions that signal "comparison/contrast" order. Does the essay seem well organized overall? Is the internal order of the essay clearly signaled by the use of transitions that show "importance" order? Offer suggestions.

_____

_____

7. Does the writer also use appropriate "linking" transitions that show the relationship between ideas? Where would you add more? Where would you omit some?

_____

_____

8. Does the concluding paragraph wrap up the essay effectively and clarify which lifestyle you prefer? What ideas do you have about writing a more effective conclusion?

_____

9. Does the title intrigue you and really catch your attention as a reader? Think of recent movie titles. What suggestions do you have for a more interesting, creative title?

_____

_____

10. What is the most powerful part of this essay? Be as specific as possible.

_____

_____

Peer Editors' Initials: ____ ____ ____ ____ (This verifies the paper is ready for a Revised Copy.)

Holt, Rinehart and Winston

Submitting the Final Copy

Once you have had your paper edited, you should revise your paper once again. Remember that experienced writers constantly revise their work to make sure it communicates exactly what they meant to say. Before you write the final copy of your paper, your instructor or tutor may want to skim over your revised draft. Then write your final copy in ink on notebook paper or type it on a typewriter or a computer. Make sure you follow the rules of manuscript form located in the Appendix.

After writing the final copy of your paper, exchange it with other members of your editing group to proofread for spelling, punctuation, and grammar errors. Ask your peer editors to initial your final copy to indicate that it has been through the final editing process. When your edited paper is returned to you, make the final corrections and submit your final copy along with your rough draft and completed Editing Sheet. Stapling the whole packet together will allow your instructor to check your progress during each stage of the writing process.

Holt, Rinehart and Winston

Reading Assignment 6: "Reparation Candy"

Prereading

Our upbringing—whether it be in a traditional family that reflects the majority culture, an immigrant family, a single parent family, or a stepfamily—can have a lasting impact on our lives. Since the family unit is our own little world, it is the source of much of the attitudes, ideas, and perspectives we develop later as adults.

In "Reparation Candy," Maxine Hong Kingston writes about the generation gap between immigrant parents, who are reluctant to give up their old values, and their children, who pick up the values of their new culture. As you read this dramatization, reflect on your own family's experiences and think about the ways in which conflicting attitudes and values affect the family unit.

What are some family conflicts between generations you or your friends have experienced? Do you think the older generation is necessarily the wisest, or can children often see issues more clearly than their parents?

Reparation Candy
Maxine Hong Kingston

We were working at the laundry when a delivery boy came from the Rexall drugstore around the corner. He had a pale blue box of pills, but nobody was sick. Reading the label we saw that it belonged to another Chinese family, Crazy Mary's family. "Not ours," said my father. He pointed out the name to the Delivery Ghost,[1] who took the pills back. My mother muttered for an hour, and then her anger boiled over. "That ghost! That dead ghost! How dare he come to the wrong house?" She could not concentrate on her marking and pressing. "A mistake! Huh!" I was getting angry myself. She fumed. She made her press crash and hiss. "Revenge. We've got to avenge this wrong on our future, on our health, and on our lives. Nobody's going to sicken my children and get away with it." We brothers and sisters did not look at one another. She would do something awful, something embarrassing. She'd already been hinting that during the next eclipse we slam pot lids together to scare the frog from swallowing the moon. (The word for "eclipse" is *frog-swallowing-the-moon*.) When we had not banged lids at the last eclipse and the shadow kept receding anyway, she'd said "The villagers must be banging and clanging very loudly back home in China."

("On the other side of the world, they aren't having an eclipse, Mama. That's just a shadow the earth makes when it comes between the moon and the sun."

"You're always believing what those Ghost Teachers tell you. Look at the size of the jaws!")

"Aha!" she yelled. "You! The biggest." She was pointing at me. "You go to the drugstore."

"What do you want me to buy, Mother?" I said.

[1]Kingston uses the word "ghost" here to refer to a non-Chinese person.

Holt, Rinehart and Winston

"Buy nothing. Don't bring one cent. Go and make them stop the curse."

"I don't want to go. I don't know how to do that. There are no such things as curses. They'll think I'm crazy."

"If you don't go, I'm holding you responsible for bringing a plague on this family."

"What am I supposed to do when I get there?" I said, sullen, trapped. "Do as I say, 'Your delivery boy made a wrong delivery'?"

"They know he made a wrong delivery. I want you to make them rectify their crime."

I felt sick already. She'd make me swing stinky censers around the counter, at the druggist, at the customers. Throw dog blood on the druggist. I couldn't stand her plans.

"You get reparation candy," she said. "You say, 'You have tainted my house with sick medicine and must remove the curse with sweetness.' He'll understand."

"He didn't do it on purpose. And no, he won't, Mother. They don't understand stuff like that. I won't be able to say it right. He'll call us beggars."

"You just translate." She searched me to make sure I wasn't hiding any money. I was sneaky and bad enough to buy the candy and come back pretending it was a free gift.

"Mymotherseztagimmesomecandy," I said to the druggist. Be cute and small. No one hurts the cute and small.

"What? Speak up. Speak English," he said, big in his white druggist coat.

"Tatatagimme somecandy."

The druggist leaned way over the counter and frowned. "Some free candy," I said. "Sample candy."

"We don't give sample candy, young lady," he said.

"My mother said you have to give us candy. She said that is the way the Chinese do it."

"What?"

"That is the way the Chinese do it."

"Do what?"

"Do things." I felt the weight and immensity of things impossible to explain to the druggist.

"Can I give you some money?" he asked.

"No, we want candy."

He reached into a jar and gave me a handful of lollipops. He gave us candy all year round, year after year, every time we went into the drugstore. When different druggist or clerks waited on us, they also gave us candy. They had talked us over. They gave us Halloween candy in December, Christmas candy around Valentine's day, candy hearts at Easter, and Easter eggs at Halloween. "See?" said our mother. "They understand. You kids just aren't very brave." But I knew they did not understand. They thought we were beggars without a home who lived in back of the laundry. They felt sorry for us. I did not eat their candy. I did not go inside the drugstore or walk past it unless my parents forced me to. Whenever we had a prescription filled, the druggist put candy into the medicine bag. This is what Chinese druggists normally do, except they give raisins. My mother thought she taught the Druggist Ghosts a lesson in good manners (which is the same word as "traditions").

We have so many secrets to hold in. Out sixth-grade teacher, who liked to explain things to children, let us read our files. My record shows that I flunked kindergarten and in first grade had no IQ—a zero IQ. I did remember the first-grade teacher calling out during a test, while students marked X's on a girl or a boy or a dog, which I covered with black. First grade was when I discovered eye control; with my seeing I could shrink the teacher down to a height of one inch, gesticulating and mouthing on the horizon. I lost this power in sixth grade for lack of practice, the teacher a generous man. "Look at your family's old addresses and think about how you've moved," he said. I looked at my parents' aliases and their birthdays, which variants I knew. But when I saw Father's occupation I exclaimed, "Hey, he wasn't a farmer, he was a . . ." He had been a gambler. My throat cut off the word—silence in front of the most understanding teacher. There were secrets never to be said in front of the ghosts, immigration secrets whose telling could get us sent back to China.

Sometimes I hated the ghosts for not letting us talk; sometimes I hated the secrecy of the Chinese. "Don't tell," said my parents, though we couldn't tell if we wanted to because we didn't know. Are there really secret trials with our own judges and penalties? Are there really flags in Chinatown signaling what stowaways have arrived in San Francisco Bay, their names, and which ships they came on? "Mother, I heard some kids say there are flags like that. Are there? What colors are they? Which buildings do they fly from?"

"No. No, there aren't any flags like that. They're just talking-story. You're always believing talking-story."

"I won't tell anybody, Mother. I promise. Which building are the flags on? Who flies them? The benevolent associations?"

"I don't know. Maybe the San Francisco villagers do that; our villagers don't do that."

Holt, Rinehart and Winston

"What do our villagers do?"

They would not tell us children because we had been born among ghosts, were taught by ghosts, and were ourselves ghostlike. They called us a kind of ghost. Ghosts are noisy and full of air; they talk during meals. They talk about anything.

"Do we send up signal kites? That would be a good idea, huh? We could fly them from the school balcony." Instead of cheaply stringing dragonflies by the tail, we could fly expensive kites, the sky splendid in Chinese colors, distracting ghost eyes while the new people sneak in. Don't tell. "Never tell."

Occasionally the rumor went about that the United States immigration authorities had set up headquarters in the San Francisco or Sacramento Chinatown to urge wetbacks and stowaways, anybody here on fake papers, to come to the city and get their files straightened out. The immigrants discussed whether or not to turn themselves in. "We might as well," somebody would say. "Then we'd have our citizenship for real."

"Don't be a fool," somebody else would say. "It's a trap. You go in there saying you want to straighten out your papers, they'll deport you."

"No, they won't. They're promising that nobody is going to go to jail or get deported. They'll give you citizenship as a reward for turning yourself in, for your honesty."

"Don't you believe it. So-and-so trusted them, and he was deported. They deported his children too."

"Where can they send us now? Hong Kong? Taiwan? I've never been to Hong Kong or Taiwan. The Big Six? Where?" We don't belong anywhere since the Revolution. The old China has disappeared while we've been away.

"Don't tell," advised my parents. "Don't go to San Francisco until they leave."

Lie to Americans. Tell them you were born during the San Francisco earthquake. Tell them your birth certificate and your parents were burned up in the fire. Don't report crimes; tell them we have no crimes and no poverty. Give a new name every time you get arrested; the ghosts won't recognize you. Pay the new immigrants twenty-five cents an hour and say we have no unemployment. And, of course, tell them we're against Communism. Ghosts have no memory anyway and poor eyesight. And the Han people won't be pinned down.

Holt, Rinehart and Winston

Reading Assignment 6: "Reparation Candy"

Double-Entry Question Journal

Note: Some students find it easier to do the double-entry journal as they are reading. Others find the process more effective after they have finished reading the entire piece. You should experiment to find the method that works best for you.

In the left column, jot down at least five "What?" "Why?" or "How?" questions. Then in the right column, jot down some possible answers and responses. If further questions come up, jot them down also. One purpose of this exercise is to learn how to think critically, so you might end up with several answers or possibilities. Go ahead, take a risk!

1.   1.

2.   2.

3.   3.

4.   4.

5.   5.

Brief Summary: _____

_____

_____

_____

_____

Note: Please refer to the Appendix if you need help in writing a summary.

Holt, Rinehart and Winston

Reading Assignment 6: "Reparation Candy"

A Closer Look

1. What is the reason behind the mother's anger at the delivery boy's mistake?

_____

_____

_____

2. Why is the daughter so reluctant to go to the druggist to ask for candy?

_____

_____

_____

3. How do you account for the difference between the mother's response and the daughter's response when the druggist not only agrees to the request for candy, but supplies the family with candy for years afterward?

_____

_____

_____

4. Why is the daughter taught to lie to the American authorities and keep secrets from them?

_____

_____

_____

CENTRAL IDEA (THEME)

What does the story "Reparation Candy" tell you about the younger and older generations in a family as well as about the basic values and beliefs of each generation (good or bad)?

_____

_____

_____

Holt, Rinehart and Winston

Writing Assignment 6: Argument Essay

An argument essay attempts to persuade your reader to agree with your own point of view on an issue, either for or against it. This type of essay takes a firm stand on an issue, making a clear, decisive judgment. Once you have asserted your judgment on an issue, you will need to come up with several good reasons to support your point of view. Lastly, for each of your supporting reasons, you will need to present convincing evidence, in the form of specific examples, facts, and so forth, to help support your point of view.

An argument paper will rely heavily on transitional phrases like "One reason," "Another important reason," and "The most important reason" as it builds its argument to a strong conclusion, which can be signaled by terms such as "Therefore" or "Consequently." Argument papers answer questions such as *"Why do you believe that? Can you prove it to me? What are the reasons for your judgment? What is the evidence for your judgment?"*

A Student Model

The following essay was written by a college English student. Its purpose is to show you how another student, like yourself, responded to this writing assignment. Continue to explore ways to develop your own thinking and individual style of writing.

Erika Valdez
English 501: Ms. Zipperian
Essay 6: Argument
July 14, 1997

The Older Generation

Many of the people I know today are struggling as parents. They come to me with stories of teenage daughters having babies, drug use in their children's school, and disobedient kids who ignore their parents and do whatever they want to do. Just the other day, a close friend of mine told me her high school-aged daughter has decided she no longer needs school. She just goes to the mall every day to meet her friends, and when her mother tries to force her to go to school, she threatens to leave home and live elsewhere. Even though
I am a representative of today's generation of parents, I admire the previous generation much more as parents.

One of the reasons I admire the older generation is for the strong values they lived by and taught their children. Children a generation ago were much more respectful of their parents, and, because of this, they would listen carefully to their parents' advice. They knew that their parents had more experience with life. Parents were not afraid to tell their children when they were wrong, and children knew there would be serious consequences if they did something bad like shoplifting or playing hooky from school. Moreover, children back in those days were raised to be respectful and polite. They would address the adults as "Ma'am" and "Sir." They would treat their teachers with respect instead of ignoring them or talking back to them. Because the older

Holt, Rinehart and Winston

generation considered respect, honesty and discipline to be very important, their children learned the importance of these fundamental values.

Another reason for my admiration is the older generation's desire to maintain a family together in harmony. Older generation families were conservative, but united, constantly helping one another. For example, if one of our family members grew crops, he would take some to the relatives to share. Knowing the value of a family kept the older generation from being selfish. They constantly sacrificed their own personal needs to keep their family strong. No matter how tired they were after a long day of work, they would always spend the evenings with us, reading to us or playing games like Checkers. They would always put their children first, and this made us respect them all the more. Our family lived and worked together as one.

Also, if the older generation had to face a bad situation, the family bonded together to support each other and find a good solution. One year my father lost his job and we had to survive on my mother's salary. It was a very difficult time for him, but we learned to make do with less until he finally got another job. It took a long time, but we figured out as a family how to stick to a budget and entertain ourselves with simple pleasures, like organizing family baseball games or camping together in the nearby mountains. As I look back, it seems as if all of the bad times made us into an even stronger, more united family, thanks to the values of the older generation.

The most important lesson I learned from the older generation in my family is to do what is best for the children. For instance, back in those days not everybody was able to have an education, to have a car, or even to go shopping with friends. Neither of my parents went to college because they were too busy earning a living and paying the bills in order to provide us with a decent childhood. Nonetheless, they did all they could to give us a good education and even encouraged us to go on to college. They knew that an education would help us all our lives.

Even though my parents may have lacked money, they possessed a valuable treasure. That treasure was their solid moral values. To me, that is the best gift in the world.

Writing Assignment 6: Argument Essay

Writing Task: Maxine Hong Kingston wrote "Reparation Candy" to dramatize the conflict between the older and younger generations in a family. As a response to "Reparation Candy," examine your own family's experiences, arguing for either the values of an older generation or a younger generation. You may also include examples from families you have observed in situations around you.

Finding a Topic

As a response to the story, think of your own family's different generations or those of other families that you know well. Do the values of the older and younger generations come into conflict? Exactly what are those values? Which seems to you to offer the best way to deal with today's world? Are the older generation's ideas and values still valid or do they need to be changed? Having a backup topic is a good idea in case your first choice does not work out.

Possible Topics:

_____

_____

Prewriting

Use any invention strategy (clustering, listing, freewriting, or asking journalistic questions) to discover ideas about the topic that is most interesting to you. Jot down whatever comes to mind until you come up with enough ideas to write your cause and effect essay.

Your Topic: _____

Holt, Rinehart and Winston

The Thesis Statement

Now that you have had some practice in writing thesis statements, you should be able to see the similarities between a thesis statement in an essay and a topic sentence in a paragraph. A thesis statement expresses the central idea that the essay as a whole will explore in each of its supporting paragraphs.

Examples of Thesis Statements

The older generation's strong sense of values is what held their families together.

Because the older generation had a strong sense of what was important, families back then raised their children much better than families do today.

Even though I am a representative of today's generation of parents, I admire the previous generation much more as parents.

The thesis statement is the most important sentence in your essay because it is the central idea that holds all of the supporting paragraphs in the entire essay together. Thus, the ideas expressed in each of the topic sentences in the body of the essay must be closely related to the thesis statement.

Finally, like the topic sentence in a paragraph, the thesis is generally located near the beginning of your essay. It is often placed at the end of an introductory paragraph that is designed to get your reader's attention.

Writing the Thesis Statement

Make sure your thesis statement communicates the central idea of your essay and forecasts the way your paper will be developed.

Tentative Thesis Statement (Central Idea):

_____

_____

Does your thesis statement clearly state a firm judgment on an issue?

Note: Please refer to Reviewing the Basics if you need further help in writing a thesis statement.

Holt, Rinehart and Winston

Writing Assignment 6: Argument Essay

TRANSITIONAL WORDS

Before you begin writing your rough draft, you will need to be familiar with the use of transitions that are useful in an argument essay.

"Argument" Transitions

one reason	the first reason	first	one of the reasons
another reason	also	second	another reason
furthermore	yet another reason	third	besides that
the main reason	the biggest reason	most significantly	the strongest reason
as a result	therefore	consequently	thus

EXERCISE

Look back at the student model, "The Older Generation" by Erika Valdez. Notice that the transitions she uses tell us that she is using "importance" order in her argument. Circle any transitional words or phrases that indicate another stage in the development of her argument. List a few of her "argument" transitions in the space below:

_____   _____

_____   _____

Note: Please refer to Reviewing the Basics if you need further help in using transitions that signal order.

Holt, Rinehart and Winston

Writing a Rough Draft

Now take your prewriting one step further by creating a rough draft on notebook paper. Begin with an introductory paragraph that ends with a thesis statement. Then draft the body paragraphs, making sure that each one begins with a topic sentence. Select the best ideas from your prewriting, and write until you have thoroughly developed your ideas. Add "argument" transitions to make sure your reader is clear about the developing order of your persuasive piece of writing.

Being Specific

A piece of writing is not really finished until it contains specific examples and vivid details that make it complete and whole. Your first draft may seem complete to you, but often it is necessary to revise your writing to provide your readers with additional information in the form of specific examples and vivid, descriptive, exact details.

For example, in Erika Valdez's essay, "The Older Generation," she gives us an anecdote from her own family's experiences to provide evidence for her reasons:

> One year my father lost his job and we had to survive on my mother's salary. It was a very difficult time for him, but we learned to make do with less until he finally got another job. It took a long time, but we figured out as a family how to stick to a budget and entertain ourselves with simple pleasures, like organizing family baseball games or camping together in the nearby mountains.

Details like these breathe life into her writing. Reread your rough draft of Writing Assignment 6, watching out for general words, phrases, and sentences. Underline the parts of your writing that might benefit from being more specific. Write a new draft, changing the passages you have underlined into more interesting, exact, and detailed writing. Use specific examples wherever you can.

Remember that experienced writers constantly revise their work to make sure it communicates exactly what they want it to say.

The Concluding Paragraph

A concluding paragraph should provide a graceful exit for your reader and bring closure to the essay. It should also reinforce the central idea of the essay. In her argument essay, "The Older Generation," Erika Valdez concludes by reminding us of the main idea and restating it clearly and firmly for the reader. She is careful not to introduce a new topic. Instead, she stays on focus and emphasizes the main idea she has been arguing for in this assignment. Because she has already made her judgment clear throughout her essay, she simply concludes with three sentences at the end of the last supporting paragraph. These three sentences restate clearly what her judgment is:

> Even though my parents may have lacked money, they possessed a valuable treasure. That treasure was their solid moral values. To me that is the best gift in the world.

Holt, Rinehart and Winston

Revising

Revision is an ongoing process in which you delete words, add phrases, and rearrange sentences to make your meaning clear to your reader. Thus, it may occur at any point in the writing process. After you have written your rough draft, reread it carefully, being as objective as possible. Underline all words, phrases, or sentences that could benefit from more specifics, details, and examples.

Peer Editing

Using your revised copy, read your paper out loud to a peer editor. Likewise, listen as your peer editor reads his or her paper back to you. When both papers have been read aloud, exchange papers, using the Editing Sheet provided for this assignment to write helpful comments to each other. In some cases it might be more appropriate to exchange papers at the start and have each peer editor read silently before completing the editing sheet. Another option would be to use the Editing Sheet as a checklist for oral feedback. A final option would be for your instructor to create peer editing groups of three or four members for collaborative learning.

Whatever option you choose, the Editing Sheet that follows will provide useful guidelines for this assignment. Only one set of Editing Sheets is provided, which is sufficient if you are using collaborative groups. However, if you are using two individual editors, you will need to obtain a photocopy of the Editing Sheet. Please check with your instructor.

Holt, Rinehart and Winston

Name_____ Date _____

Writing Assignment 6: Argument

Editing Sheet (to be completed by peer editors)

Directions: Either pair up and exchange papers with another student in class, or form editing groups of three or four members. Papers may be read silently or aloud. Every paper requires at least two peer editors who will work collaboratively to complete an Editing Sheet. The completed Editing Sheet should be attached to the rough draft and returned to the writer for reference during the revision process.

Some peer editors may prefer to write comments directly on a student's rough draft, using the Editing Sheet as more of a checklist. Check with your instructor to see which method works best for your situation.

1. Has the writer selected a topic that is interesting, sufficiently narrowed, and appropriate for an argument essay? If the topic is weak, suggest prewriting strategies (clustering, listing, freewriting, or asking journalistic questions) to generate enough ideas for a new topic.

_____

_____

2. Does the introductory paragraph "hook" you or seem powerful and engaging? If not, offer suggestions.

_____

_____

3. Draw a double line under the thesis statement. If it is missing, ask the writer, "So what? What is the point of this essay?" Suggest ways to make the thesis statement more effective, if necessary.

_____

_____

4. Draw a circle around the directing words in the topic sentences. Does each body paragraph have a clear topic sentence that points out the main idea of the paragraph?

_____

_____

5. Draw a wavy line under words or phrases that would benefit from detailed examples. Has the writer included enough examples and specific details and anecdotes (interesting little stories with a point) in each body paragraph for a fully developed essay?

_____

Holt, Rinehart and Winston

6. Is dialogue used? If not, would the use of dialogue (direct quotations) make this essay more realistic and interesting? If dialogue is used, does it express a particular emotion? If necessary, make suggestions for improvement.

_____

_____

7. Underline the transitional expressions that signal "argument" order. Does the essay seem well organized? Is the overall order of the essay clearly signaled by the use of transitions that show the development of the argument? Offer suggestions.

_____

_____

8. Does the writer also use appropriate "linking" transitions that show the relationship between ideas in a sentence? Where would you add more? Where would you omit some?

_____

_____

9. Does the concluding paragraph wrap up the essay effectively or leave a lasting impression on you? What ideas do you have about writing a more effective conclusion?

_____

_____

10. Does the title intrigue you and really catch your attention as a reader? Think of recent movie titles. What suggestions do you have for a more interesting, creative title?

_____

_____

11. What is the most powerful part of this essay? Be as specific as possible.

_____

_____

Peer Editors' Initials: ____   ____   ____   ____   (This verifies the paper is ready for a Revised Copy.)

Holt, Rinehart and Winston

Submitting the Final Copy

Once you have had your paper edited, you should revise your paper once again. Remember that experienced writers constantly revise their work to make sure it communicates exactly what they meant to say. Before you write the final copy of your paper, your instructor or tutor may want to skim over your revised draft. Then write your final copy in ink on notebook paper or type it on a typewriter or a computer. Make sure you follow the rules of manuscript form located in the Appendix.

After writing the final copy of your paper, exchange it with other members of your editing group to proofread for spelling, punctuation, and grammar errors. Ask your peer editors to initial your final copy to indicate that it has been through the final editing process. When your edited paper is returned to you, make the final corrections and submit your final copy along with your rough draft and completed Editing Sheet. Stapling the whole packet together will allow your instructor to check your progress during each stage of the writing process.

Holt, Rinehart and Winston

3

Society: Our Values

The readings in Chapter 3 focus on our complex society and its great cultural diversity. These readings will help you to discover how writers explore the culture and traditions of the society in which they live, and to think about your own unique role in our society as well as the roles of others who are different from you. The ideas you get by reading and responding to these selections will serve as springboards for you to examine your place in our fascinating and diverse culture.

In this chapter you will continue to use prewriting strategies to help you begin writing. In writing these essays you will also have the opportunity to practice the various revision strategies covered in previous chapters. Throughout this section, your reading, thinking, and writing will be in some way connected to the theme of "Society: Our Values." The readings in this chapter were carefully selected to help prepare you for the writing assignments based on the theme of society.

Reading Assignment 7: "The Storm" by Kate Chopin

Writing Assignment 7: An Essay

Reading Assignment 8: "To a Child Trapped in a Barber Shop" by Philip Levine

Writing Assignment 8: An Essay

Reading Assignment 9: "The Lottery" by Shirley Jackson

Writing Assignment 9: An Essay

Holt, Rinehart and Winston

Reading Assignment 7: "The Storm" by Kate Chopin

Prereading

In "The Storm," Kate Chopin writes about a brief extramarital affair that profoundly affects each of the characters. This story, though shocking to some readers, seems to be making a comment on society's values concerning marriage and fidelity. What is your position on honoring the vows of marriage? Is having an affair always detrimental to all parties concerned?

The Storm
Kate Chopin

I

The leaves were so still that even Bibi thought it was going to rain. Bobinôt, who was accustomed to converse on terms of perfect equality with his little son, called the child's attention to certain sombre clouds that were rolling with sinister intention from the west, accompanied by a sullen, threatening roar. They were at Friedheimer's store and decided to remain there till the storm had passed. They sat within the door on two empty kegs. Bibi was four years old and looked very wise.

"Mama'll be 'fraid, yes," he suggested with blinking eyes.

"She'll shut the house. Maybe she got Sylvie helpin' her this evenin'," Bobinôt responded reassuringly.

"No; she ent got Sylvie. Sylvie was helpin' her yistiday," piped Bibi.

Bobinôt arose and going across to the counter purchased a can of shrimps, of which Calixta was very fond. Then he returned to his perch on the keg and sat stolidly holding the can of shrimps while the storm burst. It shook the wooden store and seemed to be ripping great furrows in the distant field. Bibi laid his little hand on his father's knee and was not afraid.

II

Calixta, at home, felt no uneasiness for their safety. She sat at a side window sewing furiously on a sewing machine. She was greatly occupied and did not notice the approaching storm. But she felt very warm and often stopped to mop her face on which the perspiration gathered in beads. She unfastened her white sacque at the throat. It began to grow dark, and suddenly realizing the situation she got up hurriedly and went about closing windows and doors.

Out on the small front gallery she had hung Bobinôt's Sunday clothes to air and she hastened out to gather them before the rain fell. As she stepped outside, Alcée Laballière rode in at the gate. She had not seen him very often since her marriage, and never alone. She stood there with Bobinôt's coat in her hands, and the big rain drops began to fall. Alcée rode his horse under the shelter of a side projection where the chickens had huddled and there were plows and a harrow piled up in the corner.

"May I come and wait on your gallery till the storm is over, Calixta?" he asked.

"Come 'long in, M'sieur Alcée."

His voice and her own startled her as if from a trance, and she seized Bobinôt's vest. Alcée, mounting to the porch, grabbed the trousers and snatched Bibi's braided jacket that was about to be carried away by a sudden gust of wind. He expressed an intention to remain outside, but it was soon apparent that he might as well have been out in the open: the water beat in upon the boards in driving sheets, and he went inside, closing the door after him. It was even necessary to put something beneath the door to keep the water out.

"My! what a rain! It's good two years sence it rain' like that," exclaimed Calixta as she rolled up a piece of bagging and Alcée helped her to thrust it beneath the crack.

She was a little fuller of figure than five years before when she married; but she had lost nothing of her vivacity. Her blue eyes still retained their melting quality; and her yellow hair, dishevelled by the wind and rain, kinked more stubbornly than ever about her ears and temples.

The rain beat upon the low, shingled roof with a force and clatter that threatened to break an entrance and deluge them there. They were in the dining room—the sitting room—the general utility room. Adjoining was her bed room, with Bibi's couch along side her own. The door stood open, and the room with its white, monumental bed, its closed shutters, looked dim and mysterious.

Alcée flung himself into a rocker and Calixta nervously began to gather up from the floor the lengths of a cotton sheet which she had been sewing.

"If this keeps up, *Dieu sait* [1] if the levees goin' to stan' it!" she exclaimed.

"What have you got to do with the levees?"

"I got enough to do! An' there's Bobinôt with Bibi out in that storm—if he only didn't left Friedheimer's!"

"Let us hope, Calixta, that Bobinôt's got sense enough to come in out of a cyclone."

She went and stood at the window with a greatly disturbed look on her face. She wiped the frame that was clouded with moisture. It was stiflingly hot. Alcée got up and joined her at the window, looking over her shoulder. The rain was coming down in sheets obscuring the view of far-off cabins and enveloping the distant wood in a

[1] God knows.

gray mist. The playing of the lightning was incessant. A bolt struck a tall chinaberry tree at the edge of the field. It filled all visible space with a blinding glare and the crash seemed to invade the very boards they stood upon.

Calixta put her hands to her eyes, and with a cry, staggered backward. Alcée's arm encircled her, and for an instant he drew her close and spasmodically to him.

"Bonté!" [2] she cried, releasing herself from his encircling arm and retreating from the window, "the house'll go next! If I only knew w'ere Bibi was!" She would not compose herself; she would not be seated. Alcée clasped her shoulders and looked into her face. The contact of her warm, palpitating body when he had unthinkingly drawn her into his arms, had aroused all the old-time infatuation and desire for her flesh.

"Calixta," he said, "don't be frightened. Nothing can happen. The house is too low to be struck, with so many tall trees standing about. There! aren't you going to be quiet? say, aren't you?" He pushed her hair back from her face that was warm and steaming. Her lips were as red and moist as pomegranate seed. Her white neck and a glimpse of her full, firm bosom disturbed him powerfully. As she glanced up at him the fear in her liquid blue eyes had given place to a drowsy gleam that unconsciously betrayed a sensuous desire. He looked down into her eyes and there was nothing for him to do but to gather her lips in a kiss. It reminded him of Assumption.

"Do you remember—in Assumption, Calixta?" he asked in a low voice broken by passion. Oh! she remembered; for in Assumption he had kissed her and kissed and kissed her; until his senses would well nigh fail, and to save her he would resort to a desperate flight. If she was not an immaculate dove in those days, she was still inviolate; a passionate creature whose very defenselessness had made her defense, against which his honor forbade him to prevail. Now—well, now—her lips seemed in a manner free to be tasted, as well as her round, white throat and her whiter breasts.

They did not heed the crashing torrents, and the roar of the elements made her laugh as she lay in his arms. She was a revelation in that dim, mysterious chamber; as white as the couch she lay upon. Her firm, elastic flesh that was knowing for the first time its birthright, was like a creamy lily that the sun invites to contribute its breath and perfume to the undying life of the world.

The generous abundance of her passion, without guile or trickery, was like a white flame which penetrated and found response in depths of his own sensuous nature that had never yet been reached.

When he touched her breasts they gave themselves up in quivering ecstasy, inviting his lips. Her mouth was a fountain of delight. And when he possessed her, they seemed to swoon together at the very borderland of life's mystery.

[2] "Goodness!"

Holt, Rinehart and Winston

He stayed cushioned upon her, breathless, dazed, enervated, with his heart beating like a hammer upon her. With one hand she clasped his head, her lips lightly touching his forehead. The other hand stroked with a soothing rhythm his muscular shoulders.

The growl of the thunder was distant and passing away. The rain beat softly upon the shingles, inviting them to drowsiness and sleep. But they dared not yield.

The rain was over; and the sun was turning the glistening green world into a palace of gems. Calixta, on the gallery, watched Alcée ride away. He turned and smiled at her with a beaming face; and she lifted her pretty chin in the air and laughed aloud.

III

Bobinôt and Bibi, trudging home, stopped without at the cistern to make themselves presentable.

"My! Bibi, w'at will yo' mama say! You ought to be ashame'. You oughtn' put on those good pants. Look at 'em! An' that mud on yo' collar! How you got that mud on yo' collar, Bibi? I never saw such a boy!" Bibi was the picture of pathetic resignation. Bobinôt was the embodiment of serious solicitude as he strove to remove from his own person and his son's the signs of their tramp over heavy roads and through wet fields. He scraped the mud off Bibi's bare legs and feet with a stick and carefully removed all traces from his heavy brogans. Then, prepared for the worst—the meeting with an over-scrupulous housewife, they entered cautiously at the back door.

Calixta was preparing supper. She had set the table and was dripping coffee at the hearth. She sprang up as they came in.

"Oh, Bobinôt! You back! My! but I was uneasy. W'ere you been during the rain? An Bibi? he ain't wet? he ain't hurt?" She had clasped Bibi and was kissing him effusively. Bobinôt's explanations and apologies which he had been composing all along the way, died on his lips as Calixta felt him to see if he were dry, and seemed to express nothing but satisfaction at their safe return.

"I brought you some shrimps, Calixta," offered Bobinôt, hauling the can from his ample side pocket and laying it on the table.

"Shrimps! Oh, Bobinôt! you too good fo' anything!" and she gave him a smacking kiss on the cheek that resounded. *"J'vous réponds,[3]* we'll have a feas' tonight! umph-umph."

Bobinôt and Bibi began to relax and enjoy themselves, and when the three seated themselves at the table they laughed much and so loud that anyone might have heard them as far away as Laballière's.

[3] "I tell you."

Holt, Rinehart and Winston

IV

Alcée Laballière wrote to his wife, Clarisse, that night. It was a loving letter, full of tender solicitude. He told her not to hurry back, but if she and the babies liked it at Biloxi, to stay a month longer. He was getting on nicely; and though he missed them, he was willing to bear the separation a while longer—realizing that their health and pleasure were the first things to be considered.

V

As for Clarisse, she was charmed upon receiving her husband's letter. She and the babies were doing well. The society was agreeable; many of her old friends and acquaintances were at the bay. And the first free breath since her marriage seemed to restore the pleasant liberty of her maiden days. Devoted as she was to her husband, their intimate conjugal life was something which she was more than willing to forego for a while.

So the storm passed and everyone was happy.

Reading Assignment 7: "The Storm"

Double-Entry Question Journal

Note: Some students find it easier to do the double-entry journal as they are reading; others find the process more effective after they have finished reading the entire piece. Please experiment to find the method that works best for you.

In the left column, jot down at least five "What?" "Why?" or "How?" questions. Then in the right column, jot down some possible answers and responses. If further questions come up, jot them down also. One purpose of this exercise is to learn how to think critically, so you might end up with several answers. Go ahead, take a risk!

1.   1.

2.   2.

3.   3.

4.   4.

5.   5.

Brief Summary: _____

_____

_____

_____

_____

_____

Note: Please refer to the Appendix if you need help in writing a summary.

Holt, Rinehart and Winston

Reading Assignment 7: "The Storm"

A Closer Look

1. What role, if any, does the weather play in this story?

_____

_____

_____

2. What was the nature of Calixta and Alcée's prior relationship?

_____

_____

_____

_____

3. How would you characterize Calixta as a wife and mother before the storm?

_____

_____

_____

_____

4. What effect does the brief affair have on both Calixta's and Alcée's marriages?

_____

_____

_____

_____

CENTRAL IDEA (THEME)

What does "The Storm" tell us about society's attitudes toward sex, love, and marriage?

_____

_____

Holt, Rinehart and Winston

Writing Assignment 7: An Essay

A Student Model

The following essay was written by a college English student. Its purpose is to show you how another student, like yourself, responded to this writing assignment. Try to develop your own thinking and individual style of writing.

Theresa White
English 101: Hawkins
Assignment 7
Sept. 24, 1997

Love and Marriage

Until a couple of months ago, I thought I had an excellent family life. I had two parents who seemed to be in love with each other and would live happily ever after. I also had a little brother and a Cocker Spaniel named Sandy. We all lived together in a pretty big house with a huge back yard. I had a great boyfriend and tons of friends. I even had my own car, lots of clothes, and my very own phone line, all the material things a teenage girl could want. None of that seems important now.

My family used to be really close. We did everything together. We went on family picnics and ate dinner together every night. Then all of a sudden I found out that my parents had been fighting for years, and it had just gotten worse. Of course, all of this did not just happen overnight, but I was a self-absorbed teenager and I never paid attention to all the clues that were there. Suddenly, bills were not being paid, and my mother started complaining. All the little things, like my dad not being romantic enough, started to become big things in my mother's eyes.

My mom had been a housewife, and I never dreamed that she was unhappy. After twenty years of marriage, wasn't that almost a guarantee that my parents would stay together? My mom started acting like a stranger. She would go out and not tell anyone where she was going. I remember asking her about it one time, and she told me to mind my own business. This shocked me since we were really close, and she had never spoken to me like that before. She stopped cleaning the house and doing the traditional "mom-stuff" that used to come so naturally to her. I could tell that her new behavior hurt my dad a lot, but I was mad at both of them for doing this to me. I wondered why my father couldn't just make it right somehow.

Perhaps we had all been naive and spoiled. When I looked back, I could see that I took my mother for granted although it was hard for me to admit that. I certainly had looked at my parents' marriage as if they were the main characters in a fairy tale. Looking at my own life and my future plans, I could see that I used to think that the institution of marriage was something sacred. I had learned somewhere along the line that marriage and happiness went hand-in-hand. What had gone wrong?

One day toward the end of my senior year, my mom had a long talk with me. She told me, "Theresa, I am going to leave your father."

"You can't!" I cried. They had been going to marriage counseling sessions, and I

Holt, Rinehart and Winston

thought that things were getting better. However, I saw the look on her face and I said the only thing that could be said.

I told her, "I hope you are happy." I knew I had said the right thing, but I ran into my room and burst into tears. My attitude toward love and marriage was shattered.

After that night, I thought my mom would leave, but she stayed through the holidays. She probably thought it would be easier for my brother and me, but it was miserable. Nobody cooked or put up decorations. The house looked drab, and nobody even felt festive. I tried once or twice to put on an act for my little brother, but I was too wrapped up in my own feelings about not having the perfect family.

When she finally did leave, it was over very quickly. As the movers carried the last piece of furniture out the door, I knew my life would never be the same. When my dad came home and saw the empty house, he burst into tears. I had to be the one to comfort him and tell him that things would be all right. I started having to do all the things that my mom used to do, like cook and clean and do all the shopping. I was forced to grow up overnight. Instead of focusing on myself and my own comfort, I had to think about my little brother and my dad. Right now I am hoping that my relationship with my mom will improve as I grow older. My dad and I are twice as close as we used to be, and I would not trade that for the world. Still, my attitude toward love and marriage has changed. I used to be a hopeless romantic, but now I realize that a marriage contract is not a lifetime warranty.

Holt, Rinehart and Winston

Writing Assignment 7: An Essay

Writing Task: Kate Chopin's story, "The Storm," examines society's attitude toward the institution of marriage. As a response to "The Storm," write an essay about an issue that concerns you about the institution of marriage in today's world. You may use any of the modes we have practiced in previous assignments (narration, description, cause/effect, comparison/contrast, or argument).

Your Topic: _____

Prewriting

Use any invention strategy (clustering, listing, freewriting, or asking journalistic questions) to discover ideas about the topic that is most significant for you. Jot down whatever comes to mind until you have enough ideas to write your essay.

Writing the Thesis Statement

Make sure your thesis statement communicates the central idea of your essay and forecasts the way your paper will be developed.

Tentative Thesis Statement (Central Idea):

_____

_____

Note: Please refer to Reviewing the Basics if you need further help in writing a thesis statement.

Holt, Rinehart and Winston

Writing Assignment 7: An Essay

Writing a Rough Draft

Now take your prewriting one step further by creating a first draft. Select the best ideas, details, evidence, experiences, and reflections from your prewriting. Begin with your thesis statement and write until you have covered your topic well. Use whatever mode (narration, description, cause/effect, contrast, or argument) you feel is most appropriate to your purpose as you examine the attitudes of our society toward the institution of marriage. Through your writing you should be able to explore either the truth or inaccuracy of what "The Storm" tells us about marriage.

Being Specific

Reread your rough draft of Writing Assignment 7, watching out for general words, phrases, and sentences. Underline the parts of your writing that might benefit from being more specific. Write a new draft, changing the passages you have underlined into more interesting, exact, and detailed writing. Use specific examples wherever you can.

The Concluding Paragraph

A concluding paragraph should provide a graceful exit for your reader and bring closure to the essay. It should also reinforce the central idea of the essay. In her essay, "Love and Marriage," Theresa White concludes by reminding us of the main idea and restating it clearly for the reader. She is careful not to introduce a new topic. Instead, she stays focused on the topic and shows how she has been affected by the breakup of her parents:

> Still, my attitude toward love and marriage has changed. I used to be a hopeless romantic, but now I realize that a marriage contract is not a lifetime warranty.

Revising

Remember that experienced writers constantly revise their work to make sure it communicates exactly what they want it to say. Revision is an ongoing process requiring you to delete words, add phrases, and rearrange sentences to make your meaning clear to your reader.

Peer Editing

Using your revised copy, read your paper out loud to a peer editor. Likewise, listen as your peer editor reads his or her paper back to you. When both papers have been read aloud, exchange papers, using the Editing Sheet provided for this assignment to write helpful comments to each other. In some cases it might be more appropriate to exchange papers at the start and have each peer editor read silently before completing the Editing Sheet. Another option would be to use the Editing Sheet as a checklist for oral feedback. A final option would be for your instructor to create peer editing groups of three or four members for collaborative learning.

Holt, Rinehart and Winston

Whatever option you choose, the editing sheet that follows will provide useful guidelines for this assignment. Only one set of editing sheets is provided, which is sufficient if you are using collaborative groups. However, if you are using two individual editors, you will need to obtain a photocopy of the editing sheet. Please check with your instructor.

Holt, Rinehart and Winston

Writing Assignment 7: An Essay

Editing Sheet (to be completed by peer editors)

Directions: Either pair up and exchange papers with another student in class, or form editing groups of three or four members. Papers may be read silently or aloud. Every paper requires at least two peer editors who will work collaboratively to complete an Editing Sheet. The completed Editing Sheet should then be attached to the rough draft and returned to the writer for reference during the revision process.

Some peer editors may prefer to write comments directly on a student's rough draft, using the editing sheet as more of a checklist. Check with your instructor to see which method works best for your situation.

1. Has the writer selected a topic that is interesting, sufficiently narrowed, and suitable for the writing task? If the topic is weak, suggest prewriting strategies (clustering, listing, freewriting, or asking journalistic questions) to generate enough ideas for a new topic.

_____

_____

_____

2. Does the introductory paragraph "hook" you or seem powerful and engaging? If not, offer suggestions.

_____

_____

_____

3. Draw a double line under the thesis statement. If it is missing, ask the writer, "So what? What is the point of this essay?" Suggest ways to make the thesis statement more effective, if necessary.

_____

_____

4. Draw a circle around the directing words in the topic sentences. Does each body paragraph have a clear topic sentence that points out the main idea of the paragraph?

_____

_____

Holt, Rinehart and Winston

5. Draw a wavy line under words or phrases that would benefit from detailed examples. Has the writer included enough examples and specific details and anecdotes (interesting little stories with a point) in each body paragraph for a fully developed essay?

_____

_____

6. Underline the transitional expressions that signal the type of order used in this essay. Does the essay seem well organized? Offer suggestions.

_____

_____

7. Does the writer also use appropriate "linking" transitions that show the relationship between ideas in a sentence? Where would you add more? Where would you omit some?

_____

_____

8. Does the concluding paragraph wrap up the essay effectively or leave a lasting impression on you? What ideas do you have about writing a more effective conclusion?

_____

_____

9. Does the title intrigue you and really catch your attention as a reader? Think of recent movie titles. What suggestions do you have for a more interesting, creative title?

_____

_____

10. What is the most powerful part of this essay? Be as specific as possible.

_____

_____

Peer Editors' Initials: ____ ____ ____ ____ (This verifies the paper is ready for a Revised Copy.)

Holt, Rinehart and Winston

Submitting the Final Copy

Once you have had your paper edited, you should revise your paper once again. Remember that experienced writers constantly revise their work to make sure it communicates exactly what they meant to say. Before you write the final copy of your paper, your instructor or tutor may want to skim over your revised draft. Then write your final copy in ink on notebook paper or type it on a typewriter or a computer. Make sure you follow the rules of manuscript form located in the Appendix.

After writing the final copy of your paper, exchange it with other members of your editing group to proofread for spelling, punctuation, and grammar errors. Ask your peer editors to initial your final copy to indicate that it has been through the final editing process. When your edited paper is returned to you, make the final corrections and submit your final copy along with your rough draft and completed editing sheet. Stapling the whole packet together will allow your instructor to check your progress during each stage of the writing process.

Holt, Rinehart and Winston

Reading Assignment 8: "To a Child Trapped in a Barber Shop" by Philip Levine

Prereading

In his poem "To a Child Trapped in a Barber Shop," Philip Levine describes the situation of a crying six-year-old who finds himself "trapped" inside a barber shop. In the poem the narrator tells the child, "We've all been here before . . . and we stopped crying," implying that in one way or another the child's traumatic experience is a universal experience that will soon pass. At some point we must all learn the difficult lessons of our society, including its rules and regulations. While our first confrontations with society can be troubling, they can also, as Levine points out, help us to mature and grow. As you read the following poem, think about your own childhood experiences that ultimately made you a stronger person.

To a Child Trapped in a Barber Shop
Philip Levine

(1928–   )

You've gotten in through the transom
and you can't get out
till Monday morning or, worse,
till the cops come.

That six-year-old red face
calling for mama
is yours; it won't help you
because your case

is closed forever, hopeless.
So don't drink
the Lucky Tiger, don't
fill up on grease

because that makes it a lot worse,
that makes it a crime
against property and the state
and that costs time.

We've all been here before,
we took our turn
under the electric storm
of the vibrator

Holt, Rinehart and Winston

and stiffened our wills to meet
the close clippers
and heard the true blade mowing
back and forth

on a strip of dead skin,
and we stopped crying.
You think your life is over?
It's just begun.

Holt, Rinehart and Winston

Name_____ Date _____

Reading Assignment 8: "To a Child Trapped in a Barber Shop"

Double-Entry Question Journal

Note: Some students find it easier to do the double-entry journal as they are reading; others find the process more effective after they have finished reading the entire piece. Please experiment to find the method that works best for you.

In the left column, jot down at least five "What?" "Why?" or "How?" questions. Then in the right column, jot down some possible answers and responses. If further questions come up, jot them down also. One purpose of this exercise is to learn how to think critically, so you might end up with several answers. Go ahead, take a risk!

1.   1.

2.   2.

3.   3.

4.   4.

5.   5.

Brief Summary: _____

_____

_____

_____

_____

Note: Please refer to the Appendix if you need help in writing a summary.

Holt, Rinehart and Winston

Reading Assignment 8: "To a Child Trapped in a Barber Shop"

A Closer Look

1. What is the six-year-old child doing in the barber shop in the first place?

_____

_____

_____

2. What does the poet mean when he says, "That makes it a lot worse, / that makes it a crime / against property and the state"?

_____

_____

_____

3. Explain what the poet means when he says, "We've all been here before, / we took our turn . . . / and we stopped crying."

_____

_____

_____

4. What is the author's emotional tone (humorous, angry, sad, etc.) in the last two lines of the poem: "You think your life is over? / It's just begun."?

_____

_____

_____

CENTRAL IDEA (THEME)

What do you feel is the main message of the poem? What is the poet trying to say about life?

_____

_____

Holt, Rinehart and Winston

Writing Assignment 8: An Essay

A Student Model

The following essay was written by a college English student. Its purpose is to show you how another student, like yourself, responded to this writing assignment. Try to develop your own thinking and individual style of writing.

Linda Bonilla
English 101: Hawkins
Assignment 8
Sept. 24, 1997

Fitting In

For me, school had always been a hop, skip, and a jump. I was a pretty good student, and I always had one or two best friends. We always looked forward to recess. It was not all fun and games, though. One memory stands out above all the rest. It was the time when I first learned how it felt to be different. Before that one incident, I do not think I knew how it felt to be prejudged by others.

"Ms. Chang, room 301," the hall monitor told me. It was my first day to attend a new reading group. "Upstairs, third floor. Come with me," she ordered. I followed her. When I entered the classroom, I was greeted by stares and whispers. Apparently, the students thought I was in the wrong class. I looked around and realized that I was the only Hispanic student amongst an all-Korean class.

Ms. Chang silenced them as she led me to my desk. She gave me the assignment in English. The girl sitting to my right leaned over to another student and said loudly, "I don't know why the teacher bothers to translate for her since she is probably too lazy and stupid to do it." Everyone laughed. By the looks they gave me, they all seemed to agree. They shifted their desks away from mine and then ignored me. Ms. Chang ignored them as well as me. I was completely shunned. Besides that, the assignment was difficult. The way the class was treating me did not make it any easier.

"Read the stories and define all unknown terms as well as the vocabulary at the end of the text," Ms. Chang ordered in a voice like a robot. "Then write sentences for each word, and do this for at least three of the stories." She never smiled.

Besides that, I had to make up work since I had entered the reading group late, all in one period. I was glad the reading class lasted only an hour of my day. I could hardly wait to leave, but the time passed so slowly. I had to endure the deafening silence, the distanced glares, and the overall misery I felt by being there. When the class was over, I fled to my homeroom, trying to hold back the tears that had gathered in my eyes. All I could see was the classroom I had left behind. I could not forget the rude comments, the ugly gestures, and the oriental eyes that seemed to slice right through me. Mostly, I remember feeling shame even though it was not my fault that I was different.

I was so happy to be back with my class. There were a lot of familiar faces and wel-

Holt, Rinehart and Winston

coming smiles from my friends as they worked on their projects. Yet they all seemed to be at one end of the room, as if they were keeping far away from someone. I wondered why our teacher did not seem to notice. A desk away I saw the reason for the distance: a Korean boy. I made up my mind not to talk to him either. I thought that the class was rejecting him just as his classmates had treated me, and it made me feel good. Hate seemed to build inside of me as I looked at him with a mean stare.

He looked back at me, and what I saw was a shock. It was a mirror of the expression I had worn while I was in the reading class! My heart sank. He had also been discriminated against without reason. The class had looked down on him and hated him just for looking different. Did my parents raise me to think that way? I did recall hearing some racist remarks from them from time to time.

Right then and there I hated myself for being part of them. I did not fit in, neither with the Korean children nor the Hispanic children that hated others who were not like them. I did not fit in with the adults that stood there, unwilling to change a thing. I was not like them either, nor did I want to be. I hated them all—all except the boy who was sitting in my classroom alone. He seemed to be different in the same way that I was. With that realization, I reached out to him, knowing he would understand. We became friends and faced the world together, as we found it, in third grade.

Holt, Rinehart and Winston

Writing Assignment 8: An Essay

Writing Task: Usually an experience like getting a haircut is one of the first ventures of life outside the family unit. A place like the barbershop in the poem gives a child a hint about how difficult it is to venture outside the safety of the home into a foreign place full of dangers and new rules and regulations. Write about an incident or a place that first introduced you to the idea that a different world exists outside the comfort zone provided by your family and your home.

Your Topic: _____

Prewriting

Prewrite (cluster, list, freewrite, or ask journalistic questions) in the space below, jotting down whatever comes to mind about your topic. Prewrite until you come up with enough convincing evidence to support your point of view.

Writing the Thesis Statement

Make sure your thesis statement communicates the central idea of your essay and forecasts the way your paper will be developed.

Tentative Thesis Statement (Central Idea):

_____

_____

_____

Note: Please refer to Reviewing the Basics if you need further help in writing a thesis statement.

Holt, Rinehart and Winston

Writing Assignment 8: An Essay

Writing a Rough Draft

Now take your prewriting one step further by creating a first draft. Select the best ideas, details, evidence, experiences, and reflections from your prewriting. Begin with your topic sentence and write until you have covered your topic well. Use whatever mode (narration, description, cause/effect, contrast, or argument) you feel is most appropriate to your purpose as you write about your experiences of venturing outside that comfort zone you got used to as a child.

Being Specific

Reread your rough draft of Writing Assignment 8, watching out for general words, phrases, and sentences. Underline the parts of your writing that might benefit from being more specific. Write a new draft, changing the passages you have underlined into more interesting, exact, and detailed writing. Use specific examples wherever you can.

The Concluding Paragraph

A concluding paragraph should provide a graceful exit for your reader and bring closure to the essay. It should also reinforce the central idea of the essay. In her essay, "Fitting In," Linda Bonilla concludes by reminding us of the main idea and restating it clearly for the reader. She is careful not to introduce a new topic. Instead, she stays on focus, and in her last two lines she emphasizes the main idea she has been supporting in this assignment:

> With that realization, I reached out to him, knowing he would understand. We became friends and faced the world together, as we found it, in third grade.

Revising

Remember that experienced writers constantly revise their work to make sure it communicates exactly what they want it to say. Revision is an ongoing process requiring you to delete words, add phrases, and rearrange sentences to make your meaning clear to your reader.

Peer Editing

Using your revised copy, read your paper out loud to a peer editor. Likewise, listen as your peer editor reads his or her paper back to you. When both papers have been read aloud, exchange papers, using the Editing Sheet provided for this assignment to write helpful comments to each other. In some cases it might be more appropriate to exchange papers at the start and have each peer editor read silently before completing the Editing Sheet. Another option would be to use the Editing Sheet as a checklist for oral feedback. A final option would be for your instructor to create peer editing groups of three or four members for collaborative learning.

Whatever option you choose, the editing sheet that follows will provide useful guidelines for this assignment. Only one set of editing sheets is provided, which is sufficient if you are using collaborative groups. However, if you are using two individual editors, you will need to obtain a photocopy of the Editing Sheet. Please check with your instructor.

Holt, Rinehart and Winston

Writing Assignment 8: An Essay

Editing Sheet (to be completed by peer editors)

Directions: Either pair up and exchange papers with another student in class, or form editing groups of three or four members. Papers may be read silently or aloud. Every paper requires at least two peer editors who will work collaboratively to complete an Editing Sheet. The completed Editing Sheet should then be attached to the rough draft and returned to the writer for reference during the revision process.

Some peer editors may prefer to write comments directly on a student's rough draft, using the editing sheet as more of a checklist. Check with your instructor to see which method works best for your situation.

1. Has the writer selected a topic that is interesting, sufficiently narrowed, and appropriate for the writing task? If the topic is weak, suggest prewriting strategies (clustering, listing, freewriting, or asking journalistic questions) to generate enough ideas for a new topic.

_____

_____

_____

2. Does the introductory paragraph "hook" you or seem powerful and engaging? If not, offer suggestions.

_____

_____

_____

3. Draw a double line under the thesis statement. If it is missing, ask the writer, "So what? What is the point of this essay?" Suggest ways to make the thesis statement more effective, if necessary.

_____

_____

_____

4. Draw a circle around the directing words in the topic sentences. Does each body paragraph have a clear topic sentence that points out the main idea of the paragraph?

_____

_____

Holt, Rinehart and Winston

5. Draw a wavy line under words or phrases that would benefit from detailed examples. Has the writer included enough examples and specific details and anecdotes (interesting little stories with a point) in each body paragraph for a fully developed essay?

_____

_____

6. Underline the transitional expressions that signal the overall order used in this essay. Does the essay seem well organized? Offer suggestions.

_____

_____

7. Does the writer also use appropriate "linking" transitions that show the relationship between ideas in a sentence? Where would you add more? Where would you omit some?

_____

_____

8. Does the concluding paragraph wrap up the essay effectively or leave a lasting impression on you? What ideas do you have about writing a more effective conclusion?

_____

_____

9. Does the title intrigue you and really catch your attention as a reader? Think of recent movie titles. What suggestions do you have for a more interesting, creative title?

_____

_____

_____

10. What is the most powerful part of this essay? Be as specific as possible.

_____

_____

_____

Peer Editors' Initials: ____ ____ ____ ____ (This verifies the paper is ready for a Revised Copy.)

Holt, Rinehart and Winston

Submitting the Final Copy

Once you have had your paper edited, you should revise your paper once again. Remember that experienced writers constantly revise their work to make sure it communicates exactly what they meant to say. Before you write the final copy of your paper, your instructor or tutor may want to skim over your revised draft. Then write your final copy in ink on notebook paper or type it on a typewriter or a computer. Make sure you follow the rules of manuscript form located in the Appendix.

After writing the final copy of your paper, exchange it with other members of your editing group to proofread for spelling, punctuation, and grammar errors. Ask your peer editors to initial your final copy to indicate that it has been through the final editing process. When your edited paper is returned to you, make the final corrections and submit your final copy along with your rough draft and completed Editing Sheet. Stapling the whole packet together will allow your instructor to check your progress during each stage of the writing process.

Holt, Rinehart and Winston

Reading Assignment 9: "The Lottery" by Shirley Jackson

Prereading

Our culture provides us with many time-tested traditions and guidelines that can help us to live richer, more satisfying lives. Every society has its own holidays, celebrations, and rituals in which its members find satisfaction and meaning. Such activities can help to remind us that we are a part of a larger community. These rituals, such as celebrating the Fourth of July, New Year's Eve, religious holidays, or even a championship game, can cause us to feel that we share important, deeply held values and beliefs with other members of our society. Shirley Jackson's short story, "The Lottery," forces us to examine and compare the values we learn from our society with those of our private conscience. As you read "The Lottery," think about some rituals in which you may have participated, right or wrong.

The Lottery
Shirley Jackson

The morning of June 27th was clear and sunny, with the fresh warmth of a full-summer day; the flowers were blossoming profusely and the grass was richly green. The people of the village began to gather in the square, between the post office and the bank, around ten o'clock; in some towns there were so many people that the lottery took two days and had to be started on June 26th, but in this village, where there were only about three hundred people, the whole lottery took less than two hours, so it could begin at ten o'clock in the morning and still be through in time to allow the villagers to get home for noon dinner.

The children assembled first, of course. School was recently over for the summer, and the feeling of liberty sat uneasily on most of them; they tended to gather together quietly for a while before they broke into boisterous play, and their talk was still of the classroom and the teacher, of books and reprimands. Bobby Martin had already stuffed his pockets full of stones, and the other boys soon followed his example, selecting the smoothest and roundest stones; Bobby and Harry Jones and Dickie Delacroix—the villagers pronounced this name "Dellacroy"—eventually made a great pile of stones in one corner of the square and guarded it against the raids of the other boys. The girls stood aside, talking among themselves, looking over their shoulders at the boys, and the very small children rolled in the dust or clung to the hands of their older brothers or sisters.

Soon the men began to gather, surveying their own children, speaking of planting and rain, tractors and taxes. They stood together, away from the pile of stones in the corner, and their jokes were quiet and they smiled rather than laughed. The women, wearing faded house dresses and sweaters, came shortly after their menfolk. They greeted one another and exchanged bits of gossip as they went to join their husbands. Soon the women, standing by their husbands, began to call to their children,

Holt, Rinehart and Winston

and the children came reluctantly, having to be called four or five times. Bobby Martin ducked under his mother's grasping hand and ran, laughing, back to the pile of stones. His father spoke up sharply, and Bobby came quickly and took his place between his father and his oldest brother.

The lottery was conducted—as were the square dances, the teen-age club, the Halloween program—by Mr. Summers, who had time and energy to devote to civic activities. He was a round-faced, jovial man and he ran the coal business, and people were sorry for him, because he had no children and his wife was a scold. When he arrived in the square, carrying the black wooden box, there was a murmur of conversation among the villagers, and he waved and called, "Little late today, folks." The postmaster, Mr. Graves, followed him, carrying a three-legged stool, and the stool was put in the center of the square and Mr. Summers set the black box down on it. The villagers kept their distance, leaving a space between themselves and the stool, and when Mr. Summers said, "Some of you fellows want to give me a hand?" there was a hesitation before two men, Mr. Martin and his oldest son, Baxter, came forward to hold the box steady on the stool while Mr. Summers stirred up the papers in it.

The original paraphernalia for the lottery had been lost long ago, and the black box now resting on the stool had been put to use even before Old Man Warner, the oldest man in town, was born. Mr. Summers spoke frequently to the villagers about making a new box, but no one liked to upset even as much tradition as was represented by the black box. There was a story that the present box had been made with some pieces of the box that had preceded it, the one that had been constructed when the first people settled down to make a village here. Every year, after the lottery, Mr. Summers began talking again about a new box, but every year the subject was allowed to fade off without anything's being done. The black box grew shabbier each year; by now it was no longer completely black but splintered badly along one side to show the original wood color, and in some places faded or stained.

Mr. Martin and his oldest son, Baxter, held the black box securely on the stool until Mr. Summers had stirred the papers thoroughly with his hand. Because so much of the ritual had been forgotten or discarded, Mr. Summers had been successful in having slips of paper substituted for the chips of wood that had been used for generations. Chips of wood, Mr. Summers had argued, had been all very well when the village was tiny, but now that the population was more than three hundred and likely to keep on growing, it was necessary to use something that would fit more easily into the black box. The night before the lottery, Mr. Summers and Mr. Graves made up the slips of paper and put them in the box, and it was then taken to the safe of Mr. Summers' coal company and locked up until Mr. Summers was ready to take it to the square next morning. The rest of the year, the box was put away, sometimes one place, sometimes another; it had spent one year in Mr. Graves's barn and another year underfoot in the post office, and sometimes was set on a shelf in the Martin grocery and left there.

There was a great deal of fussing to be done before Mr. Summers declared the lottery open. There were the lists to make up—of heads of families, heads of households in each family, members of each household in each family. There was the proper

Holt, Rinehart and Winston

swearing-in of Mr. Summers by the postmaster, as the official of the lottery; at one time, some people remembered, there had been a recital of some sort, performed by the official of the lottery, a perfunctory, tuneless chant that had been rattled off duly each year; some people believed that the official of the lottery used to stand just so when he said or sang it, others believed that he was supposed to walk among the people, but years and years ago this part of the ritual had been allowed to lapse. There had been, also, a ritual salute, which the official of the lottery had had to use in addressing each person who came up to draw from the box, but this also had changed with time, until now it was felt necessary only for the official to speak to each person approaching. Mr. Summers was very good at all this; in his clean white shirt and blue jeans, with one hand resting carelessly on the black box, he seemed very proper and important as he talked interminably to Mr. Graves and the Martins.

Just as Mr. Summers finally left off talking and turned to the assembled villagers, Mrs. Hutchinson came hurriedly along the path to the square, her sweater thrown over her shoulders, and slid into place in the back of the crowd. "Clean forgot what day it was," she said to Mrs. Delacroix, who stood next to her, and they both laughed softly. "Thought my old man was out back stacking wood," Mrs. Hutchinson went on, "and then I looked out the window and the kids were gone, and then I remembered it was the twenty-seventh and came a-running." She dried her palms on her apron, and Mrs. Delacroix said, "You're in time, though. They're still talking away up there."

Mrs. Hutchinson craned her neck to see through the crowd and found her husband and children standing near the front. She tapped Mrs. Delacroix on the arm as a farewell and began to make her way through the crowd. The people separated good-humoredly to let her through; two or three people said, in voices just loud enough to be heard across the crowd, "Here comes your Missus, Hutchinson," and "Bill, she made it after all." Mrs. Hutchinson reached her husband, and Mr. Summers, who had been waiting, said cheerfully, "Thought we were going to have to get on without you, Tessie." Mrs. Hutchinson said, grinning, "Wouldn't have me leave m'dishes in the sink, now, would you, Joe?," and soft laughter ran through the crowd as the people stirred back into position after Mrs. Hutchinson's arrival.

"Well, now," Mr. Summers said soberly, "guess we better get started, get this over with, so's we can go back to work. Anybody ain't here?"

"Dunbar," several people said. "Dunbar, Dunbar."

Mr. Summers consulted his list. "Clyde Dunbar," he said. "That's right. He's broke his leg, hasn't he? Who's drawing for him?"

"Me, I guess," a woman said, and Mr. Summers turned to look at her. "Wife draws for her husband," Mr. Summers said. "Don't you have a grown boy to do it for you, Janey?" Although Mr. Summers and everyone else in the village knew the answer perfectly well, it was the business of the official of the lottery to ask such questions formally. Mr. Summers waited with an expression of polite interest while Mrs. Dunbar answered.

"Horace's not but sixteen yet," Mrs. Dunbar said regretfully. "Guess I gotta fill in for the old man this year."

"Right," Mr. Summers said. He made a note on the list he was holding. Then he asked, "Watson boy drawing this year?"

A tall boy in the crowd raised his hand. "Here," he said. "I'm drawing for m'mother and me." He blinked his eyes nervously and ducked his head as several voices in the crowd said things like "Good fellow, Jack," and "Glad to see your mother's got a man to do it."

"Well," Mr. Summers said, "guess that's everyone. Old Man Warner make it?"

"Here," a voice said, and Mr. Summers nodded.

A sudden hush fell on the crowd as Mr. Summers cleared his throat and looked at the list. "All ready?" he called. "Now, I'll read the names—heads of families first—and the men come up and take a paper out of the box. Keep the paper folded in your hand without looking at it until everyone has a turn. Everything clear?"

The people had done it so many times that they only half listened to the directions; most of them were quiet, wetting their lips, not looking around. Then Mr. Summers raised one hand high and said, "Adams." A man disengaged himself from the crowd and came forward. "Hi, Steve," Mr. Summers said, and Mr. Adams said, "Hi, Joe." They grinned at one another humorlessly and nervously. Then Mr. Adams reached into the black box and took out a folded paper. He held it firmly by one corner as he turned and went hastily back to his place in the crowd, where he stood a little apart from his family, not looking down at his hand.

"Allen," Mr. Summers said. "Anderson. . . . Bentham."

"Seems like there's no time at all between lotteries any more," Mrs. Delacroix said to Mrs. Graves in the back row. "Seems like we got through with the last one only last week."

"Time sure goes fast," Mrs. Graves said.

"Clark. . . . Delacroix."

"There goes my old man," Mrs. Delacroix said. She held her breath while her husband went forward.

"Dunbar," Mr. Summers said, and Mrs. Dunbar went steadily to the box while one of the women said, "Go on, Janey," and another said, "There she goes."

"We're next," Mrs. Graves said. She watched while Mr. Graves came around from the side of the box, greeted Mr. Summers gravely, and selected a slip of paper from the

Holt, Rinehart and Winston

box. By now, all through the crowd there were men holding the small folded papers in their large hands, turning them over and over nervously. Mrs. Dunbar and her two sons stood together, Mrs. Dunbar holding the slip of paper.

"Harburt. . . . Hutchinson."

"Get up there, Bill," Mrs. Hutchinson said, and the people near her laughed.

"Jones."

"They do say," Mr. Adams said to Old Man Warner, who stood next to him, "that over in the north village they're talking of giving up the lottery."

Old Man Warner snorted. "Pack of crazy fools," he said. "Listening to the young folks, nothing's good enough for *them*. Next thing you know, they'll be wanting to go back to living in caves, nobody work any more, live *that* way for a while. Used to be a saying about 'Lottery in June, corn be heavy soon.' First thing you know, we'd all be eating stewed chickweed and acorns. There's *always* been a lottery," he added petulantly. "Bad enough to see young Joe Summers up there joking with everybody."

"Some places have already quit lotteries," Mrs. Adams said.

"Nothing but trouble in *that*," Old Man Warner said stoutly. "Pack of young fools."

"Martin." And Bobby Martin watched his father go forward. "Overdyke. . . . Percy."

"I wish they'd hurry," Mrs. Dunbar said to her older son. "I wish they'd hurry."

"They're almost through," her son said.

"You get ready to run tell Dad," Mrs. Dunbar said.

Mr. Summers called his own name and then stepped forward precisely and selected a slip from the box. Then he called, "Warner."

"Seventy-seventh year I been in the lottery," Old Man Warner said as he went through the crowd. "Seventy-seventh time."

"Watson." The tall boy came awkwardly through the crowd. Someone said, "Don't be nervous, Jack," and Mr. Summers said, "Take your time, son."

"Zanini."

After that, there was a long pause, a breathless pause, until Mr. Summers, holding his slip of paper in the air, said, "All right, fellows." For a minute, no one moved, and then all the slips of paper were opened. Suddenly, all the women began to speak at once, saying, "Who is it?," "Who's got it?," "Is it the Dunbars?," "Is it the Watsons?" Then the voices began to say, "It's Hutchinson. It's Bill," "Bill Hutchinson's got it."

"Go tell your father," Mrs. Dunbar said to her older son.

People began to look around to see the Hutchinsons. Bill Hutchinson was standing quiet, staring down at the paper in his hand. Suddenly, Tessie Hutchinson shouted to Mr. Summers, "You didn't give him time enough to take any paper he wanted. I saw you. It wasn't fair!"

"Be a good sport, Tessie," Mrs. Delacroix called, and Mrs. Graves said, "All of us took the same chance."

"Shut up, Tessie," Bill Hutchinson said.

"Well, everyone," Mr. Summers said, "that was done pretty fast, and now we've got to be hurrying a little more to get done in time." He consulted his next list. "Bill," he said, "you draw for the Hutchinson family. You got any other households in the Hutchinsons?"

"There's Don and Eva," Mrs. Hutchinson yelled, "Make *them* take their chance!"

"Daughters draw with their husbands' families, Tessie," Mr. Summers said gently. "You know that as well as anyone else."

"It wasn't *fair*," Tessie said.

"I guess not, Joe," Bill Hutchinson said regretfully. "My daughter draws with her husband's family, that's only fair. And I've got no other family except the kids."

"Then, as far as drawing for families is concerned, it's you," Mr. Summers said in explanation, "and as far as drawing for households is concerned, that's you, too. Right?"

"Right," Bill Hutchinson said.

"How many kids, Bill?" Mr. Summers asked formally.

"Three," Bill Hutchinson said. "There's Bill, Jr., and Nancy, and little Dave. And Tessie and me."

"All right, then," Mr. Summers said. "Harry, you got their tickets back?"

Mr. Graves nodded and held up the slips of paper. "Put them in the box, then," Mr. Summers directed. "Take Bill's and put it in."

"I think we ought to start over," Mrs. Hutchinson said, as quietly as she could. "I tell you it wasn't *fair*. You didn't give him time enough to choose. *Every*body saw that."

Holt, Rinehart and Winston

Mr. Graves had selected the five slips and put them in the box, and he dropped all the papers but those onto the ground, where the breeze caught them and lifted them off.

"Listen, everybody," Mrs. Hutchinson was saying to the people around her.

"Ready, Bill?" Mr. Summers asked, and Bill Hutchinson, with one quick glance around at his wife and children, nodded.

"Remember," Mr. Summers said, "take the slips and keep them folded until each person has taken one. Harry, you help little Dave." Mr. Graves took the hand of the little boy, who came willingly with him up to the box. "Take a paper out of the box, Davy," Mr. Summers said. Davy put his hand into the box and laughed. "Take just *one* paper," Mr. Summers said. "Harry, you hold it for him." Mr. Graves took the child's hand and removed the folded paper from the tight fist and held it while little Dave stood next to him and looked at him wonderingly.

"Nancy next," Mr. Summers said. Nancy was twelve, and her school friends breathed heavily as she went forward, switching her skirt, and took a slip daintily from the box. "Bill, Jr.," Mr. Summers said, and Billy, his face red and his feet overlarge, nearly knocked the box over as he got a paper out. "Tessie," Mr. Summers said. She hesitated for a minute, looking around defiantly, and then set her lips and went up to the box. She snatched a paper out and held it behind her.

"Bill," Mr. Summers said, and Bill Hutchinson reached into the box and felt around, bringing his hand out at last with the slip of paper in it.

The crowd was quiet. A girl whispered, "I hope it's not Nancy," and the sound of the whisper reached the edges of the crowd.

"It's not the way it used to be," Old Man Warner said clearly. "People ain't the way they used to be."

"All right," Mr. Summers said. "Open the papers. Harry, you open little Dave's."

Mr. Graves opened the slip of paper and there was a general sigh through the crowd as he held it up and everyone could see that it was blank. Nancy and Bill, Jr., opened theirs at the same time, and both beamed and laughed, turning around to the crowd and holding their slips of paper above their heads.

"Tessie," Mr. Summers said. There was a pause, and then Mr. Summers looked at Bill Hutchinson, and Bill unfolded his paper and showed it. It was blank.

"It's Tessie," Mr. Summers said, and his voice was hushed. "Show us her paper, Bill."

Bill Hutchinson went over to his wife and forced the slip of paper out of her hand. It had a black spot on it, the black spot Mr. Summers had made the night before with the heavy pencil in the coal-company office. Bill Hutchinson held it up, and there was a stir in the crowd.

"All right, folks," Mr. Summers said. "Let's finish quickly."

Although the villagers had forgotten the ritual and lost the original black box, they still remembered to use stones. The pile of stones the boys had made earlier was ready; there were stones on the ground with the blowing scraps of paper that had come out of the box. Mrs. Delacroix selected a stone so large she had to pick it up with both hands and turned to Mrs. Dunbar. "Come on," she said. "Hurry up."

Mrs. Dunbar had small stones in both hands, and she said, gasping for breath, "I can't run at all. You'll have to go ahead and I'll catch up with you."

The children had stones already, and someone gave Davy Hutchinson a few pebbles.

Tessie Hutchinson was in the center of a cleared space by now, and she held her hands out desperately as the villagers moved in on her. "It isn't fair," she said. A stone hit her on the side of the head.

Old Man Warner was saying, "Come on, come on, everyone." Steve Adams was in the front of the crowd of villagers, with Mrs. Graves beside him.

"It isn't fair, it isn't right," Mrs. Hutchinson screamed, and then they were upon her.

Holt, Rinehart and Winston

Reading Assignment 9: "The Lottery"

Double-Entry Question Journal

Note: Some students find it easier to do the double-entry journal as they are reading; others find the process more effective after they have finished reading the entire piece. Please experiment to find the method that works best for you.

In the left column, jot down at least five "What?" "Why?" or "How?" questions. Then in the right column, jot down some possible answers and responses. If further questions come up, jot them down also. One purpose of this exercise is to learn how to think critically, so you might end up with several answers. Go ahead, take a risk!

1.   1.

2.   2.

3.   3.

4.   4.

5.   5.

Brief Summary: _____

_____

_____

_____

_____

_____

Note: Please refer to the Appendix if you need help in writing a summary.

Holt, Rinehart and Winston

Reading Assignment 9: "The Lottery"

A Closer Look

1. Why does the town continue to use the old black box that grows "shabbier each year" for the lottery?

_____

_____

_____

_____

2. Why does Old Man Warner think that only "a pack of crazy fools" would want to give up the lottery?

_____

_____

_____

_____

3. How would you characterize Bill Hutchinson's reaction to the fact that his family is selected as finalists in the lottery?

_____

_____

4. What is the real purpose of the lottery? Can they gain anything from continuing its practice?

_____

_____

CENTRAL IDEA (THEME)

What do you think Shirley Jackson's message is in "The Lottery"? What is the purpose of the story?

_____

_____

_____

Holt, Rinehart and Winston

Writing Assignment 9: An Essay

A Student Model

The following essay was written by a college English student. Its purpose is to show you how another student, like yourself, responded to this writing assignment. Try to develop your own thinking and individual style of writing.

Heather Gaertner
English 300: Allegre
Assignment 9
Nov. 7, 1997

The Ritual of the Tree

This year, as we do every year, we are buying our Christmas tree a week before Christmas. My sister and I have been waiting impatiently all week to make this trip. This has always been our favorite event of the holidays. We stop by to pick up our mother, and we are all in a good mood. When we arrive at our destination, however, something is different, a lot different. There are trees, but no tree farm.

The smell of the trees takes me back to a time when I was about eight or nine years old. I remember sitting in the back seat of our big van with my sister. We were both anxiously waiting to get to the tree farm. With my dad driving and my mom in the passenger seat, I thought to myself how lucky I was to have both parents for the holidays. Some of my friends had only one parent. Somehow their lives seemed more complicated than mine, with two parents to teach me everything I needed to know about life.

My dad interrupted my thoughts when he announced that we were approaching the tree farm. As our van pulled into the parking lot, the back seat came alive with laughter as my sister and I argued loudly over who could pick the best tree. We jumped out of the van and ran toward the many rows of pine trees. With my excitement level on high, I began looking for the best tree. After picking up a saw to cut the tree down, my Dad would always find a way to catch up with me and help me look. My mom usually helped my sister. Between the four of us, we would always manage to find the perfect Christmas tree. As I ran through the rows, I could smell the fresh pine scent. Checking the shape of each trees, I would search for the perfect tree. Suddenly, there it was! With a distinctive triangle shape, it stood about five and a half feet tall. It looked green and healthy. Besides that, it smelled wonderful. So excited, I rushed back to find the others. In what seemed like ritual to me, my dad had me stand by the tree so that no other family would come and take it. Then he went to find my mom and my sister. It's quite funny now, but I would always seem to find myself talking to our perfect tree, telling it how beautiful it was-showing off its millions of green branches, and smelling so fresh and clean. How could it not be perfect, like our lives?

It was like a game. After my dad found my mom and my sister, it was then my turn to be found. I made noises loud enough for them to hear me clear across the tree farm. After what seemed to take forever, they finally found me. My dad began to saw the tree down, and I almost felt sorry for it, knowing that it had grown up to be tall and straight only to be cut down and decorated, and then soon after, taken to the garbage dump.

Finally, my dad dragged it back to the car, with the rest of our family not too far behind. Knowing that our tree-cutting ceremony was coming to an end, my sister and I played a quick game of hide-and-seek through the trees on our way back to the parked van. As we climbed back into our van, my dad shoved our tree in behind us. Immediately, the van was filled with the fragrance of pine. Driving away with the whole family in the van again, I quietly said my farewell to the trees left at the tree farm: "Be back next year, I promise."

Some years have passed since those early days of picking out a Christmas tree, and a lot of things have changed. Now as we drive into the parking lot, I notice that there are trees everywhere, stacks and stacks of them. The trees are all different shapes and sizes, and they have names like Blue Spruce, Silver Tip, Fir, and Monterey Pine. They are already cut and ready to be taken off the lot. Christmas music fills the air, and the Christmas lights are blinking. There is even a Santa Claus on the lot, waiting for children to sit on his lap and tell him what they want for Christmas.

I look around, but nothing interesting catches my eye, so I leave the tree-picking decision to my mother and my sister. They choose a tree which is small, but plump and perfectly shaped. We struggle to get the tree into the car, which is still almost too small for the tree. I have to remind myself that it is not the size of the tree or where we get it that matters. It is still a family tradition. Whether we all live under the same roof or not, what matters is the time I spend with my family.

Writing Assignment 9: An Essay

Writing Task: Write an essay that examines how we learn our societal values. Do you think it starts with family? You might want to focus on how values are shaped by your family or your environment. You might also choose to examine a modern-day ceremony or holiday ritual. Another option would be to write about an initiation ritual, like hazing, that may have outgrown its use.

Your Topic: _____

Prewriting

Prewrite (cluster, list, freewrite, or ask journalistic questions) in the space below, jotting down whatever comes to mind about your topic. Prewrite until you come up with enough convincing evidence to support your point of view.

Writing the Thesis Statement

Make sure your thesis statement communicates the central idea of your essay and forecasts the way your paper will be developed.

Tentative Thesis Statement (Central Idea):

_____

_____

Note: Please refer to Reviewing the Basics if you need further help in writing a thesis statement.

Holt, Rinehart and Winston

Writing Assignment 9: An Essay

Writing a Rough Draft

Now take your prewriting one step further by creating a first draft. Select the best ideas, details, evidence, experiences, and reflections from your prewriting. Begin with your topic sentence and write until you have covered your topic well. Use whatever mode (narration, description, cause/effect, contrast, or argument) you feel is most appropriate to your purpose as you examine a ceremony or ritual or any other activity that shows how your values are shaped by your family or your environment.

Being Specific

Reread your rough draft of Writing Assignment 9, watching out for general words, phrases, and sentences. Underline the parts of your writing that might benefit from being more specific. Write a new draft, changing the passages you have underlined into more interesting, exact, and detailed writing. Use specific examples wherever you can.

The Concluding Paragraph

A concluding paragraph should provide a graceful exit for your reader and bring closure to the essay. It should also reinforce the central idea of the essay. In her essay, "The Ritual of the Tree," Heather Gaertner concludes by reminding us of the main idea and restating it clearly for the reader. She is careful not to introduce a new topic. Instead, she stays on focus, and in her last two lines she emphasizes the main idea she has been supporting in this assignment.

> I have to remind myself that it is not the size of the tree or where we get it that matters. It is still a family tradition. Whether we all live under the same roof or not, what matters is the time I spend with my family.

Revising

Remember that experienced writers constantly revise their work to make sure it communicates exactly what they want it to say. Revision is an ongoing process requiring you to delete words, add phrases, and rearrange sentences to make your meaning clear to your reader.

Peer Editing

Using your revised copy, read your paper out loud to a peer editor. Likewise, listen as your peer editor reads his or her paper back to you. When both papers have been read aloud, exchange papers, using the Editing Sheet provided for this assignment, to write helpful comments to each other. In some cases it might be more appropriate to exchange papers at the start and have each peer editor read silently before completing the Editing Sheet. Another option would be to use the Editing Sheet as a checklist for oral feedback. A final option would be for your instructor to create peer editing groups of three or four members for collaborative learning.

Whatever option you choose, the editing sheet that follows will provide useful guidelines for this assignment. Only one set of editing sheets is provided, which is sufficient if you are using collaborative groups. However, if you are using two individual editors, you will need to obtain a photocopy of the Editing Sheet. Please check with your instructor.

Holt, Rinehart and Winston

Writing Assignment 9: An Essay

Editing Sheet (to be completed by peer editor)

Directions: Either pair up and exchange papers with another student in class, or form editing groups of three or four members. Papers may be read silently or aloud. Every paper requires at least two peer editors who will work collaboratively to complete an Editing Sheet. The completed Editing Sheet should then be attached to the rough draft and returned to the writer for reference during the revision process.

Some peer editors may prefer to write comments directly on a student's rough draft, using the Editing Sheet as more of a checklist. Check with your instructor to see which method works best for your situation.

1. Has the writer selected a topic that is interesting, sufficiently narrowed, and appropriate for the writing task? If the topic is weak, suggest prewriting strategies (clustering, listing, freewriting, or asking journalistic questions) to generate enough ideas for a new topic.

_____

_____

_____

2. Does the introductory paragraph "hook" you or seem powerful and engaging? If not, offer suggestions.

_____

_____

_____

3. Draw a double line under the thesis statement. If it is missing, ask the writer, "So what? What is the point of this essay?" Suggest ways to make the thesis statement more effective, if necessary.

_____

_____

_____

4. Draw a circle around the directing words in the topic sentences. Does each body paragraph have a clear topic sentence that points out the main idea of the paragraph?

_____

_____

Holt, Rinehart and Winston

5. Draw a wavy line under words or phrases that would benefit from detailed examples. Has the writer included enough examples and specific details and anecdotes (interesting little stories with a point) in each body paragraph for a fully developed essay?

_____

_____

6. Underline the transitional expressions that signal the overall order used in this essay. Does the essay seem well organized? Offer suggestions.

_____

_____

_____

7. Does the writer also use appropriate "linking" transitions that show the relationship between ideas in a sentence? Where would you add more? Where would you omit some?

_____

_____

8. Does the concluding paragraph wrap up the essay effectively or leave a lasting impression on you? What ideas do you have about writing a more effective conclusion?

_____

_____

_____

9. Does the title intrigue you and really catch your attention as a reader? Think of recent movie titles. What suggestions do you have for a more interesting, creative title?

_____

_____

10. What is the most powerful part of this essay? Be as specific as possible.

_____

_____

Peer Editors' Initials: ____ ____ ____ ____ (This verifies the paper is ready for a Revised Copy.)

Holt, Rinehart and Winston

Submitting the Final Copy

Once you have had your paper edited, you should revise your paper once again. Remember that experienced writers constantly revise their work to make sure it communicates exactly what they meant to say. Before you write the final copy of your paper, your instructor or tutor may want to skim over your revised draft. Then write your final copy in ink on notebook paper or type it on a typewriter or a computer. Make sure you follow the rules of manuscript form located in the Appendix.

After writing the final copy of your paper, exchange it with other members of your editing group to proofread for spelling, punctuation, and grammar errors. Ask your peer editors to initial your final copy to indicate that it has been through the final editing process. When your edited paper is returned to you, make the final corrections and submit your final copy along with your rough draft and completed editing sheet. Stapling the whole packet together will allow your instructor to check your progress during each stage of the writing process.

Holt, Rinehart and Winston

4

The World around Us:
Issues and Choices

The readings in Chapter 4 will enable you to branch out and begin to grapple with larger social issues and help you to explore your own individual values. The critical thinking skills you have practiced throughout the book will be fine-tuned as you examine the issues in these readings and begin to see how your personal choices are unavoidably interconnected with the world around you. The readings are about both the individual's struggle and the collective struggles of humankind to understand the world or to create a better world.

In "The Secret," for instance, Alberto Moravia writes about a man who is tortured by his decision to leave the scene of an accident and avoid taking responsibility for causing a person's death. Sometimes our moral decisions involve criminal acts and, therefore, have earth-shaking consequences, yet at other times they may seem insignificant in comparison because they involve taking a stand without taking any physical action. In this chapter you will discover how others have used writing to explore ideas and issues that deeply affect all of us, enabling us to make informed choices about the world in which we live.

However, as indicated by each of the readings, this freedom of choice does not come easily, and certainly not without some pain and suffering. Indeed, it is often difficult to make ethical choices, but the ideas you get by reading and responding to the selections in this chapter will serve as springboards for you to examine and re-examine the ideas and issues that are important to you. The final paper, the Information Essay, is divided into three parts. For this final essay, you will be asked to complete Writing Assignments 10, 11, and 12. These three assignments will introduce you to some basic research skills to help you explore the ideas of others and develop them more thoroughly.

Reading Assignment 10: "The Secret" by Alberto Moravia

Writing Assignment 10: Information Essay, Part I

Reading Assignment 11: "Footbinding" by John King Fairbank

Writing Assignment 10: Information Essay, Part II

Reading Assignment 12: "Rites of Passage"

Writing Assignment 10: Information Essay, Part III

Holt, Rinehart and Winston

Reading Assignment 10: "The Secret" by Alberto Moravia

Prereading

"The Secret" by Alberto Moravia is about a terrible secret held by a truck driver who kills a man on a motor bike. The truck driver, guilty of this hit-and-run accident, freely admits that it is his fault. Yet, he cannot seem to justify his actions and is tortured by his guilt for a long time afterward. As you read the story, try to think of how you would have reacted in that situation. Can you give any explanations of your own about why he does not stop to give whatever aid he could give after the accident? Do you think he is prepared for the girl's reaction when he finally tells his secret? Why do you think it is so important to him that she tell him whether his actions are "right or wrong"? Do you feel there are some decisions in our lives for which we, alone, have to take ultimate responsibility?

The Secret
Alberto Moravia

Don't talk to me about secrets! I had one—and it was the kind that weighs on your conscience like a nightmare.

I am a truck driver. One beautiful spring morning, while hauling a load of lava rock from a quarry near Campagnano to Rome, I ran square into a man who was coming in the opposite direction on a motor bike. It was right at the 25 Kilometer marker on the old Cassia road. Through no fault of his, either. I had kept going on the wrong side of the road long after having passed a car, and I was speeding; he was on the right, where he belonged, and going slow. The truck hit him so hard that I barely had time to see something black fly through the blue air and then fall and lie still and black against the soft whiteness of a daisy field. The motor bike lay on the other side of the road, its wheels in the air, like a dead bug.

Lowering my head, I stepped down hard on the gas. I tore down the road to Rome and dropped my load at the yard. ·

The next day the papers carried the news: So-and-so, forty-three years old, a jobber by trade, leaving a wife and several children, had been run down at Kilometer 25 of the Cassia road and instantly killed. Nobody knew who had struck him. The hit-and-run driver had fled the scene of the accident like a coward. That's exactly what the paper said: *like a coward*. Except for those three little words that burned a hole in my brain, it didn't take more than four lines to report on what was, after all, only the death of a man.

During the next couple of days, I could think of nothing else. I know that I am only a truck driver, but who can claim that truck drivers have no conscience? A truck driver has a lot of time to mull over his own private business, during the long hours behind the wheel or lying in the truck's sleeping berth. And when, as in my case, that private business is not all it ought to be, thinking can get to be really pretty tough.

Holt, Rinehart and Winston

One thing in particular kept nagging at me. I just couldn't understand why I hadn't stopped, why I hadn't tried to help the poor guy. I lived the scene over and over again. I would be gauging the distances again before passing that car; I would feel my foot pressing down hard on the accelerator. Then the man's body would come flying up in front of my windshield . . . and at this point I would deliberately block out the picture, as you do at the movies, and I would think, "Now, jam on your brakes, jump down, run into the field, pick him up, put him in the bed of the truck and rush him to Santa Spirito Hospital. . . ."

But, you poor fool, you're just dreaming again. I had *not* stopped, I had driven straight on, with head lowered like a bull after a goring. To make a long story short, the more I thought about that split second when I had stepped on the gas instead of jamming on the brakes, the less I could make it out. Cowardice—that was the word fot it all right. But why does a man who has, or at least thinks he has guts, turn into a coward without a moment's warning? That stumped me. Yet the cold hard facts were there: the dead man was really dead; that split second when I might have stopped had passed and was now sinking farther and farther away and no one would ever be able to bring it back. I was no longer the Gino who had passed that car but another Gino who had killed a man and then had run away.

I lay awake nights over it. I grew gloomy and silent and after a while everybody shied away from me at the yard and after work: nobody wants to pass the time with a kill-joy. So I carried my secret around as if it were a hot diamond that you can't entrust to anyone or plant anywhere.

Then, after a while, I began thinking about it less and less and I can even say that there came a time when I didn't think about it at all. But the secret was still stowed away deep down inside me and it weighed on my conscience and kept me from enjoying life. I often thought that I would have felt better if I could have told somebody about it. I wasn't exactly looking for approval—I realized there was no pardon for what I had done—but if I could have told this secret of mine I would have thrown off part of its dead weight onto somebody else who would have helped me carry it. But who could I tell it to? To my friends at the yard? They had other things to worry about. To my family? I had none, being a foundling. My girl friend? She would have been the logical person because, as everybody knows, women are good at understanding you and giving you sympathy when you need it, but unfortunately, I had no girl friend.

II

One Sunday in May I went walking outside the Rome city gates with a girl I had met some time before when I had given her and one of her friends a lift in my truck. She had told me her name and address, and I had seen her again a couple of times. We had enjoyed each other's company, and she had made it clear that she liked me and would be willing to go out with me.

Her name was Iris. She was a lady's maid in the house of some wealthy woman who had lots of servants. I had fallen from the start for her serious little oval face and those great big sad gray eyes of hers. In short, here was just the girl for me in the present circumstances. After we had had a cup of coffee at the Exposition Grounds, with all those columns around us, she finally agreed in her shy, silent, and gentle way to go and sit with me in a meadow not far from St. Paul's Gate, where you get a good view of the Tiber and of the new apartment houses lined up on the opposite bank. She had spread out a handkerchief on the grass to keep her skirt from getting dirty and she sat quietly, her legs tucked under her, her hands in her lap, gazing across at the big white buildings on the other side of the river.

I noticed that there were lots of daisies in the grass around us; and like a flash I remembered the soft whiteness of those other daisies among which, just a month earlier, I had seen lying still and the dead man I had struck down. I don't know what got into me but suddenly I couldn't hold back the urge to tell my secret. If I tell her, I thought, I'll get rid of the load on my chest. She wasn't one of those dizzy, empty-headed girls who, after you've told them a secret, make you feel so much worse than you did before, that you could kick yourself hard for having spilled all you know. She was a nice, understanding person who had doubtless had her share of knocks in life—and they must have been pretty rough knocks if the sad little look on her face meant anything. Just break the ice, I said to her, in an offhanded way:

"What are you thinking about, Iris?"

She was just raising her hand to choke back a yawn. Perhaps she was tired. She said: "Nothing."

I didn't let that answer get me down but quickly went on. "Iris, you know that I like you a lot, don't you? That's why I feel that I shouldn't hide anything from you. You've got to know everything about me. Iris, I've got a secret."

She kept on looking at the tall buildings on the other side of the river, all the while fingering a little red lump on her chin, a tiny spring pimple.

"What secret?" she asked.

With an effort I got it out. "I've killed a man."

She didn't move but kept on poking gently at her chin. Then she shivered all over, as though she had finally understood. "You've killed a man? And you tell me about it just like that?"

"And how else do you expect me to tell you?"

She said nothing. She seemed to be looking for something on the ground. I went on. "Let's get this thing straight. I didn't mean to kill him."

Suddenly she found what she wanted: picking a long blade of grass, she put it into

Holt, Rinehart and Winston

her mouth and began chewing on it, thoughtfully. Then, hurriedly, but without hiding anything, I told her about the accident, bringing out the part about my cowardice. I got pretty wrought up in spite of myself, but already I was beginning to feel relieved. I concluded:

"Now tell me what you think about all this."

She kept munching on her blade of grass and didn't say a word.

I insisted. "I'll bet that now you can't stand the sight of me."

I saw her shrug her shoulders, lightly. "And why shouldn't I be able to stand the sight of you?"

"Well, I don't know. After all, it was my fault that poor guy got killed."

"And it bothers you?"

"Yes. Terribly." Suddenly, my throat closed tight as if over a hard knot of tears. "I feel as if I can't go on living. No man can go on living if he thinks he's a coward."

"Was it in the papers?"

"Yes. They gave it four lines. Just to say he had been killed and that nobody knew who had hit him."

Suddenly she asked, "What time is it?"

"Five-fifteen."

Another silence. "Listen, Iris, what does a man have to do to find out what's going on in that mind of yours?"

She shifted the blade of grass from one corner of her mouth to the other and said frankly, "Well, if you must know, there's nothing on my mind. I feel good and I'm not thinking about anything."

I couldn't believe my ears. I protested. "It can't be! You must have been thinking something about something. I'm sure of it."

I saw her smile, faintly. "Well, as a matter of fact, I was thinking about something. But if I tell you, you'll never believe it."

Hopefully, I asked, "Was it about me?"

"Good heavens, no! It had absolutely nothing to do with you!"

"What was it, then?"

She said slowly, "It was just one of those things that only women think about. I was looking at my shoes and seeing that they have holes in them. I was thinking that there is a big clearance sale on in Via Cola di Rienzo and that I've got to go there tomorrow and buy myself a pair of new shoes. There . . . are you satisfied?"

This time I shut up like a clam, my face dark and brooding. She noticed it and exclaimed: "Oh, dear! You're not mad, are you?"

I couldn't help blurting out: "Sure, I'm mad. Damn mad. Here I tell you the secret of my life, and it makes so little impression on you I wonder why I didn't keep it to myself!"

This bothered her a bit. "No," she said. "I'm glad you told me about it. It really did make an impression on me."

"Well, what kind of an impression?"

She thought it over and then said, scrupulously, "Well, I'm sorry that such a thing had to happen to you. It must have been awful."

"Is that all you've got to say?"

"I also think," she added, fingering the pimple on her chin, "that it's only right it should bother you."

"Why?"

"Well, you said so yourself. You ought to have stopped to help him but you didn't."

"Then you think I am a coward?"

"A coward? Well, yes . . . and then no. After all, a thing like that could happen to anybody."

"But you just said that I ought to have stopped!"

"You should have; but you didn't . . ."

At this point I saw her glance down at something in the daisies. "Oh, look! How pretty!"

It was an insect, a green and gold beetle, resting on the white petals of a daisy. Suddenly I felt as if I were emptied out—almost as if that secret over which I had agonized so long had vanished in the spring air, carried away, lightly, like the white butterflies that were flitting around in pairs in the sunlight.

Yet with one dogged last hope, I asked: "But tell me, Iris, in your opinion, was I right or wrong not to stop?"

"You were right and you were wrong. Of course, you ought to have stopped. After all, you had run into him. But, on the other hand, what good would it have done if you had? He was dead by that time anyway and you would probably have got into a terrible mess. You were both right and wrong."

After these words, a thought flashed through my mind. "This is the end of Iris. I'll never take her out again. I thought she was a bright, understanding girl. Instead, she is really nothing but a half-wit. Enough is enough." I jumped to my feet.

"Come on, let's go," I said. "Otherwise, we'll be late for the movies."

Once inside the theater, in the dark, she slipped her hand into mine, forcing her fingers through mine. I didn't budge. The film was a love story, a real tear-jerker. When the lights went on at the end I saw that her big gray eyes were filled with tears and that her cheeks were wet. "I just can't help it," she said, patting her face dry with a handkerchief. "Pictures like this always make me want to cry."

Afterwards we went into a bar and ordered coffee. She pressed so close to me that our bodies touched. Just as the *espresso* machine let off a loud stream of steam, she said softly, "You know that I really like you, don't you?" staring at me with those great big beautiful eyes of hers.

I felt like answering: "Fine. You really like me, but you'll let me carry the whole weight of my secret alone!" Instead, I said nothing.

Now I understood that from her, as from everybody else, I could ask only for affection, nothing more than that.

I answered with a sigh, "I like you a lot, too."

But already she had stopped listening to me. She was peering at herself in the mirror behind the bar, absorbed and concerned as she fingered the little red lump on her chin.

Holt, Rinehart and Winston

Reading Assignment 10: "The Secret"

Double-Entry Question Journal

In the left column, jot down at least five "What?" "Why?" or "How?" questions. Then in the right column, jot down some possible answers and responses. If further questions come up, jot them down also. One purpose of this exercise is to learn how to think critically, so you might end up with several answers. Go ahead, take a risk!

1.   1.

2.   2.

3.   3.

4.   4.

5.   5.

Brief Summary: _____

_____

_____

_____

_____

_____

_____

Note: Please refer to the Appendix if you need help in writing a summary.

Holt, Rinehart and Winston

Reading Assignment 10: "The Secret"

A Closer Look

1. Why does the paper's description of the truck driver fleeing the scene of the accident "like a coward" bother him so much even though he says himself that he is a coward?

_____

_____

_____

2. Do you think his decision not to tell his secret affects the quality of his life after the accident? What evidence is there in the story to support your opinion?

_____

_____

_____

3. After he finally tells his secret to the girl he met, why does she react the way she does?

_____

_____

_____

4. Ultimately, the truck driver realizes that he cannot find true forgiveness or understanding from anyone else, only "affection, nothing more than that." Why is this discovery so important to him?

_____

_____

_____

CENTRAL IDEA (THEME)

What do you think Moravia is telling us in "The Secret"? What is the purpose of the story?

_____

_____

Holt, Rinehart and Winston

Writing Assignment 10: Information Essay, Part I

This final writing assignment introduces you to some basic research skills such as locating information in books and magazines and citing your sources, using MLA documentation.

A Student Model

The following essay was written by a college English student. Its purpose is to show you how another student, like yourself, responded to this writing assignment. Remember to try to explore ways to develop your own thinking and individual style of writing.

Kevin K. Green
English 300: Mr. Isaacson
Assignment 10: Information Essay
March 21, 1997

Flashing Lights

My wife's first epileptic seizure was a frightening event in our lives. I will never forget the way she looked. First, her eyes rolled back. Then a small trickle of blood dripped out of the left side of her mouth as she bit her tongue. Finally, her back arched like the last spasm of a dying fish on a dock. For almost two years now, these seizures have been a part of our family's life, and my wife still "fades out," a term I use to describe her seizures. Today doctors are learning more about the possible causes of epilepsy, but fear and ignorance of the disease are still widespread in our society.

The Concise Medical Dictionary gives us a clear medical definition of epilepsy: "A chronic disorder characterized by paroxysmal attacks of brain dysfunction due to excessive neuronal discharge, and usually associated with some alteration of consciousness." The article goes on to mention dozens of types of seizures. These can be categorized by how the seizures are caused and by the effect of each type of seizure. Basically, epilepsy is a short circuit of the electrical activity in the brain. Also, the type of seizure depends on what area of the brain is affected and how large an area of the brain is involved. That is, small areas produce seizures called "petit mal" while large areas produce "grand mal" seizures.

In an interview with Dr. Leonora Robinson, our family doctor, I learned that epilepsy has several possible causes. It can be triggered by drug or alcohol abuse, or even by going through withdrawal from either of these drugs. It can also be the result of brain damage. While brain damage does not always develop into epilepsy, any type of scar tissue in the brain can cause a short circuit. However, Dr. Robinson also explained that sometimes there is simply no clear reason at all for the seizures. She stated, "Sometimes the brain just misfires, causing a cascading sequence of misfirings." An article in The Home Medical Encyclopedia, titled "Epilepsy," reveals that doctors can perform several procedures after a seizure for a diagnosis. The first is usually a magnetic resonance image. Later, doctors can do a computerized brain scan. These exams show the doctors the inside of the brain and any tumors or scar tissue that might be causing the seizures. If these first two procedures don't reveal anything, electrodes are placed

Holt, Rinehart and Winston

on the scalp to monitor the electrical patterns of the brain. Doctors can use this information to see if there is any abnormality in brain patterns that might be causing the seizures.

The primary treatment for epilepsy is drug therapy, according to another article in The Home Medical Encyclopedia, "Anticonvulsant Drugs." The three main drugs used today are Phenobarbital, Carbam Azepine, and Phenytoin. These drugs have been the only anticonvulsants on the market for the last sixteen years. In addition, the U.S. Food and Drug Administration has recently approved two new anticonvulsants: Felbamate and Gabapentin. However, the main problem with drug therapy is that the side effects can be just as bad as the seizure itself. The most common side effects are reduced concentration, loss of coordination, impaired memory, and fatigue. The more severe side effects can be anorexia, vomiting, nausea, headaches, and dizziness.

Perhaps the worst problem epileptics must face, however, is the ignorance and fear of other people. In his article in Epilepsy USA titled "I Am Not Defined by My Disorder," John Lovell states, "I may have a seizure anywhere, anytime. But I'm not going to limit myself in what I do. I have epilepsy, but epilepsy doesn't have me" (157). Sara Jones, in her article, "Epileptics Want Normal Lives," states that most of the limits are not set by the epileptics themselves. For example, some airlines refuse to carry epileptics because other passengers might be frightened. Also, employers often show discrimination. For instance, some employers will not hire an epileptic because they believe that an epileptic can't be trained to do a job properly or that productivity will drop due to missed days (B7). As a result, epileptics have a difficult time in their careers. In "Employment Issues Explored at Training Sessions," an article in Epilepsy USA, a recent survey of 2,000 Californians with epilepsy found that nearly 60 percent had some sort of college education or degree, yet less than 28 percent of college-educated epileptics worked full time or earned more than $20,000 a year (73).

Everyone needs to become better educated about the causes of epilepsy. They also need to learn what treatments are available, so they can be aware of the problems anyone suffering from this disease will face. Hopefully, when people are better informed about the truth of epilepsy, discrimination against epileptics will end.

Holt, Rinehart and Winston

Works Cited

"Anticonvulsant Drugs." The Home Medical Encyclopedia. 3rd ed. 1996.

"Employment Issues Explored at Training Sessions." Epilepsy USA. 14 Nov. 1996: 124-136.

"Employment Issues Explored at Training Sessions." Epilepsy USA. 5 May 1996: 29-34.

"Epilepsy." The Home Medical Encyclopedia. 3rd. ed. 1996.

"Epilepsy." The Concise Medical Dictionary. 9th ed. 1994.

Jones, Sara. "Epileptics Want Normal Lives." Santa Maria Tribune. 19 April 1997: B7.

Lovell, John. "I Am Not Defined By My Disorder." Epilepsy USA. 9 April 1995: 13-37.

Robinson, Lenora, Dr. Personal interview. March 3, 1997.

Holt, Rinehart and Winston

Writing Assignment 10: Information Essay, Part I

Searching for Information

Writing Task: Write a research paper that uses other people's words and ideas to support your argument on a social issue that is important to you.

For this paper your instructor will probably require you to use at least three sources of information: a book, a current magazine or newspaper article, and an authority on your subject that you can interview. Your instructor may also ask you to use the Internet to search for information as well.

Exploring a Topic

Writing is one way that we can take a stand on important issues in our society. Speaking out through writing can bring about positive changes and possibly transform the world we live in. Answer the following questions in the space provided.

Do you have any fears or concerns about something happening in the world today?

_____

_____

What are some contemporary issues you would really like to examine more closely?

_____

_____

_____

What are some significant topics that affect the world at large?

_____

_____

Do you have strong feelings about today's most controversial issues, for example, violence in schools, welfare reform, the right to die, health issues, or the immigration crisis?

_____

_____

_____

Holt, Rinehart and Winston

Writing Assignment 10: Information Essay, Part I

Writing an effective information essay requires having a topic that is exactly right for you. As with Kevin Green, having some personal connection with your topic can be a critical first step. In Kevin's essay, "Flashing Lights," it is obvious that he has a great stake in the topic of epilepsy, for this is a serious condition with which he and his wife must learn to live. By learning more about epilepsy for his report, Kevin is not only able to educate his readers about this disorder, but, more importantly, he is also able to discover a great deal of helpful information for himself.

Writing Task: Research is an activity in which we must involve ourselves throughout our lives, for information is power, and with it we can face challenging situations and issues much more positively and productively.

Finding a Topic

Choosing the right topic for you personally is the first big step in this process. Select a topic that you genuinely need to know about. Make a list of several broad topics or issues with which you have some personal experience and genuinely need to know more about in order to better understand them. Try to come up with three to five potential topics. Having a backup topic or two is a good idea in case you cannot find enough information on your first choice.

Possible Topics:

_____

_____

_____

_____

_____

_____

Select the most promising topic on your list and write it below:

General Topic: _____

Once you have a general topic, you will have to narrow it. For example, if Kevin Green's general topic were "Life-Threatening Diseases," it would be impossible to write a meaningful short paper on this huge topic. Instead of trying to write an essay on such a broad topic, he narrows it down to one that has an impact on his family's life: epilepsy. Likewise, you will need to narrow the focus of your research to something manageable.

Holt, Rinehart and Winston

The Thesis Statement

One way of narrowing your topic is to write a thesis that carefully defines the scope of what your essay will examine. In your previous essay writing assignments you learned that the thesis statement is the most important sentence in your entire essay. Without it your paper would have no purpose and no direction.

Example:

> Today doctors are learning more about the possible causes of epilepsy, but fear and ignorance of the disease are still widespread in our society.

Remember: The thesis statement names the topic (epilepsy) and often forecasts the essay's overall development (the causes and treatment of epilepsy and the unjust way its victims are treated).

Tentative Thesis Statement

Make sure your thesis statement communicates the central idea (topic) of your paper and forecasts the way in which your topic will be developed.

_____

_____

_____

Holt, Rinehart and Winston

Reading Assignment 11: "Footbinding" by John King Fairbank

Prereading

As you read John King Fairbank's' essay, "Footbinding," try to imagine what it would have been like to have lived in a time and place that required women to mutilate a part of their bodies in order to to fit in to their culture and be accepted. As you reflect on this extraordinary custom, you might think of the ways in which members of our culture, both male and female, are required to conform in order to be accepted. What is the price of such conformity? What do we give up? What do we gain? Are women still treated unfairly in our world?

Footbinding
John King Fairbank

Of all the many unexplored facets of China's ancient history, the subjection of women has been the least studied. Women were fitted into the social and cosmic order (which were a continuum) by invoking the principles of Yang and Yin. All things bright, warm, active, male, and dominant were Yang while all things dark, cold, passive, female, and yielding were Yin. This dualism, seen in the alternation of night and day or the contrast of the sun and moon, was a ready-made matrix in which women could be confined. The subjection of women was thus a sophisticated and perfected institution like the other Chinese achievements, not a mere accident of male biceps or female childbearing as might be more obviously the case in a primitive tribe. The inequality between the sexes was buttressed with philosophical underpinnings and long-continued social practices. Symbolic of woman's secondary status was her bridal night; she expected to be deflowered by a stranger, a husband selected by her family whom she had never seen before. Even though the facts may often have been less stark, the theory was hard-boiled.

Out of all this complex of theory and custom by which the Chinese world was given an enduring and stable order, the most neglected aspect is the institution of footbinding. This custom arose at court in the tenth century during the late Tang and spread gradually among the upper class during the succeeding Sung period. By the Ming and Ch'ing eras after 1368 it had penetrated the mass of the Han Chinese population. It became so widespread that Western observers in the nineteenth century found it almost universal, not only among the upper class but throughout the farming population.

Footbinding spread as a mark of gentility and upper class status. Small feet became a prestige item to such an extent that a girl without them could not achieve a good marriage arrangement and was subjected to the disrespect and taunts of the community. In short, bound feet became *de rigueur*, the only right-thinking thing to do for a daughter, an obligation on the part of a mother who cared about her daughter's eventual marriage and success in life. The bound foot was a must. Only tribal peoples

Holt, Rinehart and Winston

and exceptional groups like the Manchu conquerors or the Hakka Chinese migrant groups in South China or finally the mean people, that lowest and rather small group who were below the social norms of civility, could avoid binding their daughters' feet.

The small foot was called a "golden lotus" or "golden lily" (*chin lien*) and was much celebrated in poems and essays by male enthusiasts. Here is the early Sung poet Su Tung-p'o (1036–1101):

> Anointed with fragrance, she takes lotus steps;
> Though often sad, she steps with swift lightness.
> She dances like the wind, leaving no physical trace.
> Another stealthily but happily tries on the palace style,
> But feels such distress when she tries to walk!
> Look at them in the palms of your hands,
> so wondrously small that they defy description.

The Sung philosophers stressed women's inferiority as a basic element of the social order. The great Chu Hsi (1130–1200) codified the cosmology of China as magistrally as his near contemporary Thomas Aquinas (d. 1274) codified that of Western Christendom. When he was a magistrate in Fukien province, Chu Hsi promoted footbinding to preserve female chastity and as "a means of spreading Chinese culture and teaching the separation of men and women."

By the Ming period the overwhelming majority of Han Chinese women all over the country had artificially small feet. The Manchu emperors many times inveighed against it in hortatory edicts, but to no avail. Male romanticizing on the subject continued unabated as in this poem of the fourteenth century:

> Lotus blossoms in shoes most tight,
> As if she could stand on autumnal waters!
> Her shoe tips do not peek beyond the skirt,
> Fearful lest the tiny embroideries be seen.[1]

There can be no doubt that footbinding was powered by a sexual fetish. Chinese love manuals are very specific about the use of bound feet as erogenous areas. All the different ways of taking hold of the foot, rubbing it with the hands, and using the mouth, tongue, and lips are explicitly catalogued. Many cases are recorded with the verisimilitude of high class pornography. Meanwhile, the aesthetic attractiveness of the small shoes with their bright embroidered colors was praised in literature, while the tottering gait of a bound foot woman was considered very fetching as a symbol of feminine frailty, which indeed it was. In fact, of course, bound feet were a guarantee of chastity because they kept women within the household and unable to venture far abroad. Lily feet, once formed, could not be unlocked like a chastity belt. By leaving only men able-bodied, they ensured male domination in a very concrete way.

Thus the prevalence of footbinding down to the 1920s, while the movement against it began only in the 1890s, vividly index the speed and scope of China's modern social

Holt, Rinehart and Winston

revolution. This may be less comprehensible to white American males than to white women, or especially to black Americans, for Chinese women within the present century have had an emancipation from veritable slavery.

While footbinding is mentioned in so many foreign books about China, it is usually passed by as a curious detail. I don't think it was. It was a major erotic invention, still another achievement in Chinese social engineering. Girls painfully deformed themselves throughout their adolescence in order to attract desirable husbands who, on their part, subscribed to a folklore of self-fulfilling beliefs: for example, that footbinding made a vagina more narrow and muscular and that lotus feet were major foci of erotic sensitivity, the erogenous zones, a net addition of 50 percent to the female equipment. Normal feet, we are now told by purveyors of sexual comfort, are an underdeveloped area sensually, but one must admit they are a bit hard to handle—whereas small lotus feet could be grasped, rubbed, licked, sucked, nibbled, and bitten. The garrulous Jesuit Father Ripa, who spent a decade at the court of K'ang-hsi in the early 1700s, reported that "Their taste is perverted to such an extraordinary degree that I knew a physician who lived with a woman with whom he had no other intercourse but that of viewing and fondling her feet."[2] Having compacted all their nerve endings in a smaller area, golden lilies were far more sensitive than, for example, the back of the neck that used to bewitch Japanese samurai. After all, they had been created especially for male appreciation. When every proper girl did it, what bride would say that her sacrifice, suffering, and inconvenience were not worth it? A bride without small feet in the old China was like a new house in today's America without utilities—who would want it? Consequently in the 1930s and '40s one still saw women on farms stumping about on their heels as they worked, victims of this old custom.

A girl's foot was made small, preferably only three inches long, by pressing the four small toes under the sole or ball of the foot (plantar) in order to make it narrower. At the same time it was made shorter by forcing the big toe and heel closer together so that the arch rose in a bowed shape. As a result the arch was broken and the foot could bear no weight except on the heel. If this process was begun at age five, the experience was less severe than if a little girl, perhaps in a peasant household, had been left with normal feet until age eight or ten so that she could be of more use in the household.

> When I was seven [said one woman to Ida Pruitt], my mother . . . washed and placed alum on my feet and cut the toenails. She then bent my toes toward the plantar with a binding cloth ten feet long and two inches wide, doing the right foot first and then the left. She . . . ordered me to walk but when I did the pain proved unbearable. That night . . . my feet felt on fire and I couldn't sleep; mother struck me for crying. On the following days, I tried to hide but was forced to walk on my feet . . . after several months all toes but the big one were pressed against the inner surface . . . mother would remove the bindings and wipe the blood and pus which dripped from my feet. She told me that only with removal of the flesh

[1]Howard Levy, *Chinese Footbinding: The History of a Curious Erotic Custom* (New York: Walton Rawls, 1966), p. 47.

Holt, Rinehart and Winston

could my feet become slender . . . every two weeks I changed to new shoes. Each new pair was one-to-two-tenths of an inch smaller than the previous one. . . . In summer my feet smelled offensively because of pus and blood; in winter my feet felt cold because of lack of circulation . . . four of the toes were curled in like so many dead caterpillars . . . it took two years to achieve the three-inch model . . . my shanks were thin, my feet became humped, ugly and odoriferous.[3]

After the first two years the pain lessened. But constricting the feet to a three-inch size was only the beginning of trouble. By this time they were very private parts indeed and required daily care, washing and manicuring at the same time that they had to be kept constantly bound and shod night and day. Unmanicured nails could cut into the instep, binding could destroy circulation, blood poisoning or gangrene could result. Massage and applications of hot and cold water were used to palliate the discomfort, but walking any distance remained difficult. It also produced corns on the bent-under toes, which had to be pared with a knife. Once deformed to taste, bound feet were of little use to stand on. Since weight was carried entirely on the heels, it had to be constantly shifted back and forth. Since the bound foot lacked the resilience of a normal foot, it was a tiring and unsteady support.

Footbinding, in short, had begun as an ostentatious luxury, which made a girl less useful in family work and more dependent on help from others. Yet, once the custom had spread among the populace, lotus feet were considered essential in order to get a good husband. Marriages, of course, were arranged between families and often by professional matchmakers, in whose trade the length of the lily foot was rated more important than beauty of face or person. When the anti-footbinding movement began at the end of the nineteenth century, many mothers and daughters, too, stubbornly clung to it to avoid the public shame of having large feet. The smallness of the foot, in short, was a source of social pride both to the family and to the victim. First and last one may guess that at least a billion Chinese girls during the thousand-year currency of this social custom suffered the agony of footbinding and reaped its rewards of pride and ecstasy, such as they were.

There are three remarkable things about footbinding. First, that it should have been invented at all—it was such a feat of physio-psychosociological engineering. Second, that once invented it should have spread so pervasively and lasted so long among a generally humane and practical-minded farming population. We are just at the beginning of understanding this phenomenon. The fact that an upper-class erotic luxury permeated the peasantry of Old China, for whom it could only lower productivity, suggests that the old society was extraordinarily homogeneous.

Finally, it was certainly ingenious how men trapped women into mutilating themselves for an ostensibly sexual purpose that had the effect of perpetuating male domination. Brides left their own homes and entered their husband's family in the lowest status, servants of their mothers-in-law. Husbands were chosen for them sight unseen, and

[2]Fortunato Prandi, ed. and trans., *Memoirs of Father Ripa* (London: John Murray, 1855), p. 58.

Holt, Rinehart and Winston

might find romance in extra-marital adventures or, if they could afford it, bring in secondary wives. But a woman once betrothed, if her husband-to-be died even as a child, was expected to remain a chaste widow thereafter. Mao remarked that "women hold up half the sky," but in old China they were not supposed to lift their heads. The talent that one sees in Chinese women today had little chance to grow and express itself. This made a weak foundation for a modern society.

Holt, Rinehart and Winston

[3]Ida Pruitt, *A Daughter of Han: The Autobiography of a Chinese Working Woman* (Yale University Press, 1945), p. 22.

Reading Assignment 11: "Footbinding"

Double-Entry Question Journal

In the left column, jot down at least five "What?" "Why?" or "How?" questions. Then in the right column, jot down some possible answers and responses. If further questions come up, jot them down also. One purpose of this exercise is to learn how to think critically, so you might end up with several answers. Go ahead, take a risk!

1.   1.

2.   2.

3.   3.

4.   4.

5.   5.

Brief Summary: _____

_____

_____

_____

_____

_____

Note: Please refer to the Appendix if you need help in writing a summary.

Holt, Rinehart and Winston

Reading Assignment 11: "Footbinding"

A Closer Look

1. How were the feet of Chinese women made small?

_____

_____

_____

2. Even though the custom originated with wealthy, upper-class Chinese, why did footbinding become generally accepted in all walks of life?

_____

_____

_____

_____

3. What does the essay tell you about the role of women during this period of China's history?

_____

_____

_____

4. What are the basic explanations the author gives for subjecting women to the practice of footbinding?

_____

_____

_____

CENTRAL IDEA (THEME)

What do you think Fairbank is trying to tell us in "Footbinding"? What is the purpose of the essay?

_____

_____

Holt, Rinehart and Winston

Writing Assignment 10: Information Essay, Part II

Direct and Indirect Quotations

For Writing Assignment 10 you will be required to use both direct and indirect quotations to support the ideas in your essay. Whether you use exact quotations or put information in your own words, you must give credit to every source.

Direct Quotations

If you copy information word-for-word out of a book, magazine, or World Wide Web site, use quotation marks around the quoted material. You will need to include the page number of the book or magazine from which you took the information in parentheses ( ) just before the period. Also, book titles are underlined, while article or essay titles are in quotation marks.

>   Example of a quotation from a book:
>
>   In The California Indian Journal William Warner states, "The Chumash took from their environment only what they needed for survival, nothing more, nothing less (79)."
>
>   Example of a quotation from a magazine article:
>
>   In "The Face of White Mountain," Inez Castillo writes, "The women stayed far away from the burial grounds, which were alive with the wandering spirits of their ancestors. Only the men were strong enough to ward off any evil" (127).
>
>   Example of a quotation from a daily newspaper:
>
>   In the *Santa Barbara Independent*, Pedro Lopes states, "Local Native Americans are eager to prevent real estate and oil development from impacting ancient burial and village sites" (A3).

Indirect Quotations

You must give credit to your source if you take information out of a book, or magazine, or World Wide Web site even if you paraphrase or summarize it. Notice that no quotation marks are used when you put the information in your own words. You will need to include the page number from which you took the information from the book or magazine in parentheses ( ) just before the period. Also, book titles are underlined, while article or essay titles are in quotation marks.

>   Example of an indirect quotation from a book:
>
>   In The California Indian Journal William Warner states that the Chumash were very careful not to take more than they actually needed from their environment (79).

Holt, Rinehart and Winston

Example of an indirect quotation from a magazine article:

In "The Face of White Mountain," Inez Castillo writes about the attitude toward women, who avoided the burial grounds because they were regarded as too weak to fight off evil (127).

Example of an indirect quotations from a newspaper:

In the *Santa Barbara Independent,* Pedro Lopez states that Native Americans in this region want to preserve significant cultural sites from unnecessary development (A3).

The Works Cited Page

Kevin Green's essay, "Epilepsy," is followed by a Works Cited page, which is an alphabetized, unnumbered list of the various sources of information. The Works Cited page is necessary to let your reader know the exact sources of information.

As you have learned above, whenever you use another writer's information in direct or indirect quotes (or even an idea, fact, or statistic) you must thoroughly document its original source in the following ways:

1. Provide the author's name and the name of the book or magazine article along with the information you are using.
2. Place the page number or numbers in parentheses before the period in the sentence you use the information. (This is usually unnecessary in encyclopedias or documents such as a World Wide Web site with unnumbered pages.)

Also, you must provide your readers with exact publication information on the Works Cited page, which serves as the final page of your essay. This information should enable your reader to locate the source of information, if necessary.

Documenting your sources on the Works Cited page can often get very complicated, but for this paper you will probably only be concerned with using books, magazine articles, newspapers, encyclopedias, personal interviews, and Internet sites. Each of these is done in a different, but exact, way according to the rules that are set by the Modern Language Association. (Your instructor will help you with documenting special cases or unusual sources of information). Note carefully how the lines after the first line are indented and that the punctuation in each instance is different.

Examples of Works Cited Listings

1. A Book: author's last and first name, book title, place of publication, name of publishing company, and the year of publication.
   Jones, Martha. <u>The Truth About the Modoc Wars</u>. San Francisco: New World Press, 1968.
2. A Magazine Article: author's last and first name (if they are available), title of article, title of magazine, date of publication, and the page numbers.
   Castillo, Inez. "The Face of White Mountain." <u>California History</u>. 3 March 1993: 127–134.
3. A Daily Newspaper Article: author's last and first name (if they are available), title of article, title of newspaper, date of publication, the section letter or number, and the page number.
   Lopez, Pedro. "Ancient Sites Threatened." *Santa Barbara Independent*. 25 June 1997: A3.

Holt, Rinehart and Winston

4. An Encyclopedia: the title of the article, the title of the encyclopedia, the edition, and its year of publication.

   "California." <u>American Heritage Encyclopedia</u>. 10th ed. 1978.

5. A Personal Interview: the last name and first name of the person interviewed, the title "Personal Interview," and the date of the interview.

   Sanchez, Manuel. Personal interview. 17 November 1997.

6. A World Wide Web Site: author's last and first name (if they are available), the full title of the work in quotation marks, the title of the whole work (if available), the document date (if available), the complete http address (URL), and the date you actually visited the site.

   Costa, Sandra. "Ancient Herbal Remedies." <u>Native American Research Project Homepage</u>. 1996. http://www.narph.ucsd.net/essay/ (19 April 1997).

Works Cited Page Format

1. Write "Works Cited" (centered and without quotation marks) at the top of the list as its title.

2. Double space the entire page.

3. Indent all lines after the first one in each entry. (This is called a hanging indentation.)

4. Alphabetize each entry according to the last name of the author. If no author is given, use the first word in the first line (not counting articles such as "The," "An," or "A" as first words).

5. Do not number the entries.

6. Paginate the "Works Cited" page in the upper right-hand corner. As in the body of your essay, use your last name followed by the consecutive page number.

Writing Assignment 10: Information Essay, Part II

Exercise on Citing Sources

1. Using Fairbank's essay, "Footbinding," find a sentence that proves that the author thinks footbinding was a means for men to control their women. Making sure you cite the source of the quote (author and title of the essay), write it in the space below as a direct quotation:

_____

_____

_____

_____

2. Rewrite the previous quotation as an indirect quotation. Make sure you cite your source.

_____

_____

_____

_____

3. Find a sentence that proves that having small feet was a sign of prestige in Chinese society. Making sure you cite the source of the quote (author and title of the essay), write it in the space below as a direct quotation.

_____

_____

_____

_____

4. Rewrite the previous quotation as an indirect quotation. Make sure you cite your source.

_____

_____

_____

_____

Writing Assignment 10: Information Essay, Part II

5. Find a sentence that indicates Chinese women went along with the practice of footbinding. Making sure you cite the source of the quote (author and title of the essay), write it in the space below as a direct quotation.

_____

_____

_____

6. Rewrite the previous quotation as an indirect quotation. Make sure you cite your source.

_____

_____

_____

_____

Holt, Rinehart and Winston

Searching for Information
Paraphrasing and Summarizing

1. Find at least one current book, magazine article, newspaper item, or Internet site that gives you important information on your topic. Use the space below to write the name of your book, article, or Internet site:

_____

2. Use the space below to paraphrase (put in your own words) one section of your book, magazine article, newspaper item, or Internet site that supports or clarifies your essay's point of view:

_____

_____

_____

_____

_____

_____

_____

_____

_____

_____

_____

_____

_____

_____

_____

_____

_____

Feel free to use notebook paper to paraphrase additional sections for your essay.

Holt, Rinehart and Winston

Writing Assignment 10: Information Essay, Part II

3. Use the space below to summarize (Restate only the main ideas) one section of your book, magazine article, newspaper item, or Internet site that supports or clarifies your essay's point of view:

_____

_____

_____

_____

_____

_____

_____

_____

_____

_____

_____

_____

Feel free to use notebook paper to summarize additional sections for your essay.

4. Find one passage in your book, magazine article, newspaper item, or Internet site that proves or supports one of the main ideas of your essay. Write it as a direct quotation below:

_____

_____

_____

5. Find an additional passage in your book, magazine article, newspaper item or Internet site that proves or supports one of the main ideas of your essay. Write it as an indirect quotation below:

_____

_____

_____

Holt, Rinehart and Winston

Writing Assignment 10: Information Essay, Part II

Interviewing

Now that you have researched your topic by finding a book, magazine article, newspaper article, and/or Internet site, what questions do you still have about your topic? Interviewing someone who is an authority on the subject or an expert in the field would add valuable first-hand information to your essay. Make an appointment to meet with a person who knows something about your topic. Prepare for the interview by reviewing your notes on your topic and by jotting down some questions. Use the space below to write five genuine questions.

1. _____

_____

_____

2. _____

_____

_____

3. _____

_____

_____

4. _____

_____

_____

5. _____

_____

_____

Holt, Rinehart and Winston

Reading Assignment 12: "Rites of Passage" by Sharon Olds

Prereading

In "Rites of Passage" Sharon Olds describes a scene in her young son's birthday party, and, in doing so, she explores the curiously confrontational relationships among the six- and seven-year-old boys as they gather at the start of the party. She notices a barely hidden strand of violence in the boys' body language and words. The title, "Rites of Passage," implies that someone is being tested to see if he or she can be accepted by a group or achieve a new level of growth and maturity. Why does Olds call the poem "Rites of Passage"? Who is being tested? Why?

Rites of Passage
Sharon Olds

As the guests arrive at my son's party
they gather in the living room—
short men, men in first grade
with smooth jaws and chins.
Hands in pockets, they stand around
jostling, jockeying for place, small fights
breaking out and calming. One says to another
How old are you? Six, I'm seven. So?
They eye each other, seeing themselves
tiny in the other's pupils. They clear their
throats a lot, a room of small bankers,
they fold their arms and frown. I could beat you
up, a seven says to a six,
the dark cake, round and heavy as a
turret, behind them on the table. My son,
freckles like specks of nutmeg on his cheeks,
chest narrow as the balsa keel of a
model boat, long hands
cool and thin as the day they guided him
out of me, speaks up as a host
for the sake of the group.
We could easily kill a two-year-old,
he says in his clear voice. The other
men agree, they clear their throats
like Generals, they relax and get down to
playing war, celebrating my son's life.

Holt, Rinehart and Winston

Reading Assignment 12: "Rites of Passage"

Double-Entry Question Journal

In the left column, jot down at least five "What?" "Why?" or "How?" questions. Then in the right column, jot down some possible answers and responses. If further questions come up, jot them down also. One purpose of this exercise is to learn how to think critically, so you might end up with several answers. Go ahead, take a risk!

1.   1.

2.   2.

3.   3.

4.   4.

5.   5.

Brief Summary: _____

_____

_____

_____

_____

_____

Note: Please refer to the Appendix if you need help in writing a summary.

Holt, Rinehart and Winston

Reading Assignment 12: "Rites of Passage"

A Closer Look

1. What does Olds mean when she says, "They eye each other, seeing themselves tiny in the other's pupils"?

_____

_____

_____

2. Why does the narrator refer to the boys at the party as "small bankers"?

_____

_____

_____

3. What does Olds mean when she describes the birthday cake as "the dark cake, round and heavy as a / turret"?

_____

_____

_____

4. Why would the birthday boy tell his friends, "We could easily kill a two-year-old"? What is he trying to achieve with this remark?

_____

_____

_____

CENTRAL IDEA (THEME)

The last lines of the poem state that the boys at the party "get down to / playing war, celebrating my son's life." What do you think Sharon Olds's purpose is in writing the poem? What is she trying to teach us?

_____

_____

Holt, Rinehart and Winston

Reading Assignment 12: "Rites of Passage"

Use the lines that follow to write a letter to the author, Sharon Olds. Tell her what you think about the boys and their behavior in her poem, "Rites of Passage." Are they just normal boys and there is nothing to be concerned about, or should Olds try to make changes in how she is raising her son?

Dear _____:

_____

_____

_____

_____

_____

_____

_____

_____

_____

_____

_____

_____

_____

_____

_____

_____

Sincerely,

_____

Holt, Rinehart and Winston

Writing Assignment 10: Information Essay (continued)

Prewriting

Prewrite (using clustering, listing, freewriting, or asking journalistic questions) in the space below, jotting down the main ideas that you want to include in your research paper. Also include ideas from your paraphrases, summaries, quotations, as well as information from your interview. Prewrite until you come up with enough convincing evidence to support your point of view. Now is the time to think of the overall plan for your essay. You might prefer to make a brief outline or create a flow chart for your whole essay.

Revising Your Thesis Statement

By now you have done quite a bit of research and critical thinking on your topic. Have you changed or redefined the direction of your research paper in any way? At this point, you should feel free to revise your thesis statement for Assignment 10, if necessary. Make sure your thesis statement communicates the central idea (purpose) of your paper and forecasts how your paper will be developed.

_____

_____

_____

Holt, Rinehart and Winston

Writing a Rough Draft

Now that you have researched your topic, you are ready to write the rough draft. Begin with a brief introductory paragraph that ends with your thesis statement. Then draft the body paragraphs, making sure that each begins with a topic sentence. This essay should include information from your outside sources in the form of paraphrased and summarized material as well as direct and indirect quotations. Make sure you name the title and author of the sources you use. Use transitions to signal the order of your essay, and make sure each paragraph is fully developed with specific examples. Finally, make sure your essay has an effective concluding paragraph that brings your argument to a close.

Being Specific

Reread your rough draft of Writing Assignment 10, watching out for general words, phrases, and sentences. Underline the parts of your writing which might benefit from being more specific. Write a new draft, changing the passages you have underlined into more interesting, exact, and detailed writing. Use specific examples wherever you can.

Revising

Remember that experienced writers constantly revise their work to make sure it communicates exactly what they want it to say. Revision is an ongoing process requiring you to delete words, add phrases, and rearrange sentences to make your meaning clear to your reader.

Peer Editing

Using your revised copy, read your paper out loud to a peer editor. Likewise, listen as your peer editor reads his or her paper back to you. When both papers have been read aloud, exchange papers, using the Editing Sheet provided for this assignment, to write helpful comments to each other. In some cases it might be more appropriate to exchange papers at the start and have each peer editor read silently before completing the Editing Sheet. Another option would be to use the Editing Sheet as a checklist for oral feedback. A final option would be for your instructor to create peer editing groups of three or four members.

Whatever option you choose, the Editing Sheet that follows will provide useful guidelines for this assignment. Only one set of Editing sheets is provided, which is sufficient if you are using collaborative groups. However, if you are using two individual editors, you will need to obtain a photocopy of the Editing Sheet. Please check with your instructor.

Holt, Rinehart and Winston

Writing Assignment 10: Information Essay, Part III

Editing Sheet (to be completed by peer editors)

Directions: Either pair up and exchange papers with another student in class, or form editing groups of three or four members. Papers may be read silently or aloud. Every paper requires at least two peer editors who will work collaboratively to complete an Editing Sheet. The completed Editing Sheet should then be attached to the rough draft and returned to the writer for reference during the revision process.

Some peer editors may prefer to write comments directly on a student's rough draft, using the editing sheet as more of a checklist. Check with your instructor to see which method works best for your situation.

1. Has the writer selected a topic that is interesting, sufficiently narrowed, and suitable for a research project? If the topic is weak, suggest prewriting strategies (clustering, listing, freewriting, or asking journalistic questions) to generate enough ideas for a new topic.

_____

_____

_____

2. Does the introductory paragraph hook you or seem powerful and engaging? If not, offer specific suggestions.

_____

_____

3. Draw a double line under the thesis statement. If it is missing, ask the writer, "So what? What is the point of this essay?" Suggest ways to make the thesis statement more effective, if necessary.

_____

_____

_____

4. Draw a circle around the directing words in the topic sentences. Does each body paragraph have a clear topic sentence that points out the main idea of the paragraph?

_____

_____

Holt, Rinehart and Winston

5. Underline the transitional expressions that signal the type of overall order used in this essay. Does the essay seem well organized? Offer suggestions.

_____

_____

6. Do you think the writer uses appropriate linking transitions to show the relationships between sentences?

_____

_____

7. Draw a wavy line under words or phrases that would benefit from detailed examples. Has the writer included enough examples and specific details and anecdotes (interesting little stories with a point) in each body paragraph for a fully developed essay?

_____

8. Are direct and indirect quotations used effectively for support? Are they correctly formatted, following the rules of the Modern Language Association (MLA)?

_____

_____

9. Does the concluding paragraph wrap up the essay effectively or leave a lasting impression on you? What ideas do you have about writing a more effective conclusion?

_____

10. Does the Works Cited page list all the sources used in writing the paper? Is the format exact in terms of spacing, punctuation, authors' names, dates, and publication information?

_____

11. Does the title intrigue you and really catch your attention as a reader? Think of recent movie titles. What suggestions do you have for a more interesting, creative title?

_____

Peer Editors' Initials: ____ ____ ____ ____ (This verifies the paper is ready for a Revised Copy.)

Holt, Rinehart and Winston

Writing Assignment 10: Information Essay, Part III

Submitting the Final Copy

Now that you have had your paper edited, you should revise your paper once again. When you feel your paper communicates exactly what you want it to, you are ready to write your final copy in ink on notebook paper or type it on a typewriter or a computer. Before you write the final copy of your paper, your instructor or tutor may want to skim over your revised draft. Follow the rules of manuscript form found in the Appendix.

After writing the final copy of your paper, exchange it with another student to proofread for spelling, punctuation, and grammar errors. Ask your peer editors to initial your final copy to indicate that it has been through the final editing process. When your edited paper is returned to you, make the final corrections and turn in your final copy with your rough draft and completed Editing Sheet. Stapling the whole packet together will allow your instructor to check your progress during each stage of the writing process.

Holt, Rinehart and Winston

Additional Readings

Fiction

- "Can-Can" by Arturo Vivante
- "Blue Day" by Joel Antonio Villalón
- "I See You Never" by Ray Bradbury

Poetry

- "Sindhi Woman" by Jon Stallworthy
- "Homage to My Hips" by Lucille Clifton
- "Marks" by Linda Pastan
- "Hazel Tells LaVerne" by Katharyn Howd Machan

Essays

- "Shame" by Dick Gregory
- "Mother Tongue" by Amy Tan
- "Home Is a Freeway" by Neil Morgan
- "The Jeaning of America" by Carin Quinn

Can-Can
Arturo Vivante

"I'm going to go for a drive," he said to his wife. "I'll be back in an hour or two."

He didn't often leave the house for more than the few minutes it took him to go to the post office or to a store, but spent his time hanging around, doing odd jobs—Mr. Fix-it, his wife called him—and also, though not nearly enough of it, painting—which he made his living from.

"All right," his wife said brightly, as though he were doing her a favor. As a matter of fact, she didn't really like him to leave; she felt safer with him at home, and he helped look after the children, especially the baby.

"You're glad to be rid of me, aren't you?" he said.

"Uh-huh," she said with a smile that suddenly made her look very pretty—someone to be missed.

She didn't ask him where he was going for his drive. She wasn't the least bit inquisitive, though jealous she was in silent, subtle ways.

As he put his coat on, he watched her. She was in the living room with their elder daughter. "Do the can-can, mother," the child said, at which she held up her skirt and did the can-can, kicking her legs up high in his direction.

He wasn't simply going out for a drive, as he had said, but going to a café, to meet Sarah, whom his wife knew but did not suspect, and with her go to a house on a lake his wife knew nothing about—a summer cottage to which he had the key.

"Well, goodbye," he said.

"Bye," she called back, still dancing.

This wasn't the way a husband expected his wife—whom he was about to leave at home to go to another woman—to behave at all, he thought. He expected her to be sewing or washing, not doing the can-can, for God's sake. Yes, doing something uninteresting and unattractive, like darning the children's clothes. She had no stockings on, no shoes, and her legs looked very white and smooth, secret, as though he had never touched them or come near them. Her feet, swinging up and down high in the air, seemed to be nodding to him. She held her skirt bunched up, attractively. Why was she doing that of all times *now*? He lingered. Her eyes had mockery in them, and she laughed. The child laughed with her as she danced. She was still dancing as he left the house.

He thought of the difficulties he had arranging this *rendezvous*—going out to a call box; phoning Sarah at her office (she was married, too); her being out; his calling her again; the busy signal; the coin falling out of sight, his opening the door of the phone box in order to retrieve it; at last getting her on the line; her asking him to call again next week, finally setting a date.

Waiting for her at the café, he surprised himself hoping that she wouldn't come. The appointment was at three. It was now ten past. Well, she was often late. He looked at the clock, and at the picture window for her car. A car like hers, and yet not hers—no luggage rack on it. The smooth hardtop gave him a peculiar pleasure. Why? It was 3:15 now. Perhaps she wouldn't come. No, if she was going to come at all, this was the most likely time for her to arrive. Twenty past. Ah, now there was some hope. Hope? How strange he should be hoping for her absence. Why had he made the appointment if he was hoping she would miss it? He didn't know why, but simpler, simpler if she didn't come. Because all he wanted now was to smoke that cigarette, drink that cup of coffee for the sake of them, and not to give himself something to do. And he wished he could go for a drive, free and easy, as he had said he would. But he waited, and at 3:30 she arrived. "I had almost given up hope," he said.

They drove to the house on the lake. As he held her in his arms he couldn't think of her; for the life of him he couldn't.

"What are you thinking about? she said afterwards, sensing his detachment.

For a moment he didn't answer, then he said, "You really want to know what I was thinking of?"

"Yes," she said, a little anxiously.

He suppressed a laugh, as though what he was going to tell her was too absurd or silly. "I was thinking of someone doing the can-can."

"Oh," she said, reassured. "For a moment I was afraid you were thinking of your wife."

Blue Day
Joel Antonio Villalón

The day was blue, and the young man carrying a briefcase smiled to the sun. His steps bobbed as shadows of leaves dappled his face, and he wanted to dance, because white buds had once again appeared on the trees outside his bedroom window now that the snows had melted. He hated the empty feeling that winter left in him, and today, that emptiness, that loneliness, which accompanied winter was gone. Today felt new to the young man, the air clean and cold, and he hummed loudly strolling on the street. "What a great day," he thought. "Spring every year should start on days like today; bright, brisk, clear days."

The thought of the season changing filled his memory with a warm surge of images: the penetrating smells of thawing earth, the bright whites of flowering dogwoods and the resonating sounds of returning robins. A very cold wind grazed the young man, and he picked up his pace. He shivered and smiled at his impatience with winter lingering the way it was, and he stopped and set his briefcase down. As he buttoned his heavy overcoat, he noted a child on the sidewalk standing against a red brownstone. "What a tiny thing," the young man thought. "Should he be here alone?" The tiny child examined the young man with soulful eyes; his legs were crossed, his palms seemed stuck to bricks on each side of him. His coat was well padded and buttoned, and he looked, to the young man, like a furry, round ball.

"Smnpht . . . tript . . . crt . . . treet," the child mumbled.

The young man walked to the child. "What?" he said.

The child peered at his feet, lifted his arm and pointed, "Mnpt . . . crot treet."

The man straightened and looked up the steps to the brownstone. He saw no one; then turning, he squinted his eyes and scanned the roadway. Cars came from both directions. No one walked on the sidewalks.

"Where are your parents?" he looked down at the child. "Do they know where you are?"

"Mmpt . . . cropt," he whispered.

"I don't understand you. What do you want?" The man looked around again. "Do you want to cross the street? Is that it? Is that what you want?" The child pointed a stubby finger to the corner and mumbled, but the man did not comprehend his sounds. "Do you want to cross?" the young man said louder.

The child slid two steps sideways from the man into the shade of the stoop and looked down.

The man chuckled, shook his head, picked up his briefcase and started off again. He had taken two steps when he heard a scream, "Aaagh!" He swerved, off balance, looking to the street. He then turned and saw the child standing to his side. The child pointed with both hands to the corner and shouted, "Treet . . . preeth!"

"Where are your parents?" the man yelled. "You scared me to death, you know that?"

"Treeth!" the child screamed.

"C'mon, . . . I don't believe this." He took a step toward the child, and the child ran to the shadow of the stoop. "Listen," he shouted, "if you want me to help you, you're gonna have to tell me what you want."

The child took a step back further, "Spreeee!"

The young man stood shaking his head. He could see the child's breath in the shadow, and he turned and noticed a tall man approaching them down the sidewalk.

"What's the matter?" the tall man said as he neared.

"Nothing's the matter," the young man said. "I don't know who this kid is. I was just standing here . . ." He leaned toward the tall man, "Is he yours?"

"No, he's not," the man replied. "What's the matter? Is he hurt?"

"Look, I didn't touch him or anything. I don't know who he is. I was on my way to work, and he was standing here, and he started talking to me, but I can't understand a word he says." The young man took a breath, "He may want to cross the street."

The tall man's eyes remained on him. "Well," he said.

"Well, what?"

"Does he want to cross the street?"

"Oh, I don't know," the young man shrugged, "I don't know that for sure."

The tall man lowered himself on one knee before the child, smiled and looked at the child. "Hi, my name's Bob. I live around the corner. Do you live around here?" The tall man waited. The child looked at him and said nothing.

"Well . . . let's see, are you waiting for your mommy or daddy?" The child lowered his head. The tall man glanced up to the man. He slowly drew closer and gently placed his fingers on the child's shoulder and whispered, "I'm going to cross the street right now. Would you like to come with me across the street?"

The child drew a heavy breath.

"This street right here. I'm going to cross this street now. Would you like to come with me?" The child took another breath, then meekly nodded.

The tall man looked up again and said, "It's O.K., I'm not late for work. I'll take care of it."

The young man stood there, not knowing what to say, and he clumsily raised his brief-case to them and woodenly started off, but, after a few steps, he felt he should thank the other man, but he did not know why. He turned to say something, but the tall man and the child were walking away from him. The tall man was saying something to the child the young man could not hear, moving his head, swinging his briefcase. The child held onto the tall man's free arm and surveyed him quietly. The young man sullenly watched. Shadows from the new leaves fluttered across his face and another cold breeze blew down the street. He lifted the collar of his coat and continued looking at the couple. The sun shone brilliantly on them as they took very small, slow steps. Cars stopped to let them pass, and when they reached the other side, the child let the man go and awkwardly crawled up some stairs and tapped on a door. After a moment, the door creaked open, and the child quickly disappeared through the gap.

I See You Never
Ray Bradbury

The soft knock came at the kitchen door, and when Mrs. O'Brian opened it, there on the back porch were her best tenant, Mr. Ramirez, and two police officers, one on each side of him. Mr. Ramirez just stood there, walled in and small.

"Why, Mr. Ramirez!" said Mrs. O'Brian.

Mr. Ramirez was overcome. He did not seem to have the words to explain.

He had arrived at Mrs. O'Brian's rooming house more than two years earlier and had lived there ever since. He had come by bus from Mexico City to San Diego and had then gone up to Los Angeles. There he had found a clean little room, with glossy blue linoleum, and pictures and calendars on the flowered walls, and Mrs. O'Brian as the strict but kindly landlady. During the war he had worked at the airplane factory and made parts for the planes that flew off somewhere, and even now, after the war, he still held his job. From the first he had made big money. He saved some of it, and he got drunk only once a week—a privilege that to Mrs. O'Brian's way of thinking, every good workingman deserved, unquestioned and unreprimanded.

Inside Mrs. O'Brian's kitchen, pies were baking in the oven. Soon the pies would come out with complexions like Mr. Ramirez'—brown and shiny and crisp, with slits in them for the air almost like the slits of Mr. Ramirez' dark eyes. The kitchen smelled good. The policemen leaned forward, lured by the odor. Mr. Ramirez gazed at his feet, as if they had carried him into all this trouble.

"What happened, Mr. Ramirez?" asked Mrs. O'Brian.

Behind Mrs. O'Brian, as he lifted his eyes, Mr. Ramirez saw the long table laid with clean white linen and set with a platter, cool, shining glasses, a water pitcher with ice cubes floating inside it, a bowl of fresh potato salad and one of bananas and oranges, cubed and sugared. At this table sat Mrs. O'Brian's children—her three grown sons, eating and conversing, and her two younger daughters, who were staring at the policemen as they ate.

"I have been here thirty months," said Mr. Ramirez quietly, looking at Mrs. O'Brian's plump hands.

"That's six months too long," said one policeman. "He only had a temporary visa. We've just got around to looking for him."

Soon after Mr. Ramirez had arrived he bought a radio for his little room; evenings, he turned it up very loud and enjoyed it. And he bought a wrist watch and enjoyed that too. And on many nights he had walked silent streets and seen the bright clothes in the windows and bought some of them, and he had seen the jewels and bought some of them for his few lady friends. And he had gone to picture shows five nights a week for a while. Then, also, he had ridden the streetcars—all night some nights—smelling the electricity, his dark eyes moving over the advertisements, feeling the wheels rumble under him, watching the little sleeping houses and big hotels slip by. Besides that, he had gone to large restaurants, where he had eaten many-course dinners, and to the opera and the theater. And he had bought a car, which later, when he forgot to pay for it, the dealer had driven off angrily from in front of the rooming house.

"So here I am," said Mr. Ramirez now, "to tell you I must give up my room, Mrs. O'Brian. I come to get my baggage and clothes and go with these men."

"Back to Mexico?"

"Yes. To Lagos. That is a little town north of Mexico City."

"I'm sorry, Mr. Ramirez."

"I'm packed," said Mr. Ramirez hoarsely, blinking his dark eyes rapidly and moving his hands helplessly before him. The policemen did not touch him. There was no necessity for that.

"Here is the key, Mrs. O'Brian," Mr. Ramirez said. "I have my bag already."

Mrs. O'Brian, for the first time, noticed a suitcase standing behind him on the porch.

Mr. Ramirez looked in again at the huge kitchen, at the bright silver cutlery and the young people eating and the shining waxed floor. He turned and looked for a long moment at the apartment house next door, rising up three stories, high and beautiful. He looked at the balconies and fire escapes and back-porch stairs, at the lines of laundry snapping in the wind.

"You've been a good tenant," said Mrs. O'Brian.

"Thank you, thank you, Mrs. O'Brian," he said softly. He closed his eyes.

Mrs. O'Brian stood holding the door half open. One of her sons, behind her, said that her dinner was getting cold, but she shook her head at him and turned back to Mr. Ramirez. She remembered a visit she had once made to some Mexican border towns—the hot days, the endless crickets leaping and falling or lying dead and brittle like the small cigars in the shopwindows, and the canals taking river water out to the farms, the dirt roads, the scorched landscape. She remembered the silent towns, the warm beer, the hot, thick foods each day. She remembered the slow, dragging horses and the parched jack rabbits on the road. She remembered the iron mountains and the dusty valleys and the ocean beaches that spread hundreds of miles with no sound but the waves—no cars, no buildings, nothing.

"I'm sure sorry, Mr. Ramirez," she said.

"I don't want to go back, Mrs. O'Brian," he said weakly. "I like it here, I want to stay. I've worked, I've got money. I look all right, don't I? And I don't want to go back!"

"I'm sorry, Mr. Ramirez," she said. "I wish there was something I could do."

"Mrs. O'Brian!" he cried suddenly, tears rolling out from under his eyelids. He reached out his hands and took her hand fervently, shaking it, wringing it, holding to it. "Mrs. O'Brian, I see you never, I see you never!"

The policemen smiled at this, but Mr. Ramirez did not notice it, and they stopped smiling very soon.

"Goodbye, Mrs. O'Brian. You have been good to me. Oh, goodbye Mrs. O'Brian. I see you never!"

The policemen waited for Mr. Ramirez to turn, pick up his suitcase, and walk away. Then they followed him, tipping their caps to Mrs. O'Brian. She watched them go down the porch steps. Then she shut the door quietly and went slowly back to her chair at the table. She pulled the chair out and sat down. She picked up the shining knife and fork and started once more upon her steak.

"Hurry up, Mom," said one of her sons. "It'll be cold."

Mrs. O'Brian took one bite and chewed on it for a long, slow time; then she stared at the closed door. She laid down her knife and fork.

"What's wrong, Ma?" asked her son.

"I just realized," said Mrs. O'Brian—she put her hand to her face—"I'll never see Mr. Ramirez again."

El Hoyo
Mario Suarez

From the center of downtown Tucson the ground slopes gently away to Main Street, drops a few feet, and then rolls to the banks of the Santa Cruz River. Here lies the section of the city known as El Hoyo. Why it is called El Hoyo is not very clear. In no sense is it a hole as its name would imply; it is simply the river's immediate valley. Its inhabitants are chicanos who raise hell on Saturday night and listen to Padre Estanislao on Sunday morning. While the term chicano is the short way of saying Mexicano, it is not restricted to the paisanos who came from old Mexico with the territory or the last famine to work for the railroad, labor, sing, and go on relief. Chicano is the easy way of referring to everybody. Pablo Gutierrez married the Chinese grocer's daughter and now runs a meat department; his sons are chicanos. So are the sons of Killer Jones who threw a fight in Harlem and fled to El Hoyo to marry Cristina Mendez. And so are all of them. However, it is doubtful that all these spiritual sons of Mexico live in El Hoyo because they love each other-many fight and bicker constantly. It is doubtful they live in El Hoyo because of its scenic beauty-it is everything but beautiful. Its houses are simple affairs of unplastered adobe, wood, and abandoned car parts. Its narrow streets are mostly clearings which have, in time, acquired names. Except for some tall trees which nobody has ever cared to identify, nurse, or destroy, the main things known to grow in the general area are weeds, garbage piles, dark-eyed chavalos, and dogs. And it is doubtful that the chicanos live in El Hoyo because it is safe-many times the Santa Cruz has risen and inundated the area.

In other respects living in El Hoyo has its advantages. If one is born with a weakness for acquiring bills, El Hoyo is where the collectors are less likely to find you. If one has acquired the habit of listening to Octavio Perea's Mexican Hour in the wee hours of the morning with the radio on at full blast, El Hoyo is where you are less likely to be reported to the authorities. Besides, Perea is very popular and sooner or later to everyone "Smoke In The Eyes" is dedicated between the pinto beans and white flour commercials. If one, for any reason whatever, comes on an extended period of hard times, where, if not in El Hoyo, are the neighbors more willing to offer solace? When Teofila Malacara's house burned to the ground with all her belongings and two children, a benevolent gentleman carried through the gesture that made tolerable her burden. He made a list of five hundred names and solicited from each a dollar. At the end of a month he turned over to the tearful but grateful senora one hundred dollars in cold cash and then accompanied her on a short vacation. When the new manager of a local store decided that no more chicanas were to work behind the counters, it was the chicanos of El Hoyo who, on taking their individually small but collectively great buying power elsewhere, drove the manager out and the girls returned to their jobs. When the Mexican Army was en route to Baja California and the chicanos found out that the enlisted men ate only at infrequent intervals, it was El Hoyo's chicanos who crusaded across town with pots of beans and trays of tortillas to meet the train. When someone gets married celebrating is not restricted to the immediate friends of the couple. Everybody is invited. Anything calls for a celebration and a celebration calls for anything. On Memorial Day there are no less than half a dozen good fights at the

Riverside Dance Hall. On Mexican Independence Day more than one flag is sworn allegiance to amid cheers for the queen.

And El Hoyo is something more. It is this something more which brought Felipe Sanchez back from the wars after having killed a score of Vietnamese with his body resembling a patchwork quilt to marry Julia Armijo. It brought Joe Zepeda, a gunner, . . . back to compose boleros. He has a metal plate for a skull. Perhaps El Hoyo is proof that those people exist, and perhaps exist best, who have as yet failed to observe the more popular modes of human conduct. Perhaps the humble appearance of El Hoyo justifies the indifferent shrug of those made aware of its existence. Perhaps

El Hoyo's simplicity motivates an occasional chicano to move away from its narrow streets, babbling comadres and shrieking children to deny the bloodwell from which he springs and to claim the blood of a conquistador while his hair is straight and his face beardless. Yet El Hoyo is not an outpost of a few families against the world. It fights for no causes except those which soothe its immediate angers. It laughs and cries with the same amount of passion in times of plenty and of want. Perhaps El Hoyo, its inhabitants, and its essence can best be explained by telling a bit about a dish called capirotada. Its origin is uncertain. But, according to the time and the circumstance, it is made of old, new or hard bread. It is softened with water and then cooked with peanuts, raisins, onions, cheese, and panocha. It is fired with sherry wine. Then it is served hot, cold, or just "on the weather" as they say in El Hoyo. The Sermehos like it one way, the Garcias another, and the Ortegas still another. While it might differ greatly from one home to another, nevertheless it is still capirotada. And so it is with El Hoyo's chicanos. While being divided from within and from without, like the capirotada, they remain chicanos.

Sindhi Woman
Jon Stallworthy (b. 1935)

Barefoot through the bazaar,
and with the same undulant grace
as the cloth blown back from her face,
she glides with a stone jar
high on her head
and not a ripple in her tread.

Watching her cross erect
stones, garbage, excrement, and crumbs
of glass in the Karachi slums,
I, with my stoop, reflect
they stand most straight
who learn to walk beneath a weight.

Homage to My Hips
Lucille Clifton

these hips are big hips.
they need space to
move around in.
they don't fit into little
petty places. these hips
are free hips.
they don't like to be held back.
these hips have never been enslaved,
they go where they want to go
they do what they want to do.
these hips are mighty hips.
these hips are magic hips.
i have known them
to put a spell on a man and
spin him like a top!

Marks
Linda Pastan

My husband gives me an A
for last night's supper,
an incomplete for my ironing,
a B plus in bed.
My son says I'm average,
an average mother, but if
I put my mind to it
I could improve.
My daughter believes
in Pass/Fail and tells me
I pass. Wait 'til they learn
I'm dropping out.

Hazel Tells LaVerne
Katharyn Howd Machan

last night
im cleanin out my
howard johnsons ladies room
when all of a sudden
up pops this frog
musta come from the sewer
swimmin aroun an tryin ta
climb up the sida the bowl
so i goes ta flushm down
but sohelpmegod he starts talkin
bout a golden ball
an how i can be a princess
me a princess
well my mouth drops
all the way to the floor
an he says
kiss me just kiss me
once on the nose
well i screams
ya little green pervert
an i hitsm with my mop
an has ta flush
the toilet down three times
me
a princess

Shame
Dick Gregory

I never learned hate at home, or shame. I had to go to school for that. I was about seven years old when I got my first big lesson. I was in love with a little girl named Helene Tucker, a light-complected little girl with pigtails and nice manners. She was always clean and she was smart in school. I think I went to school then mostly to look at her. I brushed my hair and even got me a little old handkerchief. It was a lady's handkerchief, but I didn't want Helene to see me wipe my nose on my hand. The pipes were frozen again, there was no water in the house, but I washed my socks and shirt every night. I'd get a pot, and go over to Mister Ben's grocery store, and stick my pot down in his soda machine. Scoop out some chopped ice. By evening the ice melted to water for washing. I got sick a lot that winter because the fire would go out at night before the clothes were dry. In the morning I'd put them on, wet or dry, because they were the only clothes I had.

Everybody's got a Helene Tucker, a symbol of everything you want. I loved her for her goodness, her cleanness, her popularity. She'd walk down my street and my brothers and sisters would yell, "Here comes Helene," and I'd rub my tennis sneakers on the back of my pants and wish my hair wasn't so nappy and the white folks' shirt fit me better. I'd run out on the street. If I knew my place and didn't come too close, she'd wink at me and say hello. That was a good feeling. Sometimes I'd follow her all the way home, and shovel the snow off her walk and try to make friends with her Momma and her aunts. I'd drop money on her stoop late at night on my way back from shining shoes in the taverns. And she had a Daddy, and he had a good job. He was a paper hanger.

I guess I would have gotten over Helene by summertime, but something happened in that classroom that made her face hang in front of me for the next twenty-two years. When I played the drums in high school it was for Helene and when I broke track records in college it was for Helene and when I started standing behind microphones and heard applause I wished Helene could hear it, too. It wasn't until I was twenty-nine years old and married and making money that I finally got her out of my system. Helene was sitting in that classroom when I learned to be ashamed of myself.

It was on a Thursday. I was sitting in the back of the room, in a seat with a chalk circle drawn around it. The idiot's seat, the troublemaker's seat.

The teacher thought I was stupid. Couldn't spell, couldn't read, couldn't do arithmetic. Just stupid. Teachers were never interested in finding out that you couldn't concentrate because you were so hungry, because you hadn't had any breakfast. All you could think about was noontime, would it ever come? Maybe you could sneak into the cloakroom and steal a bite of some kid's lunch out of a coat pocket. A bit of something. Paste. You can't really make a meal of paste, or put it on bread for a sandwich, but sometimes I'd scoop a few spoonfuls out of the paste jar in the back of the room. Pregnant people get strange tastes. I was pregnant with poverty. Pregnant with dirt and pregnant with smells that made people turn away, pregnant with cold and pregnant with shoes that were never bought for me, pregnant with five other people in my bed and no Daddy in the next room, and pregnant with hunger. Paste doesn't taste too bad when you're hungry.

The teacher thought I was a troublemaker. All she saw from the front of the room was a little black boy who squirmed in his idiot's seat and made noises and poked the kids around him. I guess she couldn't see a kid who made noises because he wanted someone to know he was there.

It was on a Thursday, the day before the Negro payday. The eagle always flew on Friday. The teacher was asking each student how much his father would give to the Community Chest. On Friday night, each kid would get the money from his father, and on Monday he would bring it to the school. I decided I was going to buy me a Daddy right then. I had money in my pocket from shining shoes and selling papers, and whatever Helene Tucker pledged for her Daddy I was going to top it. And I'd hand the money right in. I wasn't going to wait until Monday to buy me a Daddy.

I was shaking, scared to death. The teacher opened her book and started calling out names alphabetically.

"Helene Tucker?"

"My Daddy said he'd give two dollars and fifty cents."

"That's very nice, Helene. Very, very nice indeed."

That made me feel pretty good. It wouldn't take too much to top that. I had almost three dollars in dimes and quarters in my pocket. I stuck my hand in my pocket and held onto the money, waiting for her to call my name. But the teacher closed her book after she called everybody else in the room.

I stood up and raised my hand.

"What is it now?"

"You forgot me."

She turned to the blackboard. "I don't have time to be playing with you, Richard."

"My Daddy said he'd . . ."

"Sit down, Richard, you're disturbing the class."

"My Daddy said he'd give . . . fifteen dollars."

She turned around and looked at me. "We are collecting this money for you and your kind, Richard Gregory. If your Daddy can give fifteen dollars you have no business being on relief."

"I got it right now, I got it right now, my Daddy gave it to me to turn in today, my Daddy said . . ."

"And furthermore," she said, looking right at me, her nostrils getting big and her lips getting thin and her eyes opening wide, "we know you don't have a Daddy."

Helene Tucker turned around, her eyes full of tears. She felt sorry for me. Then I couldn't see her too well because I was crying, too.

"Sit down, Richard."

And I always thought the teacher kind of liked me. She always picked me to wash the blackboard on Friday, after school. That was a big thrill, it made me feel important. If I didn't wash it, come Monday the school might not function right.

"Where are you going, Richard?"

I walked out of school that day, and for a long time I didn't go back very often. There was shame there.

Now there was shame everywhere. It seemed like the whole world had been inside that classroom, everyone had heard what the teacher had said, everyone had turned around and felt sorry for me. There was shame in going to the Worthy Boys Annual Christmas Dinner for you and your kind, because everybody knew what a worthy boy was. Why couldn't they just call it the Boys Annual Dinner, why'd they have to give it a name? There was shame in wearing the brown and orange and plaid mackinaw the welfare gave to 3,000 boys. Why'd it have to be the same for everybody so when you walked down the street people could see you were on relief? It was a nice warm mackinaw and it had a hood, and my Momma beat me and called me a little rat when she found out I stuffed it in the bottom of a pail full of garbage way over on Cottage Street. There was shame in running over to Mister Ben's at the end of the day and asking for his rotten peaches, there was shame in asking Mrs. Simmons for a spoonful of sugar, there was shame in running out to meet the relief truck. I hated that truck, full of food for you and your kind. I ran into the house and hid when it came. And then I started to sneak through alleys, to take the long way home so the people going into White's Eat Shop wouldn't see me. Yeah, the whole world heard the teacher that day, we all know you don't have a Daddy.

It lasted for a while, this kind of numbness. I spent a lot of time feeling sorry for myself. And then one day, I met this wino in a restaurant. I'd been out hustling all day, shining shoes, selling newspapers, and I had goo-gobs of money in my pocket. Bought me a bowl of chili for fifteen cents, and a cheeseburger for fifteen cents, and a Pepsi for five cents, and a piece of chocolate cake for ten cents. That was a good meal. I was eating when this old wino came in. I love winos because they never hurt anyone but themselves.

The old wino sat down at the counter and ordered twenty-six cents worth of food. He ate it like he really enjoyed it. When the owner, Mister Williams, asked him to pay the check, the old wino didn't lie or go through his pocket like he suddenly found a hole.

He just said: "Don't have no money."

The owner yelled: "Why in hell you come in here and eat my food if you don't have no money? That food cost me money."

Mister Williams jumped over the counter and knocked the wino off his stool and beat him over the head with a pop bottle. Then he stepped back and watched the wino bleed. Then he kicked him. And he kicked him again.

I looked at the wino with blood all over his face and I went over. "Leave him alone, Mister Williams. I'll pay the twenty-six cents."

The wino got up, slowly, pulling himself up to the stool, then up to the counter, holding on for a minute until his legs stopped shaking so bad. He looked at me with pure hate. "Keep your twenty-six cents. You don't have to pay, not now. I just finished paying for it."

He started to walk out, and as he passed me, he reached down and touched my shoulder. "Thanks, sonny, but it's too late now. Why didn't you pay it before?"

I was pretty sick about that. I waited too long to help another man.

Mother Tongue
Amy Tan

I am not a scholar of English or literature. I cannot give you much more than personal opinions on the English language and its variations in this country or others.

I am a writer. And by that definition, I am someone who has always loved language. I am fascinated by language in daily life. I spend a great deal of my time thinking about the power of language—the way it can evoke an emotion, a visual image, a complex idea, or a simple truth. Language is the tool of my trade. And I use them all—all the Englishes I grew up with.

Recently, I was made keenly aware of the different Englishes I do use. I was giving a talk to a large group of people, the same talk I had already given to half a dozen other groups. The nature of the talk was about my writing, my life, and my book, *The Joy Luck Club*. The talk was going along well enough, until I remembered one major difference that made the whole talk sound wrong. My mother was in the room. And it was perhaps the first time she had heard me give a lengthy speech, using the kind of English I have never used with her. I was saying things like, "The intersection of memory upon imagination" and "There is an aspect of my fiction that relates to thus-and-thus"—a speech filled with carefully wrought grammatical phrases, burdened, it suddenly seemed to me, with nominalized forms, past perfect tenses, conditional phrases, all the forms of standard English that I had learned in school and through books, the forms of English I did not use at home with my mother.

Just last week, I was walking down the street with my mother, and I again found myself conscious of the English I was using, the English I do use with her. We were talking about the price of new and used furniture and I heard myself saying this: "Not waste money that way." My husband was with us as well, and he didn't notice any switch in my English. And then I realized why. It's because over the twenty years we've been together I've often used the same kind of English with him, and sometimes he even uses it with me. It has become our language of intimacy, a different sort of English that relates to family talk, the language I grew up with.

So you'll have some idea of what this family talk I heard sounds like, I'll quote what my mother said during a recent conversation which I videotaped and then transcribed. During this conversation, my mother was talking about a political gangster in Shanghai who had the same last name as her family's, Du, and how the gangster in his early years wanted to be adopted by her family, which was rich by comparison. Later, the gangster became more powerful, far richer than my mother's family, and one day showed up at my mother's wedding to pay his respects. Here's what she said in part:

"Du Yusong having business like fruit stand. Like off the street kind. He is Du like Du Zong—but not Tsung-ming Island people. The local people call putong, the river east side, he belong to that side local people. That man want to ask Du Zong father take him in like become own family. Du Zong father wasn't look down on him, but didn't take seriously, until that man big like become a mafia. Now important person, very hard to inviting him. Chinese way, came only to show respect, don't stay for dinner. Respect for making big celebration, he shows up. Mean gives lots of respect. Chinese custom. Chinese social life that way. If too important won't have to stay too long. He come to my wedding. I didn't see, I heard it. I gone to boy's side, they have YMCA dinner. Chinese age I was nineteen."

You should know that my mother's expressive command of English belies how much she actually understands. She reads the *Forbes* report, listens to *Wall Street Week*, converses daily with her stockbroker, reads all of Shirley MacLaine's books with ease—all kinds of things I can't begin to understand. Yet some of my friends tell me they understand 50 percent of what my mother says. Some say they understand 80 to 90 percent. Some say they understand none of it, as if she were speaking pure Chinese. But to me, my mother's English is perfectly clear, perfectly natural. It's my mother tongue. Her language, as I hear it, is vivid, direct, full of observation and imagery. That was the language that helped shape the way I saw things, expressed things, made sense of the world.

Lately, I've been giving more thought to the kind of English my mother speaks. Like others, I have described it to people as "broken" or "fractured" English. But I wince when I say that. It has always bothered me that I can think of no way to describe it other than "broken," as if it were damaged and needed to be fixed, as if it lacked a certain wholeness and soundness. I've heard other terms used, "limited English," for example. But they seem just as bad, as if everything is limited, including people's perceptions of the limited English speaker.

I know this for a fact, because when I was growing up, my mother's "limited" English limited *my* perception of her. I was ashamed of her English. I believed that her English reflected the quality of what she had to say. That is, because she expressed them imperfectly her thoughts were imperfect. And I had plenty of empirical evidence to support me: the fact that people in department stores, at banks, and at restaurants did not take her seriously, did not give her good service, pretended not to understand her, or even acted as if they did not hear her.

My mother has long realized the limitations of her English as well. When I was fifteen, she used to have me call people on the phone to pretend I was she. In this guise, I was forced to ask for information or even to complain and yell at people who had been rude to her. One time it was a call to her stockbroker in New York. She had cashed out her small portfolio and it just so happened we were going to go to New York the next week, our very first trip outside California. I had to get on the phone and say in an adolescent voice that was not very convincing, "This is Mrs. Tan."

And my mother was standing in the back whispering loudly, "Why he don't send me check, already two weeks late. So mad he lie to me, losing me money."

And then I said in perfect English, "Yes, I'm getting rather concerned. You had agreed to send the check two weeks ago, but it hasn't arrived."

Then she began talking more loudly. "What he want, I come to New York tell him front of his boss, you cheating me?" And I was trying to calm her down, make her be quiet, while telling the stockbroker, "I can't tolerate any more excuses. If I don't receive the check immediately, I am going to have to speak to your manager when I'm in New York next week." And sure enough, the following week there we were in front of this astonished stockbroker, and I was sitting there red-faced and quiet, and my mother, the real Mrs. Tan, was shouting at his boss in her impeccable broken English.

We used a similar routine just five days ago, for a situation that was far less humorous. My mother had gone to the hospital for an appointment, to find out about a benign brain tumor a CAT scan had revealed a month ago. She said she had spoken very good English, her best English, no mistakes. Still, he said, the hospital did not apologize when they said they had lost the CAT scan and she had come for nothing. She said they did not seem to have any sympathy when she told them she was anxious to know the exact diagnosis, since her husband and son had both died of brain tumors. She said they would not give her any more information until the next time and she would have to make another appointment for that. So she said she would not leave until the doctor called her daughter. She wouldn't budge. And when the doctor finally called her daughter, me, who spoke in perfect English—lo and behold—we had assurances the CAT scan would be found, promise that a conference call on Monday would be held, and apologies for any suffering my mother had gone through for the most regrettable mistake.

I think my mother's English almost had an effect on limiting my possibilities in life as well. Sociologists and linguists probably will tell you that a person's developing language skills are more influenced by peers. But I do think that the language spoken in the family, especially in immigrant families which are more insular, plays a large role in shaping the language of the child. And I believe that it affected my results on achievement tests, IQ tests, and the SAT. While my English skills were never judged as poor, compared to math, English could not be considered my strong suit. In grade school I did moderately well, getting perhaps B's, sometimes B-pluses, in English and scoring perhaps in the sixtieth or seventieth percentile on achievement tests. But those scores were not good enough to override the opinion that my true abilities lay in math and science, because in those areas I achieved A's and scored in the ninetieth percentile or higher.

This was understandable. Math is precise; there is only one correct answer. Whereas, for me at least, the answers on English tests were always a judgment call, a matter of opinion and personal experience. Those tests were constructed around items like fill-in-the-blank sentence completion, such as, "Even though Tom was _____, Mary thought he was _____." And the correct answer always seemed to be the most bland combinations of thoughts, for example, "Even though Tom was shy, Mary thought he was charming," with the grammatical structure "even though" limiting the correct answer to some sort of semantic opposites, so you wouldn't get answers like, "Even though Tom was foolish, Mary thought he was ridiculous." Well, according to my mother, there were very few limitations as to what Tom could have been and what Mary might have thought of him. So I never did well on tests like that.

The same was true with word analogies, pairs of words in which you were supposed to find some sort of logical, semantic relationship—for example, "*Sunset* is to *nightfall* as _____ is to _____." And here you would be presented with a list of four possible pairs, one of which showed the same kind of relationship: *red* is to *stoplight*, *bus* is to *arrival*, *chills* is to *fever*, *yawn* is to *boring*. Well, I could never think that way. I knew what the tests were asking, but I could not block out of my mind the images already created by the first pair, "*sunset* is to *nightfall*"—and I would see a burst of color against a darkening sky, the moon rising, the lowering of a curtain of stars. And all the other pairs of words—red, bus, stoplight, boring—just threw up a mass of confusing images, making it impossible for me to sort out something as logical as saying: "A sunset precedes nightfall" is the same as "a chill precedes a fever." The only way I would have gotten that answer right would have been to imagine an associative situation, for example, by being disobedient and staying out past sunset, catching a chill at night which turns into feverish pneumonia as punishment, which indeed did happen to me.

I have been thinking about all this lately, about my mother's English, about achievement tests. Because lately I've been asked, as a writer, why there are not more Asian Americans represented in American literature. Why are there few Asian Americans enrolled in creative writing programs? Why do so many Chinese students go into engineering? Well, these are broad sociological questions I can't begin to answer. But I have noticed in surveys—in fact, just last week—that Asian students, as a whole, always do significantly better on math achievement tests than in English. And this makes me think that there are other Asian-American students whose English spoken in the home might also be described as "broken" or "limited." And perhaps they also have teachers who are steering them away from writing and into math and science, which is what happened to me.

Fortunately, I happen to be rebellious in nature and enjoy the challenge of disproving assumptions made about me. I became an English major my first year in college, after being enrolled as pre-med. I started writing nonfiction as a freelancer the week after I was told by my former boss that writing was my worst skill and I should hone my talents toward account management.

But it wasn't until 1985 that I finally began to write fiction. And at first I wrote using what I thought to be wittily crafted sentences, sentences that would finally prove I had mastery over the English language. Here's an example from the first draft of a story that later made its way into *The Joy Luck Club,* but without this line: "That was my mental quandary in its nascent state." A terrible line, which I can hardly pronounce.

Fortunately, for reasons I won't go into today, I later decided I should envision a reader for the stories I would write. And the reader I decided upon was my mother, because these were stories about mothers. So with this reader in mind—and in fact she did read my early drafts—I began to write stories using all the Englishes I grew up with: the English I spoke to my mother, which for lack of a better term might be described as "simple"; the English she used with me, which for lack of a better term might be described as "broken"; my translation of her Chinese, which could certainly be described as "watered down"; and what I imagine to be her translation of her Chinese if she could speak perfect English, her internal language, and for that I sought to preserve the essence, but neither an English nor a Chinese structure. I wanted to capture what language ability tests can never reveal: her intent, her passion, her imagery, the rhythms of her speech and the nature of her thoughts.

Apart from what any critic had to say about my writing, I knew I had succeeded where it counted when my mother finished reading my book and gave me her verdict: "So easy to read."

Home Is a Freeway
Neil Morgan

During the year 1966, in the pithy but unsensational little journey called *Cry California*, there was a picture story that appeared to document a novel case: a family who lived on the freeways of Los Angeles in their motor home, one of those outsized vehicles with sleeping area, kitchenette and bathroom. When their first baby had come, the story related, Marilee Farrier had given up her job. Installment payments and bills had mounted, and her husband had taken a second, nighttime job. Still they were in trouble. Rather than sell their motor home, which they enjoyed for weekend holidays, the Farriers had sold their tract home and their car.

A night photograph in the magazine showed their motor home parked in a public lot not far from the Los Angeles Music Center. At 7:00 each morning, Marilee Farrier was quoted as saying, she got up, changed the baby, plugged in the coffee, and began driving out the Hollywood Freeway. Mike Farrier noted proudly that his wife didn't wake him until they passed the Cahuenga off-ramp. They parked for a light breakfast outside the Burbank factory where he worked. Then she drove back over the Golden State and San Bernardino freeways to her mother's home, where she left the baby and went to a half-day job. Later she reversed the route to pick up her child and her husband. He drove back to downtown Los Angeles as she prepared dinner. More photographs showed the Farrier family making a deposit at a drive-in teller's window at their bank, attending a drive-in movie, and pulling into a drive-in restaurant for a dinner out.

With the story, the editor of *Cry California* produced a map of metropolitan Los Angeles freeways, tracing the Farrier family's daily route. It was a jumble of circuitous dots and arrows indicating runs totaling 128 miles. Farrier was quoted:

"One day is about the same as another: about ten gallons of gas a day. We've begun to feel that the freeways, particularly the Hollywood Freeway, belong to us. It's not the same feeling you get about a house on a lot, but it's definitely a sense of ownership. We don't have any neighbors, of course, but actually we had a few neighbors before that we were happy to leave behind."

When the story appeared, I was one of several newsmen who went to the magazine's editor, William Bronson, in an attempt to locate the Farriers. Bronson told us the story was a hoax, and that he had used friends and borrowed a motor home for the photographs. He has insisted doggedly ever since that it seemed to him to be so patent a farce that he did not think it necessary to label it. But in California the Farriers did not seem outrageous enough to lead readers to doubt them. I still do not entirely accept Bronson's disclaimer. I suspect people like the Farriers are driving about Los Angeles today.

In California the automobile assumes tribal significance. Limitless ingenuity is displayed in adapting it to man's desire. Freeway commuters grow so blasé that a Los Angeles mortuary has directed its radio and roadside advertising toward those who daydream or read, shave, study or neck while they drive along at sixty or seventy miles an hour. When traffic slows toward the stop-and-go commuter rush hours, the student can be seen grasping his slide rule or turning to an anatomy chart. Businessmen are dictating into tape recorders. Others are plugged into tutor tapes, learning languages. Women are applying lipstick, brushing their hair, hooking their dresses. The automobile serves as office, bedroom and signboard. In San Francisco, a neighborhood divorcée became the talk of the service stations by gluing her phone number in plastic tape to her car's oil stick. At Laguna Beach, a blonde's Volkswagen bore the legend "Have Pills—Will Go." When freeways and beaches grow too crowded, young people can be found embracing in their cars on the top floors of public garages. Teenagers prize ancient hearses as personal vehicles; they can be equipped to carry surfboards and sleep two. The automobile is even used as a mobile listening post to maintain the sanctity of the home. In San Diego, a photographer answered a newspaper advertisement offering a camera for sale, and discovered he had telephoned a pay booth outside a drive-in restaurant. "That's right," a voice answered, "you wanted the guy with the camera. He drove up here this morning with a book to read, parked outside the phone booth and answered the phone for about half an hour until he'd made his deal. I asked him if he didn't have a phone at home. 'Sure,' he said, 'but this way I can sell the camera and not have to sit around listening to the damn phone ring all day and night.' "

Since there is now relatively little rapid mass transit in California cities, every man's car is his mobile castle. The number of motor vehicles in the metropolitan Los Angeles area alone is approaching five million; only the states of New York, Pennsylvania and Texas have more cars than Los Angeles. In Southern California there is a car for about every two people; in New York City, there is one for every six. Close to eight million gallons of gasoline are burned each day in the Los Angeles Basin. Throughout California one finds the greatest concentration of motor vehicles in the world, and it shows no sign of diminishing. In 1968 the California Department of Motor Vehicles was seeking a new method of license plate numbering. Under the system using three letters and three digits on each plate, there were only about sixteen million possible combinations, and they were being exhausted. Officials were predicting that twenty-two million cars would be registered in California by 1980. San Francisco is choking with cars, the highest density of automobiles of any city: 7000 per square mile. The San Francisco freeways, blocked from completion because outraged citizens regarded them as eyesores on the lovely San Francisco skyline, now dump their daily burden of cars at the edges of downtown. The city awaits completion of the Bay Area Rapid Transit District, an interurban rail commuter system which has been mired in debt and debacle during its construction. Meanwhile, from off the Bayshore Freeway, the Golden Gate and the Oakland Bay Bridges, motor vehicles are funneled into the city until it seems sure to burst in an exploding aneurysm of steel, rubber and fume.

In Los Angeles, which has desperately accepted all proffered freeways—slightly or not—almost half a million cars roll each day through the central interchange known as The Slot. Only for about four hours each day, at peak commuter rushes, does the intricate freeway system overload enough to bring automobile speeds down below maximum. By the early 1980's the three Southern California counties of Los Angeles, Orange and Ventura alone will be slashed by a network of 1535 miles of freeway costing more than five billion dollars; close to one-half of it is already in existence. It is possible to drive on freeways from San Diego almost five hundred miles northward through Los Angeles and through the Great Central Valley without encountering any traffic signal, stop sign or toll station; for cars with sufficient fuel capacity and drivers of adequate durability, there is no compulsion to pause. It is not a sightseer's route.

The Jeaning of America
Carin Quinn

This is the story of a sturdy American symbol which has now spread throughout most of the world. The symbol is not the dollar. It is not even Coca-Cola. It is a simple pair of pants called blue jeans, and what the pants symbolize is what Alexis de Tocqueville called "a manly and legitimate passion for equality. . . ." Blue jeans are favored equally by bureaucrats and cowboys; bankers and deadbeats; fashion designers and beer drinkers. They draw no distinctions and recognize no classes; they are merely American. Yet they are sought after almost everywhere in the world—including Russia, where authorities recently broke up a teen-aged gang that was selling them on the black market for two hundred dollars a pair. They have been around for a long time, and it seems likely that they will outlive even the necktie.

This ubiquitous American symbol was the invention of a Bavarian-born Jew. His name was Levi Strauss.

He was born in Bad Ocheim, Germany, in 1829, and during the European political turmoil of 1848 decided to take his chances in New York, to which his two brothers already had emigrated. Upon arrival, Levi soon found that his two brothers had exaggerated their tales of an easy life in the land of the main chance. They were landowners, they had told him; instead, he found them pushing needles, thread, pots, pans, ribbons, yarn, scissors, and buttons to housewives. For two years he was a lowly peddler, hauling some 180 pounds of sundries door-to-door to eke out a marginal living. When a married sister in San Francisco offered to pay his way West in 1850, he jumped at the opportunity, taking with him bolts of canvas he hoped to sell for tenting.

It was the wrong kind of canvas for that purpose, but while talking with a miner down from the mother lode, he learned that pants—sturdy pants that would stand up to the rigors of digging—were almost impossible to find. Opportunity beckoned. On the spot, Strauss measured the man's girth and inseam with a piece of string and, for six dollars in gold dust, had [the canvas] tailored into a pair of stiff but rugged pants. The miner was delighted with the result, word got around about "those pants of Levi's," and Strauss was in business. The company has been in business ever since.

When Strauss ran out of canvas, he wrote his two brothers to send more. He received instead a tough, brown cotton cloth made in Nimes, France—called *serge de Nîmes* and swiftly shortened to "denim" (the word "jeans" derives from Gênes, the French word for Genoa, where a similar cloth was produced). Almost from the first, Strauss had his cloth dyed the distinctive indigo that gave blue jeans their name, but it was not until the 1870s that he added the copper rivets which have long since become a company trademark. The rivets were the idea of a Virginia City, Nevada, tailor, Jacob W. Davis, who added them to pacify a mean-tempered miner called Alkali Ike. Alkali, the story goes, complained that the pockets of his jeans always tore when he stuffed them with ore samples and demanded that Davis do something about it. As a kind of joke, Davis took the pants to a blacksmith and had the pockets riveted; once again, the idea worked so well that word got around; in 1873 Strauss appropriated and patterned the gimmick—and hired Davis as a regional manager.

By this time, Strauss had taken both his brothers and two brothers-in-law into the company and was ready for his third San Francisco store. Over the ensuing years the company prospered locally, and by the time of his death in 1902, Strauss had become a man of prominence in California. For three decades thereafter the business remained profitable though small, with sales largely confined to the working people of the West—cowboys, lumberjacks, railroad workers, and the like. Levi's jeans were first introduced to the East, apparently, during the dude-ranch craze of the 1930s, when vacationing Easterners returned and spread the word about the wonderful pants with rivets. Another boost came in World War II, when blue jeans were declared an essential commodity and were sold only to people engaged in defense work. From a company with fifteen salespeople, two plants, and almost no business east of the Mississippi in 1946, the organization grew in thirty years to include a sales force of more than twenty-two thousand, with fifty plants and offices in thirty-five countries. Each year, more than 250,000,000 items of Levi's clothing are sold—including more than 83,000,000 pairs of riveted blue jeans. They have become, through marketing, word of mouth, and demonstrable reliability, the common pants of America. They can be purchased pre-washed, pre-faded, and pre-shrunk for the suitable proletarian look. They adapt themselves to any sort of idiosyncratic use; women slit them at the inseams and convert them into long skirts, men chop them off above the knees and turn them into something to be worn while challenging the surf. Decorations and ornamentations abound.

The pants have become a tradition, and along the way have acquired a history of their own—so much so that the company has opened a museum in San Francisco. There was, for example, the turn-of-the-century trainman who replaced a faulty coupling with a pair of jeans; the Wyoming man who used his jeans as a towrope to haul his car out of a ditch; the Californian who found several pairs in an abandoned mine, wore them, then discovered they were sixty-three years old and still as good as new and turned them over to the Smithsonian as a tribute to their toughness. And then there is the particularly terrifying story of the careless construction worker who dangled fifty-two stories above the street until rescued, his sole support the Levi's belt loop through which his rope was hooked.

Reviewing the Basics

This chapter offers additional explanations and exercises that reinforce the lessons covered in Chapters 1–4. It also includes information and practice on fundamental revision strategies and the basic patterns of English sentences. The various exercises will help you improve areas of your writing that require additional attention or work, like grammar, punctuation, and mechanics.

Your instructor may assign either all or part of these exercises as a mandatory requirement of the course, or you may be referred to particular sections for supplementary work on specific problems, such as how to correct fragments or use commas correctly. In courses that have a writing center or a lab component, these exercises may be assigned as lab units.

Topic Sentences and Directing Words

Concluding Sentences

Transitional Words That Signal Order

Transitional Words That Link Sentences and Ideas

Being Specific

Consistency of Tense, Number, and Person

The Basic Pattern of English Sentences

Sentence Types

    The Simple Sentence

    The Compound Sentence

    The Complex Sentence

    The Compound-Complex Sentence

A Word about Fragments

Commas

Other Punctuation Marks: The Apostrophe, Colon, and Semicolon

Holt, Rinehart and Winston

Topic Sentences and Directing Words

A **topic sentence** consists of two main parts:

> 1. Your topic (what your paragraph is about)
> 2. Directing words (the point you want to make about your topic)

Exercise 1

Directing Words

For each topic sentence that follows, add two different sets of directing words.

> EXAMPLE:
>
> Reentry women <u>add personality and spice to our student population.</u>
>
> *Another direction:* Reentry women are <u>*often overwhelmed by the responsibilities of being*</u>
> <u>*a student once again.*</u>
>
> *A different direction:* Reentry women have <u>*several possibilities for financial assistance*</u>
> <u>*while in school.*</u>

1. Television talk shows <u>deal with all kinds of controversy.</u>

Another direction: Television talk shows _____

_____

A different direction: Television talk shows _____

_____

2. The parking problem on campus <u>is the result of a chain of other issues.</u>

Another direction: The parking problem on campus _____

_____

A different direction: The parking problem on campus _____

_____

Holt, Rinehart and Winston

Exercise I (continued)

3. Teachers in the public schools <u>are increasingly being faced with limited resources</u>.

Another direction: Teachers in the public schools _____

_____

A different direction: Teachers in the public schools _____

_____

4. Environmental pollution <u>is a global issue</u>.

Another direction: Environmental pollution _____

_____

A different direction: Environmental pollution _____

_____

5. Home schooling <u>has advantages as well as disadvantages</u>.

Another direction: Home schooling _____

_____

A different direction: Home schooling _____

_____

Holt, Rinehart and Winston

Exercise 2

Concluding Sentences

A **concluding sentence** completes your paragraph (or essay) and puts the final touch on it. There are no definite rules for writing a concluding sentence, but it should complete the paragraph (or essay) in one of the following ways:

1. by restating the idea in your topic sentence (or your thesis statement if you are writing an essay).
2. by making a final, overall impression on your reader.
3. by ending with a prediction for the future.
4. by using a quotation followed by a comment.
5. by suggesting a possible course of action.

The paragraph that follows does not have a concluding sentence:

> Coffeehouses of the '60s are popular again as neighborhood bars without the alcohol. For one thing, these places offer an alternative way to spend an evening. This environment often allows for intellectual arguments, social protest, intense conversation, music, or even poetry readings. For another, customers can just sit back and relax. For example, they might listen to the words of a song that has personal meaning for them, a rare occurrence in our fast-paced society. Also, patrons can read a magazine, study, chat, or even do their taxes while they sip espresso coffee. The informal atmosphere invites these types of activities. Most appealing is that these places are inexpensive, offering various kinds of coffee drinks for as little as $1.25.

Three possible concluding sentences:

> *The popularity of these coffeehouses attests to people's need for an alternate type of entertainment.*

> *People who look for a place to enjoy intellectual stimulation and an inexpensive evening will find coffeehouses attractive.*

> *As long as people continue to seek alcohol-free entertainment, coffeehouses will appear in more and more cities and towns.*

Holt, Rinehart and Winston

Exercise 2 (continued)

My father is an amazing parent. First of all, he is extremely strict, but nice about it. He always wants us to ask his permission before we go out, and he will not let us come in after midnight, even on weekends. Also, he is very trustworthy. For example, if I have a big problem, he always helps me, no matter how big the problem. I know I cannot always tell my private secrets to him, but I know that I can trust him in all other situations. That is why he makes me and my whole family feel so secure. Another thing that I admire about him is that he always wants the best for us and sacrifices his own needs for ours. When he was saving money for some new tools, he gave it to me so I could go on my senior trip. He works all week and even during the weekends so he can save extra money for what we need. In fact, he likes to help people in general, giving his clothes to people who need them. Also, when he buys fresh vegetables, he always shares them with his friends. The most important thing that he does is to give us good, sound advice. For instance, he tells us that if we have clothes that we do not use, we should give them to people who need them.

EXAMPLE:

What makes him so amazing is that my father not only teaches us by word, but also by example.

Other possible concluding sentences:

1. _____

_____

2. _____

_____

Holt, Rinehart and Winston

Exercise 2 (continued)

Getting bitten by a dog when I was five years old really changed my feelings about dogs. One Saturday morning, like all Saturdays before, I started to get ready for church. I carefully put on my baby blue dress with the little white ruffled collar. When we arrived at church, I went to my Bible class. I was restless that morning, and I had trouble listening to my Sunday school teacher. She was teaching us a lesson about being careful because there were dangers everywhere. I was young, and I had a hard time imagining that anything could happen to me. All I knew was that the sooner church was over, the sooner I could go home. After church we started on our way home. As we turned onto my street, I saw my cousin and some friends playing hide-and-seek. My mom dropped me and my sister off so we could play, warning us to be careful. I thought she was talking about our dresses. We started to play, and Diana, one of my friends, said, "Let's go hide in my back yard." I knew she had a pit bull dog, but she said it was tied up, so we went along with her. We closed the gate so the other kids could not see us. I remember standing by the wall of the house when out of nowhere came this vicious dog. Within a second, the dog jumped on top of me, and I slipped on a paint tray that was on the ground. The next thing I knew, I was bleeding from everywhere. My hands, my legs, and even my blue dress were covered with blood. Somehow I managed to get up and jump over the fenced gate we had shut earlier. My cousin grabbed me by the arm, took me into the house, and laid me on the couch. While we waited for the ambulance to arrive, my uncle poured peroxide on my face. Later, at the hospital, I received ten stitches. After that big accident, I was terrified of dogs. I would see a dog blocks away and start to panic.

EXAMPLE:

From that time on, I started listening to grown-ups when they told me to be careful.

Other possible concluding sentences:

1. _____

_____

2. _____

_____

TRANSITIONAL WORDS THAT SIGNAL ORDER

A paragraph is coherent when its sentences are arranged in logical order and when each sentence is linked to the previous one. Using **transitional words** (expressions that signal order and provide links between sentences) is one way to achieve coherence, and thereby communicate your ideas effectively within a paragraph.

Order is the logical arrangement of sentences within a paragraph. The three common types of orders are as follows:

> Time
>
> Space
>
> Importance

Because transitional words help to signal the order of a paragraph, they are usually found at the beginning of a sentence.

Transitional Words: Time Order

Paragraphs in which you might use a **time order** (first to last, past to present) include the following:

1. Instructions on how to do something (preparing for a natural disaster, borrowing money)
2. A narrative or story (about a car wreck, a job experience, a first date)
3. Facts, statistics, or data (history of baseball, spread of AIDS, population increase)

Exercise 3

Transitional Words: Time Order

The paragraphs below are arranged by time order. Choose a transitional word or words to link the sentences and write them in the blanks provided.

EXAMPLE:

Several U.S. cities offer an unusual way to spend a weekend. *In February,* Mankato, Minnesota, sponsors a sit and spit convention. Contestants aim their six spits at a spittoon some eight feet away. In Hamburg, Arkansas, the Banana Slug Festival attracts people from all over the country *during the first weekend in March.* Events include a slug sprint and a slug cook-off. The Armadillo Festival is held *in early May* in South Bend, Texas. The festivities in-clude armadillo races and beauty contests. With these activities available, people should not have to complain about boring weekends.

1. Following the directions in the booklet, Calvin completed the registration forms for spring classes. _____, he filled out the data sheet accurately. _____, he listed his classes in the space provided on the form. _____, he wrote the check for his enrollment fees. _____, he folded all the forms and inserted them into a stamped envelope. _____ when he dropped the envelope into the mailbox, he was registered for classes.

2. Making a flower lei, which is worn around a person's neck, is a painstaking, but rewarding process. _____, you must choose a variety of exotic Hawaiian flowers such as ilima, pikabe, or maunaloa, to name a few. _____, the refrigerated flowers must be sorted by color and type and cleansed thoroughly. _____, a special lei-making needle, twelve inches long, is used to thread each flower carefully through its delicate stem. _____, after you have threaded over a hundred blossoms, the ends are tied. Making a Hawaiian lei requires patience and care, but the end result is a work of art.

3. Writing a dictionary takes many years. _____, the editors must record the context of each word on cards over a period of time. Some words have hundreds of context cards with exact quota-tions on each card illustrating how the word is used. _____, the primary editor reviews the cards, sorts, discards, and determines several meanings for the word. _____, the editor writes the definitions for that word based on the illustrative quotes on the cards. As a result, the de-finitions of the word reflect its use.

Holt, Rinehart and Winston

Transitional Words: Space Order

Paragraphs in which you might use **a space order** (top to bottom, near to far, right to left) include the following:

1. Description of a place
2. Description of an object
3. Description of a person

Exercise 4

Transitional Words: Space Order

The paragraphs below are arranged by space order. Add appropriate transitional words in the blanks provided.

EXAMPLE:

In my grandparents' city of Guadalajara, the beautiful "La Plaza de lost Mariachis" is in the heart of the downtown area. *At the center of this plaza* are two beautifully carved, eight-foot-high water fountains that make the place attractive. *Next to the fountains* are chairs and small round tables nicely decorated with flowers. *Surrounding the plaza,* trees give nice shade for people to sit and enjoy the music of the mariachi bands. This well-known plaza has many buildings *on all sides.* The beautiful cathedral towers *above the whole plaza* and is the main attraction for the people sitting at the tables. My grandparents spend many wonderful hours in the plaza in the heart of the city of Guadalajara, Mexico.

1. The view from the top of Figueroa Mountain is spectacular. _____ the mountain slopes down dramatically, forming a complex and beautiful pattern of brush, pine trees, and small grassy meadows. _____ the enormous Santa Ynez Valley lies with its elegant thoroughbred ranches, large rolling hills, and majestic oak trees. _____ the coast mountains form a sheer wall of steep, brush-covered ridges, often capped by rugged outcroppings of sandstone rock. _____ _____ gleams the bright blue Pacific Ocean with its three channel islands. Figueroa's wonderful view is well worth the long drive it takes to get there.

2. Sitting at a sidewalk cafe in New Orleans' French Quarter permits me to observe a fascinating array of unusual people. _____ strange-looking tourists, dressed in their colorful Bermuda shorts and reflector sunglasses, parade up and down. Of course, they take photographs of every flower-filled balcony. _____ a bizarre-looking girl with purple hair, wire-rimmed glasses, and a formal evening gown stands. She is playing Mozart on a violin. _____ wildly costumed circus clowns race around on stilts. Few sidewalk cafes in other cities offer such a fascinating view of people.

Holt, Rinehart and Winston

Transitional Words: Importance Order

Paragraphs in which you might use importance order (least to most) include the following:

1. Reasons for something (choosing a particular college, taking a stand on an issue, selecting a particular movie)
2. Types (different kinds of medical treatments, types of parties, varieties of exercise)

Exercise 5

Transitional Words: Importance Order

The paragraphs below are organized by importance order. Fill in the blanks with appropriate transitional words.

EXAMPLE:

Millions of people today suffer from the problems associated with Alzheimer's disease. *One of the problems* is "wandering," caused by loss of memory and associative powers. All of a sudden even a walk down a neighborhood street is strange and unfamiliar for the Alzheimer sufferer. The victim becomes lost, and anything can happen. *Another problem* is the loss of survival skills. That is, a person with Alzheimer's disease often forgets to eat or to be concerned with the necessary tasks of daily living. *The biggest problem* is depression. In their good moments Alzheimer's sufferers realize the extent to which they are victims of this devastating illness, and they become depressed because they feel helpless to stop its progression. Fortunately, many self-help groups are emerging across the country to offer relief and advice for the victims and their families.

1. Allergy season is in full swing, and sufferers everywhere wonder out loud, "Why me?" _____, they search for the culprits that are causing their discomfort. For example, they might blame a host of causes in our environment: weeds, dust mites, pollen, fragrances, petroleum by-products, etc. _____, they might examine what they put inside their bodies, like what they eat or drink. Foods such as chocolate, bananas, nuts, yeast products, and milk are common sources of allergic reactions. _____ they might do some genetic research. In many cases sufferers need look no further than their own fathers and mothers. Hay fever, for instance, is the most commonly inherited allergy, and it is passed down through a person's genes. That is, children of hay fever sufferers have a 70% chance of inheriting it. Unfortunately, since the causes of allergies are so complex, many sufferers all over the world are doomed to a lifelong search for relief.

2. Contrary to popular belief, the rodeo is not cruel to bucking horses. _____ _____, if it were not for rodeos, most bucking horses would be destroyed because they are not suitable for pets or for general ranch use. The rodeo circuit saves them from their fateful ending. _____, once they are chosen for the rodeo, they receive excellent treatment. That is, they are well fed and kept in good health so that they will be in top form during rodeo performances. _____, rodeo producers take care of their animals because of the costs involved. Indeed, they are an expensive investment. Thus, in spite of what activists for animal rights say, rodeo horses are actually treated very well.

Holt, Rinehart and Winston

TRANSITIONAL WORDS THAT LINK SENTENCES AND IDEAS

In addition to using transitional words that signal the main order of your entire paper, transitional words also link the sentences within a paragraph. These transitions actually link one sentence to the next and clarify the relationship of one sentence to another.

Giving Examples

in other words   for instance
for example   as an illustration

EXAMPLES:

Mr. Chavez is an excellent teacher. *In other words,* he knows the course material, explains it clearly, and is always well prepared.

Sam Weatherstone knows how to take care of his horse. *For example,* he feeds it properly, keeps its teeth "floated," and provides plenty of fresh, clean water.

According to the Distilled Spirits Industry Council, food can slow down the absorption of alcohol. *For instance,* cheese and meats, foods high in protein, are especially good.

Contrasting Ideas

nevertheless   however   on the contrary
on the other hand   in contrast   otherwise

EXAMPLES:

J. T. dreamed of becoming a pro football player. *However,* a bad knee injury ended that dream.

For some, a New Year's resolution is no more than a conversation topic. *On the other hand,* for others it is a real commitment.

Holidays are a time for socializing. *Nevertheless,* the joy of visiting friends can turn to tragedy if alcohol is overused.

Holt, Rinehart and Winston

Giving Additional Information

in addition	furthermore	besides that	likewise
similarly	of course	moreover	

EXAMPLES:

Bob increased the value of his car by getting chrome wheels for it. *In addition,* he put in a compact disc player and custom speakers.

Rika did well in her electronics classes at San Jose State. *Besides that,* she earned good grades in her engineering course and her technical writing course.

Graffiti art, which started in New York subways during the 1970s, is embracing Los Angeles. *Furthermore,* the city's abandoned industrial spaces provide a canvas to spray paint one's way into legend.

Showing Results

as a result	consequently	therefore	thus

EXAMPLES:

John Toreno felt he could become an even better teacher if he had more education. *Therefore,* he went back to get a master's degree.

The best way to cope with children's fear of the dark is to allow them to have a small light that they can control. *As a result,* they will eventually decide they do not need the light at all.

Shy people are often overly concerned with themselves. *Consequently,* they need to be reminded to move beyond their own shyness to help others.

Holt, Rinehart and Winston

Exercise 6

Transitional Words That Link Sentences and Ideas: Giving Examples

Complete the following steps for each sentence:

      1. Add a second sentence that gives an example.

      2. Begin your sentence with an appropriate transitional word.

      3. Put a comma after the transitional word.

1. His boss was very considerate. _____

_____

2. J. T. worked hard at being a good teacher. _____

_____

Exercise 7

Transitional Words That Link Sentences and Ideas: Contrasting Ideas

Complete the following steps for each sentence:

      1. Add a second sentence that shows contrast.

      2. Begin your sentence with an appropriate transitional word.

      3. Put a comma after the transitional word.

1. A visit to the dentist terrifies some people. _____

_____

2. Irwin applied for a job as a tutor after school. _____

_____

Exercise 8

Transitional Words That Link Sentences and Ideas: Giving Additional Information

Complete the following steps for each sentence:

       1. Add a second sentence that gives additional information.
       2. Begin your sentence with an appropriate transitional word.
       3. Put a comma after the transitional word.

1. Hector spent the day preparing a special dinner for his friends. _____

_____

2. One way to prepare for a test is to review all the class notes. _____

_____

Exercise 9

Transitional Words That Link Sentences and Ideas: Showing Results

Complete the following steps for each sentence:

       1. Add a second sentence that shows results.
       2. Begin each sentence with an appropriate transitional word.
       3. Put a comma after the transitional word.

1. The child made up a convincing story about her report card. _____

_____

2. Olivia was an outstanding college softball player. _____

_____

Holt, Rinehart and Winston

Exercise 10

Transitional Words That Link Sentences and Ideas

The following paragraph is missing some transitional words or phrases. From the list below, choose a transitional word or phrase to link the sentences, and write the word or phrase in the blanks provided.

in contrast	as a result	thus
however	for example	for instance
as an illustration	besides	likewise
consequently	of course	moreover

Office workers of the '90s have found their jobs more technical and demanding. A few years ago an executive secretary needed three basic skills: to type 80 wpm, to have good phone manners, and to demonstrate a talent for organization. _____, today's office worker must be computer literate, technology conscious, and responsible. Not only do workers handle all the secretarial-clerical tasks, they also manage an office and make decisions. What has caused this increase in responsibilities? One cause is the reduction in the number of employees and the restructuring of a business. _____, the number of tasks and the levels of responsibilities for office workers has increased. Yet, while the recession of 1990–91 triggered a spate of layoffs, it had less of an impact on office workers. _____, their ranks swelled to 18.6 million in 1992 from 13.1 million in 1972. Another cause of increased responsibilities is computers and communications. _____, this technology has allowed these workers to perform more technical tasks. Thus, through corporate downsizing, the office worker of today assumes more responsibilities in a highly technical environment.

Holt, Rinehart and Winston

Exercise 11

BEING SPECIFIC

Revise the underlined passages in the following two paragraphs, making them more exact, detailed, and specific. Write your revised sentences on the lines provided.

EXAMPLE:

Our <u>place</u> lies hidden in the hills.

Our small family dairy farm lies hidden in the hills. _____

1. Our small family dairy farm lies hidden in the hills. In the center of the valley <u>runs a beautiful stream.</u> Next to the stream stands our white two-story farmhouse, a tall, leaning silo, and a small, bright red barn used for milking the cows and storing many tons of hay for the long winter months. Surrounding this small complex of old, wooden buildings, our 165 acres of hay and pasture land lies over the gently rolling hills like an intriguing checkerboard pattern with their varying yellow and green hues and colors of the grain, pasture, and other crops. On all sides, beyond the boundaries of our farm, stretches <u>a large wilderness area.</u> Our farm seems to be a small island in a vast ocean of hills in all directions.

_____

_____

_____

_____

_____

_____

_____

_____

_____

_____

_____

_____

_____

_____

Exercise 11 (continued)

Being Specific

Revise the underlined passages in the following two paragraphs, making them more exact, detailed, and specific. Write your revised sentences on the lines provided.

EXAMPLE:

The Halloween festival at my old elementary school transformed it into <u>an exciting place.</u>

The Halloween festival at my old elementary school transformed it into a wonderful, magical world for children.

2. The Halloween festival at my old elementary school transformed it into a wonderful, magical world for children. The cakewalk always created a mysterious, slow moving human maze in the kindergarten room as the costumed children and parents, dressed as clowns, pirates, and ghosts, stepped hesitantly from one numbered marker to the next. <u>Many exciting game booths</u> filled the fifth grade classroom. Best of all, the deep basement below the stage was made into a <u>haunted house,</u> one that offered young kids <u>every imaginable horror.</u> My old school's Halloween festival was always a world of fun.

_____

_____

_____

_____

_____

_____

_____

_____

_____

_____

_____

_____

_____

_____

CONSISTENCY OF TENSE, NUMBER, AND PERSON

Being **consistent** means your paper is easy to follow from beginning to end because you have avoided confusing shifts in tense, number, and person.

CONSISTENCY OF TENSE

Verb tense indicates the time of an action, indicating whether the action occurred in the past, whether it occurs in the present, or whether it will happen in the future. In general, **consistency of tense** means using the same tense throughout your paper, unless it is necessary to show an event that occurred at a different time.

Holt, Rinehart and Winston

Exercise 12

Consistency of Tense

The following sentences contain shifts in verb tense. Complete these steps for each sentence:

1. Cross out the verb with the wrong tense and write the correct verb tense above it.
2. Rewrite each sentence in the space provided.

EXAMPLE:

came

After the huddle *broke*, the football team ~~comes~~ up to the line to execute the play.

After the huddle broke, the football team came up to the line to execute the play.

1. Some people *marry* for companionship while others *decided* to marry for money.

_____

_____

2. On television today women *make* up a smaller proportion of all characters; in addition, they usually *played* a romantic role or one with a sexual context.

_____

_____

3. Several studies *indicate* that first-born children *tended* to be more frightened by the prospect of an accident or physical injury.

_____

_____

4. Some cultures *depend* on computers for survival in their society; others *functioned* quite well even without the luxury of electricity.

_____

_____

5. Everyone on the volleyball team *runs* four miles each morning, whereas the players on the football team *visited* the weight room.

_____

_____

Exercise 13

Past Tense

Change the following paragraph from present tense to past tense:

From my kitchen table I <u>watch</u> my family in action. My eleven-year-old son, Mark, <u>enters</u> the dark kitchen, muttering about the cold. He <u>shuffles</u> barefooted across the linoleum floor to the long counter, almost crashing into a kitchen chair. Our Boston terrier, Blackie, fifteen pounds of nervous energy, <u>bounces</u> up and <u>nips</u> at Mark's heels. Still muttering, Mark <u>shoves</u> aside cans and cereal boxes, looking for the hot chocolate mix. At this point, my daughter, Catheryn, <u>drags</u> into the room. Without even saying hello, Catheryn <u>grabs</u> a piece of toast from my plate and <u>plops</u> down on a chair. Blackie <u>jumps</u> up in her lap, and suddenly Catheryn <u>leaps</u> up and runs out of the room, screaming, "Dog hairs!" Mark <u>can't find</u> a clean mug, and he <u>slams</u> the cabinet door. It is just another Monday at our house.

_____

_____

_____

_____

_____

_____

_____

_____

_____

_____

_____

_____

_____

_____

_____

_____

_____

_____

Holt, Rinehart and Winston

Exercise 14

Present Tense

Change the following paragraph from past tense to present tense:

My English teacher's office <u>was located</u> down an old, musty hallway. Two wooden bookshelves on the left wall <u>were stuffed</u> with all types of books. On the far wall <u>hung</u> a poster of an Irish poet, W. B. Yeats. Beneath the poster <u>sat</u> a desk cluttered with student papers and official-looking forms. On the right wall, an ancient school clock <u>moved</u> its hands forward erratically, ticking off the minutes. Beneath the shelves <u>sat</u> a long, low shelf covered with piles of worksheets, textbooks, and old essays. Unbelievably, my English teacher <u>was</u> able to work amidst this clutter.

_____

_____

_____

_____

_____

_____

_____

_____

_____

_____

_____

_____

_____

_____

_____

_____

_____

_____

Exercise 15

Consistency of Tense

The following paragraphs contain shifts in verb tense. Complete the following steps for each paragraph:

1. Decide whether the paragraph should be in the past tense or present tense.
2. To make the paragraph consistent, cross out only the verbs with the wrong tenses and write the correct verb tenses above them.
3. Rewrite the entire paragraph in the space provided.

1. My younger brother <u>drove</u> like a <u>maniac</u> before he <u>has</u> his license revoked. For one thing, he never <u>stops</u> at red lights, only slowing down to check for police officers before roaring right through the intersection. Also, he rarely <u>pays</u> attention to other cars on the road; instead, he <u>turned</u> up his stereo and <u>allows</u> his eyes to drift aimlessly over the scenery on either side of the highway. Worst of all, he <u>drives</u> at extraordinary speeds, sometimes up to eighty or ninety miles per hour on narrow, winding roads. Fortunately, he <u>was required</u> to go through a driver's rehabilitation program before being allowed to drive again.

_____

_____

_____

_____

_____

_____

_____

_____

_____

_____

_____

_____

_____

_____

_____

_____

_____

Holt, Rinehart and Winston

Exercise 15 (continued)

2. My older sister <u>makes</u> my life miserable each and every day. In the morning she <u>greeted</u> me with blaring country music from her prized stereo. I <u>had</u> no choice but to listen to the twang of whiny steel guitars and nasal singers crying into their pillows. In the afternoon she either <u>managed</u> to lend my best cashmere sweater to a friend she just met, or she <u>promises</u> a neighbor my baby-sitting services. In the evening she and her friends <u>take</u> over the television set in the family room, flipping through the channels and imitating some senseless cartoon characters on the screen. From morning to night, my sister <u>ruins</u> my days, and I wonder why I <u>was</u> not the big sister.

Consistency of Number

Consistency of number refers to the agreement of nouns and pronouns. A pronoun (a word that can be used to take the place of a noun) must agree in number (singular or plural) with the noun to which it refers.

EXAMPLES:

The *horse* was galloping across the huge sweep of meadow at the edge of the forest. *It* was moving faster than the cars on the nearby crowded highway.

Explanation: "It" is a pronoun used to take the place of the noun "horse."

Jonathan was not the sort of person to talk behind *his* friends' backs, and *he* was widely respected for *his* integrity.

Explanation: "He" and "his" are pronouns used to take the place of "Jonathan."

Many *people* cannot afford to save enough money every year to pay *their* taxes. *They* must borrow the money every year, and *they* fall further behind financially.

Explanation: "Their" and "they" are pronouns used to take the place of "people."

If you use a singular noun, then you should stay with a singular pronoun whenever you refer to that noun. Likewise, if you use a plural noun, then you should stay with a plural pronoun whenever you refer to that noun.

Singular Pronouns	**Plural Pronouns**
I, me, my, myself	we, us, our, ourselves
you, yourself	you, your, yourselves
he, him, his, himself	they, them, their, themselves
she, her, hers, herself	
it, its, itself	

EXAMPLES

Consistent in number

Singular

Sandra was always an excellent student who never wasted any of *her* precious time. If *she* was not doing *her* homework, *she* was reading novels or writing letters to *her* many pen pals.

Plural

Australian shepherds are terrific family dogs. While *they* will often attach *themselves* to one family member in particular, *they* will also show great affection and concern for the whole family.

Holt, Rinehart and Winston

Inconsistent in number:

A *college student* today must often hold down one or two jobs as well as do homework and attend classes. *They* often must make difficult choices between *their* income and *their* course work.

Explanation: To be consistent in number, change "a college student" to "college students."

A *woman politician* of today is serving as an important female role model. *Their* success story will encourage larger numbers of females to seek careers in public service.

Explanation: To be consistent in number, change "their" to "her."

Exercise 16

Consistency of Number

Each sentence below contains at least one error in number. Cross out all errors and write the correct words above them.

EXAMPLES:

New York City is known for ~~their~~ *its* lack of low-cost housing.

Since the typical tennis *player* here is a scholar-athlete, ~~they know~~ *she knows* how to manage ~~their~~ *her* time.

Note: The verb "know" has to change to the singular verb (with the "s") to agree with "she."

1. An *instructor* can get great satisfaction from *their* teaching if *they* communicate well with *their* students.

2. Cathy was enjoying her three *classes,* and she earned A's in *it*.

3. After he painted the *window frames* a bright green, *it* gleamed in the sunlight.

4. The typical high school *student* has many pairs of expensive tennis shoes in *their* closet, and *they* use them all.

5. The *men* living in the next apartment are genuine health food people who cook and prepare *his* own meals with care; *he* wants to be careful of exactly what *he* is eating.

Holt, Rinehart and Winston

Exercise 17

Consistency of Number

In the following paragraph, cross out all errors in number and write the correct words above them. Don't forget to change verb forms, if necessary.

Central California's ground squirrel population is controlled by three distinctive predators. The coyote, a medium-sized, dog-like animal, is the squirrel's most common hunter. *Their* habitat is the entire state, and *they* even can be seen hunting squirrels in vacant lots near the edges of urban areas. A less frequently observed predator, the bobcat, is very fast and shy. Most commonly seen on the fringes of wooded and brushy rural regions, *they* often patiently stalk the ground squirrels' dens. *They* pounce on the squirrels feeding on the grasses and seeds. The rarest squirrel predator is the mountain lion. *It* has been known to attack and eat ground squirrels although *they* generally prefer to hunt deer. Together, each one of these three predators does *their* share in keeping the quickly growing squirrel population under control.

Consistency of Person

Consistency of person refers to the proper use of first, second, and third person pronouns to indicate the speaker.

EXAMPLES *(A PARTIAL LISTING):*

First person is informal, used for personal experience, and represents the writer.

Singular   Plural
I, me, my, mine, myself   we, us, our, ourselves

Second person refers directly to the reader.

Singular   Plural
you, your, yourself   you, your, yourselves

Third person is the most formal and is used to tell about someone else's experience.

Singular   Plural
he, she, it   they, them, their
his, hers, its, her   themselves
himself, herself, itself   persons, students
person, student
everyone

Shifts in Person

Shifting from one person to another within sentences or within the entire piece of writing confuses your reader. If you start a piece of writing in either the first, second, or third person point of view, then you should stay with that point of view consistently throughout your entire paragraph or essay, unless you need to shift the perspective, such as when you quote someone else's exact words.

EXAMPLES:

Consistent in person:

First Person:

My travels across the United States have given *me* the opportunity to meet many people, and *I* know that *I* am a better, more informed citizen because of those journeys.

Second Person:

You will need to spend at least two hours on *your* homework for each hour that *you* spend in class.

Holt, Rinehart and Winston

Third Person:

Eventually most *people* realize that *they* cannot lose weight without reducing *their* calorie intake.

Inconsistent in person:

All basketball *players* should meet after the game, and bring ~~your~~ *their* practice jerseys.

Explanation: Both "players" and "their" are third person.

The *government* generally tries to do too much with too little money to fund *its* space program. Therefore, ~~you are~~ *it is* often cutting corners with safety issues.

Explanation: Both "government" and "it" are third person.

Holt, Rinehart and Winston

Exercise 18

Consistency of Person

Each sentence below contains an error in person. Cross out all errors and write the correct words above them.

EXAMPLE:

Many *people* prepare *their* own tax forms; ~~you~~ *they* want to save money by not hiring an accountant.

1. Most *students* realize that *you* cannot pass the engineering midterm exam without plenty of long hours studying by *yourself*.

2. *Tourists* who visit Los Angeles for the first time are overwhelmed by the freeway system. *You* are always initially amazed by the vast numbers of cars and lanes in which *you* suddenly find *yourself*.

3. *I* am uncertain about what *we* will do for the rest of the day. *You* never know what will happen next in this family!

4. If *you* can't stand the heat, *they* should get out of the kitchen.

5. In a panic situation there are always *people* who like to give lots of advice, but *we* never seem to know when enough is enough.

Holt, Rinehart and Winston

BASIC SENTENCE PATTERNS

In this section you will learn about the basic patterns of English sentences. You will learn to convey the exact meaning you want by using a variety of sentence types. Also, through sentence combining, you will learn to create effective sentences that show clear relationships between ideas.

Subjects

Typically, a **subject** is a word or group of words that names a person, place, thing, or concept.

In sentences that have active verbs, the subject indicates who or what is doing an *action:*

> The *peacock* screamed at the intruders.

In sentences that have a linking verb or a "state-of-being" verb, the subject is the main focus of the sentence:

> *Dr. Martin Luther King Jr.* was a great civil rights leader.

The subject can be a **person:**

> *Tyrone* plays hockey. *He* is also a math major.

The subject can be a **place:**

> *New Orleans* is a fascinating city. *It* is full of coffee houses and exotic restaurants.

The subject can be a **physical thing.**

> The *flower pot* fell off the shelf. *It* shattered into a dozen pieces.

The subject can be a **nonphysical thing** such as **an idea or concept:**

> *Communism* has fallen in eastern Europe. *It* was once a common form of government.

Holt, Rinehart and Winston

Exercise 19

Basic Sentence Patterns: Subjects

Provide a subject for each of the following sentences:

Use a **person** subject: _Domenico_ scored three goals in the first half of the soccer game.

     1. _____ danced the Cotton-eyed Joe at the Crazy Horse Cafe.

     2. _____ flipped his flatbed truck in El Paso.

Use a **place** subject: _Miami_ is famous for its salsa music.

     1. _____ has green, rolling hills mixed with dense forests.

     2. _____ was voted the best place to live in America.

Use a **thing** subject: _The tennis shoes_ cost over a hundred dollars.

     1. _____ tastes great on a hot summer day.

     2. _____ are difficult to find, except in swap meets.

Use an **idea** or a **concept** (a nonphysical thing) subject: _The unknown_ makes our imaginations run wild.

     1. _____ helps people cope with unexpected tragedies.

     2. _____ raises our self-esteem and makes us believe in ourselves.

Verbs

In addition to having a subject, every sentence must have a **verb**—a word that describes an action that is performed by the subject. A verb can also indicate a state of being.

There are two kinds of verbs:

1. Action verbs
2. Linking verbs

Action verbs express physical and mental activities.

The bridge *collapsed* during the recent earthquake.

Tyrone *laughed* throughout the horror movie.

The wind *whistled* through the empty streets.

Linking verbs express a state of being or condition.

The nearly extinct California condor *is* the largest bird in the world.

Albert Einstein *was* an eccentric genius.

The Granny Smith apples *seem* smaller than usual this season.

Some common linking verbs:

is	be	feel	seem
are	being	grow	smell
was	been	look	sound
were	become	remain	taste

Helping Verbs

Sometimes the main verb needs a **helping verb.** The helping verb and the main verb together form a **verb phrase.**

The jockey *will ride* the horse into the winner's circle.

Why *were* the fans *booing* the umpire's last call?

Her courage *has helped* me to face my problem.

Some common helping verbs:

am, are, be, been, is, was, were	may, might
have, has, had	can, could
do, does, did	will, would
shall, should	must

Exercise 20

Basic Sentence Patterns: Verbs

Provide a verb for each of the following sentences.

EXAMPLE:

The African killer bees _swarmed_ across the border last year.

1. The full moon _____ over the snowcapped mountain range.

2. Grizzly bears _____ in the spring after hibernation.

3. Her courage _____ me after all her failures.

4. The volleyball player _____ the ball during the championship game.

5. The preschool children _____ in the afternoon.

Holt, Rinehart and Winston

Parts of Verbs

All verbs have four principal parts (from which the tenses are derived):

1. The present
2. The present participle
3. The past
4. The past participle

The **present tense** is the main form of the verb as it appears in the dictionary.

Her parents still *choose* her friends for her.

We *type* our final draft on a computer in the lab.

The **present participle** uses the *ing* ending plus a form of the *be* verb as a helping verb.

The young man *is buying* a lottery ticket.

The **past tense** is formed by adding *ed*.

The horse *jumped* the fence effortlessly.

The **past participle** is generally formed by adding *ed* and includes a form of the verb *to have,* such as *have, has, or had.*

Obviously the horse *had jumped* that fence many times.

Regular Verbs

Most English verbs are **regular** and form their principal parts with *ing* and *ed*.

Following are the principal parts of some regular verbs:

Present	Present Participle	Past	Past Participle
create	creating	created	created
dance	dancing	danced	danced
laugh	laughing	laughed	laughed

Irregular Verbs

Some 200 English verbs are **irregular.** These verbs often change significantly in the past tense and past participle.

Following are the principal parts of some irregular verbs:

Present	Present Participle	Past	Past Participle
do	doing	did	done
go	going	went	gone
see	seeing	saw	seen
eat	eating	ate	eaten

Holt, Rinehart and Winston

Exercise 21

Basic Sentence Patterns: Verbs

Complete the following sentences with an appropriate form of the verb. The present tense is shown in parentheses.

EXAMPLE:

The professor *shook* her head in disagreement during yesterday's lecture. (shake)

1. Agnes has _____ every one of Sandra Cisneros's books. (buy)

2. The last fifty years have _____ a virtual explosion in new drugs to combat disease and alleviate suffering. (see)

3. The Food and Drug Administration (FDA), a screening agency to which drug companies must prove their products are safe and effective, was _____ because of a 1937 tragedy involving the drug sulfanilamide. (create)

4. Desiring to capitalize on the drug's popularity, one company _____ to market a more easily administered liquid form. (seek)

5. However, the company _____ unaware that its chemist had _____ diethylene glycol, a deadly poison, as a solvent. (remain) (use).

Completers

In addition to having a subject and a verb, many sentences also contain a completer—a word or words that help to complete the meaning of the verb.

> The automotive mechanic rebuilt *the carburetor.*
>
> Alaska is *the last wilderness.*

Thus, the basic pattern of an English sentence is as follows:

> **Subject/verb:** The autumn leaves / scattered.
>
> or
>
> **Subject / verb / completer:** The musicians / are playing / mariachi music.

Holt, Rinehart and Winston

Exercise 22

Basic Sentence Patterns: Completers

Provide a completer for each of the following sentences.

EXAMPLE:

Deer mice carry *the deadly hantavirus.*

1. The history teacher acted _____

3. The rock band played _____

4. The new college student felt _____

5. The unidentified flying object (UFO) landed _____

Holt, Rinehart and Winston

SENTENCE TYPES: THE SIMPLE SENTENCE

A **simple sentence** contains one main or independent clause. A **clause** is a group of words that has a subject and a verb. An **independent clause** not only has a subject and a verb, but also expresses a complete thought. Thus, as the name suggests, an independent clause can stand by itself as a sentence.

The following are some basic patterns of simple sentences:

S/V Pattern: One subject and one verb

The quaking aspen trees / quivered in the wind.

SS/V Pattern: Two subjects and one verb

Nina and Teresita / graduated from Officer Training School.

S/VV Pattern: One subject and two verbs

Armadillos / can walk under water and float across streams.

SS/VV pattern: Two subjects and two verbs

Daryl and Delcia / left Arizona and moved to Paris.

S/VVV pattern: One subject and three verbs

The river / broke through the levee, flooded the farms, and closed the highway.

VS or VSV pattern: The verb before the subject

There are cockroaches in the cabinets.

Why is the wolf being reintroduced to Arizona?

In these examples the subjects and verbs are separated by slashes except when the verb comes before the subject.

Holt, Rinehart and Winston

Exercise 23

Sentence Types: The Simple Sentence
(S/V Pattern: The Subject before the Verb)

Write five simple sentences that contain one subject and one verb. Draw a slash mark between the subject and the verb.

EXAMPLE:

The taxi driver / delivered the baby in the middle of Fifth Avenue.

1. _____

_____

2. _____

_____

3. _____

_____

4. _____

_____

5. _____

_____

Exercise 24

Sentence Types: The Simple Sentence
(SS/V Pattern: Two Subjects and One Verb)

Write five simple sentences that contain two subjects and one verb. Complete the following steps for each sentence:

1. Draw a slash between the subjects and verb.
2. Circle the word that joins the two subjects.

EXAMPLE:

Mountain goats (and) elk / graze in separate habitats in Yellowstone National Park.

1. _____

_____

2. _____

_____

3. _____

_____

4. _____

_____

5. _____

_____

Holt, Rinehart and Winston

Exercise 25

Sentence Types: The Simple Sentence
(S/VV Pattern: One Subject and Two Verbs)

Complete the following steps for each sentence:

1. Combine each pair of sentences to form one simple sentence with one subject and two verbs.
2. Draw a slash between the subject and the verbs.
3. Circle the word that joins the two verbs.

EXAMPLE:

My grandfather plowed the bottom field. My grandfather planted barley and oats.

My grandfather / plowed the bottom field (and) planted barley and oats.

1. Ricardo works during the day at a gas station. He attends night classes at the local college.

_____

_____

2. The earthquake destroyed the garment factory. It caused the loss of many jobs.

_____

_____

3. The new Disney America will be based on historic periods. It will mix education with entertainment.

_____

_____

Holt, Rinehart and Winston

Exercise 26

Sentence Types: The Simple Sentence
(S/VV Pattern: One Subject and Two Verbs)

Write five simple sentences that contain one subject and two verbs. Complete the following for each sentence:

1. Draw a slash between the subject and the verb.
2. Circle the word that joins the two verbs.

EXAMPLE:

Rosa / writes intensely lyrical poetry (and) paints Renaissance-style portraits.

1. _____

_____

2. _____

_____

3. _____

_____

4. _____

_____

5. _____

_____

Holt, Rinehart and Winston

Exercise 27

Sentence Types: The Simple Sentence
(SS/VV Pattern: Two Subjects and Two Verbs)

Combine each group of sentences below to form one simple sentence containing two subjects and two verbs. Complete the following steps for each sentence:

1. Draw a slash between the subjects and verbs.
2. Circle the words that join the two subjects and the two verbs.

EXAMPLE:

United Way raised money.   United Way built shelters for the homeless.

Church charities raised money.   Church charities built shelters for the homeless.

United Way (and) church charities / raised money (and) built shelters for the homeless.

1. Doctors investigated the cause of   Doctors discovered much valuable information.
   Alzheimer's disease.
   Medical researchers investigated the cause of   Medical researchers discovered much valuable
   Alzheimer's disease.   information.

   _____

   _____

2. The valley oak does not reproduce itself well.   The valley oak is becoming an endangered species.
   The blue oak does not reproduce itself well.   The blue oak is becoming an endangered species.

   _____

   _____

3. Marta attends Millbrooke Community   Marta takes a women's literature class.
   College.   Her son takes a women's literature class.
   Her son attends Millbrooke Community
   College.

   _____

   _____

Exercise 28

Sentence Types: The Simple Sentence
(SS/VV Pattern: Two Subjects and Two Verbs)

Write five simple sentences that contain two subjects and two verbs. Complete the following steps for each sentence:

  1. Draw a slash between the subjects and the verbs.
  2. Circle the words that join the subjects and verbs.

  EXAMPLE:

  The philosophy instructor (and) her students / studied the history of Greek thought (and) toured the Getty Museum.

1. _____

_____

2. _____

_____

3. _____

_____

4. _____

_____

5. _____

_____

Holt, Rinehart and Winston

Exercise 29

Sentence Types: The Simple Sentence
(S/VVV Pattern: One Subject and Three Verbs)

Combine each group of sentences below to form one simple sentence that contains one subject and three verbs. Complete the following steps for each:

    1. Draw a slash between the subject and the verbs.
    2. Circle the word that joins the three verbs.

EXAMPLE:

The coach stormed into the locker room.

The coach threw down his clipboard.

The coach glared at the players.

The coach / stormed into the locker room, threw down his clipboard, (and) glared at his

players.

1. The transient walked down the street.
   The transient sat under the beech tree.
   The transient fell asleep.

   _____

   _____

   _____

2. The sand is washed ashore by the powerful waves.
   The sand blows in from the broad beach.
   The sand forms wind-sculptured dunes and hills.

   _____

   _____

   _____

3. The protesters marched to the state capitol building.
   The protesters sat on the steps to block the entrance.
   The protesters refused to leave without speaking to the governor.

   _____

   _____

   _____

Exercise 30

Sentence Types: The Simple Sentence
(S/VVV Pattern: One Subject and Three Verbs)

Write five simple sentences that contain one subject and three verbs. Complete the following steps for each sentence:

1. Draw a slash between the subject and verbs.
2. Circle the word that joins the three verbs.
3. Insert commas to set off verbs in a series.

EXAMPLE:

The tired househusband / planned the menu, invited the guests, (and) cooked the dinner.

1. _____

_____

2. _____

_____

3. _____

_____

4. _____

_____

5. _____

_____

Holt, Rinehart and Winston

Exercise 31

Sentence Types: The Simple Sentence
(VS or VSV Pattern: Verb before the Subject)

Write five simple sentences that follow the VS or VSV pattern. Complete the following steps for each sentence:

    1. Write V over the verb.
    2. Write S over the subject.

    EXAMPLES:

           V   S
    There are many homeless people in the United States.

           V   S   V
    Why are the students keeping a journal in class?

1. _____

   _____

2. _____

   _____

3. _____

   _____

4. _____

   _____

5. _____

   _____

Exercise 32

Review of Simple Sentence Patterns

Write a simple sentence that follows the pattern indicated for each number.

1. For the subject before the verb patterns, draw a slash between the subject(s) and verb(s).

2. For the verb before the subject patterns, mark V above the verb and S above the subject.

EXAMPLES:

S/V   *Ghost stories / frighten me.* _____

VS   *Where is the all-night party for the senior citizens?* _____

S/V   1. _____

SS/V   2. _____

S/VV   3. _____

S/VVV   4. _____

VS   5. _____

VSV   6. _____

Holt, Rinehart and Winston

SENTENCE TYPES: THE COMPOUND SENTENCE

A **compound sentence** has two or more simple sentences (main clauses) joined to form one sentence that contains two or more related ideas.

Why do we use compound sentences?

1. To combine closely related ideas into one sentence.
2. To avoid a series of short, choppy sentences.
3. To create more interesting sentences.

One way to join simple sentences (main clauses) is to use a **comma** and a **coordinating conjunction.**

Two simple sentences:

> *The moviegoers / complained loudly about the long lines.*
> *They / threatened to leave.*

One compound sentence:

> *The moviegoers / complained loudly about the long lines, and they / threatened to leave.*

However, when the sentence is short, the comma is not always needed. A short compound sentence:

> *Kenny / was right and he / knew it.*

In a compound sentence the simple sentences (main clauses) are basically equal in importance.

Notice that when two simple sentences (main clauses) are joined to form a compound sentence, some changes occur:

1. The compound sentence has the pattern S/V, conjunction S/V.
2. The first word of the second clause is not capitalized.
3. A comma and a joining word (coordinating conjunction) replace the period at the end of the first sentence.

Coordinating Conjunctions

Coordinating conjunctions are words that join two main clauses to create an effective sentence.

The seven coordinating conjunctions are as follows:

and	but
for	nor
or	so
yet	

Holt, Rinehart and Winston

Exercise 33

Sentence Types: The Compound Sentence
(S/V, Conjunction S/V Pattern)

Combine each pair of sentences below to form one compound sentence. Complete the following steps for each sentence:

1. Add a comma before the coordinating conjunction.
2. Circle the conjunction.
3. Draw a slash between each subject and verb.

EXAMPLE:

Soon Jae had her math book open.

Soon Jae was not thinking about math.

Soon Jae / had her math book open, (but) she / was not thinking about math.

1.1. C. J. wanted to go to the movies with his friends.
1.2. His mother had other plans for him.

_____

_____

2.1. Boris transferred to a four-year university.
2.2. He majored in microbiology.

_____

_____

3.1 She dressed and talked like Marilyn Monroe.
3.2 Her hair was dyed platinum blonde.

_____

_____

Holt, Rinehart and Winston

Exercise 34

Sentence Types: The Compound Sentence
(S/V, Conjunction S/V Pattern)

Write five compound sentences of your own. Be sure the ideas are closely related and of equal importance. Complete the following steps for each sentence:

1. Add a comma before the coordinating conjunction.
2. Circle the conjunction.
3. Draw a slash between each subject and verb.

EXAMPLE:

The fire / raged through the mountains, (and) timber / was destroyed. _____

1. _____

_____

2. _____

_____

3. _____

_____

4. _____

_____

5. _____

_____

S/V; S/V Pattern

Using a comma and a coordinating conjunction is one way to join two simple sentences. Another way to join two simple sentences is with a **semicolon.**

Two simple sentences:

> *Margaret received a postcard from Dolores.*
>
> *It came from South America.*

One compound sentence:

> *Margaret received a postcard from Dolores; it came from South America.*

When simple sentences are joined with a semicolon, notice the following:

1. The compound sentence has the pattern S/V; S/V.
2. The semicolon replaces the period at the end of the first sentence.
3. The first word in the second clause is not capitalized (unless it is a proper name or the word "I").
4 A coordinating conjunction is not used.

Holt, Rinehart and Winston

Exercise 35

Sentence Types: The Compound Sentence (S/V; S/V Pattern)

Complete these steps for each of the sentences that follow:

1. Add a simple sentence to create a compound sentence. Be sure the ideas are closely related.
2. Add a semicolon. Make sure the word after the semicolon is not capitalized, unless necessary.

EXAMPLE:

Elephants possess the largest brain of any land animal; *they can learn up to a hundred commands.*

1. The hurricane knocked the power lines down _____

_____

2. Strong fragrances gave Mina headaches_____

_____

3. Sarah bought a brand-new computer_____

_____

4. Elephants possess the largest brain of any land animal_____

_____

_____

5. Good manners are a thing of the past _____

_____

Exercise 36

Effective Compound Sentences

Create effective compound sentences by adding a related main clause to the simple sentences below. Complete the following steps for each sentence:

1. Circle the coordinating conjunction that joins the main clauses.
2. Draw a slash between each subject and verb.

EXAMPLE:

A three-day weekend / is coming up, (but) *we / have a research project due.* _____

1. The students rented some video equipment, and _____

2. The rain had just started to fall, so _____

3. Prenatal care is important for an expectant mother, but _____

4. Incidents of rudeness are on the rise, and _____

5. The state senator did not keep his promises, nor _____

Holt, Rinehart and Winston

Exercise 37

Review of Compound Sentences

On the lines provided, combine each pair of sentences by adding the appropriate coordinating conjunction for relating the ideas. For each sentence complete the following steps:

    1. Punctuate the sentence correctly.

    2. Draw a slash between each subject and verb.

1.1 I was afraid of lightning storms.

1.2 That night I found the storm very beautiful.

_____

_____

2.1 The chemistry experiment failed.

2.2 The students were confused.

_____

_____

3.1 Alejandro wrote down the unfamiliar word.

3.2 Later, he looked it up in the dictionary.

_____

_____

4.1 My dad cautioned me not to buy that car.

4.2 I was too excited to take his advice.

_____

_____

5.1 The library book was overdue.

5.2 Lil had to pay a fine.

_____

_____

SENTENCE TYPES: THE COMPLEX SENTENCE

So far you have learned that a simple sentence contains a subject and verb that work together as a complete unit of thought. You have also learned that a compound sentence consists of two (or more) simple sentences (main clauses). The third sentence type is the **complex sentence.**

A complex sentence consists of a main clause (one that can stand alone as a complete unit of thought) plus a dependent, or subordinate, clause (one that is introduced by a **subordinator** and cannot stand alone as a sentence).

Subordinators

Here is a list of the most common subordinators:

after	because	if	unless	whenever	which
although	before	since	until	where	while
as	how	that	when	whereas	who

Complex sentences are useful not only in adding variety to your writing, but also in showing emphasis. By using subordinators effectively, you can deemphasize ideas by placing them in a secondary position (within a dependent clause). This allows your main ideas to stand out. Also, by using subordinators such as *because* or *since,* you can create complex sentences that show cause-effect relationships.

Dependent Clauses

Dependent clauses cannot stand alone as sentences. They are dependent on main clauses to complete their meaning.

The dependent clause may appear at the beginning of a complex sentence. In the following example, the dependent clause is bracketed and the subordinator is starred (*).

> EXAMPLE:
>
> [*Because the fire / was so intense], the setting sun / appeared red-orange.

Holt, Rinehart and Winston

Exercise 38

Sentence Types: The Complex Sentence (Dependent Clauses)

Using the subordinators listed below, write five dependent clauses. Draw a slash between the subject and the verb.

after   because   if   unless   when

EXAMPLE:

[*When *he / took off his hat* _____]

1. [*After _____]

2. [*Because _____]

3. [*If _____]

4. [*Unless _____]

5. [*When _____]

Exercise 39

Sentence Types: The Complex Sentence

Select two of the preceding dependent clauses and write them separately on each of the following lines. Then create two separate complex sentences by adding a main clause to each dependent clause. Complete the following steps for each of the sentences:

1. Mark each subordinator with a star.
2. Draw a slash between the subject and verb.
3. Place brackets around the dependent clause.
4. Add a comma after dependent clauses that appear at the beginning of a complex sentence.

EXAMPLE:

[*When he / took off his hat], his hair / looked like a flattened haystack.

1. _____

2. _____

Exercise 40

Sentence Types: The Complex Sentence

In the complex sentences you have written so far, the dependent clauses have been at the beginning of the sentences. However, a dependent clause may also appear at the end of a complex sentence.

EXAMPLE:

He / wore a white tuxedo [*because he / wanted to impress his girlfriend].

For this exercise, write five complex sentences with the dependent clause at the end of the sentence. Complete the following steps for each sentence:

1. Mark each subordinator with a star.
2. Draw a slash mark between each subject and verb.
3. Place brackets around each dependent clause.

1. _____

_____

2. _____

_____

3. _____

_____

4. _____

_____

5. _____

_____

Holt, Rinehart and Winston

Relative Pronouns: Who, Which, and That

Relative pronouns refer to a previous noun or pronoun, clarifying the relationship of a dependent clause to a noun in the sentence.

In using relative pronouns, remember the following:

Who refers to people or animals with names.

Which and *that* usually refer to objects, events, or animals.

Exercise 41

Sentence Types: The Complex Sentence

For this exercise, write five complex sentences with the dependent clause in the middle of a sentence. Complete the following steps for each sentence:

1. Mark each subordinator with a star.
2. Draw a slash mark between each subject and verb.
3. Place brackets around each dependent clause.

EXAMPLE:

The thoroughbred, [*which / was raised on a farm in Ireland,] / won the Kentucky Derby.

1. _____

_____

2. _____

_____

3. _____

_____

4. _____

_____

5. _____

_____

Exercise 42

Sentence Types: The Complex Sentence (Sentence Combining to Create Complex Sentences)

Using the list of common subordinators, join the following pairs of simple sentences, turning them into complex sentences. Complete the following steps for each sentence:

1. Add an appropriate subordinator, marking each one with a star.
2. Draw a slash mark between each subject and verb.
3. Place brackets around the dependent clause.
4. Use a comma (or commas), if necessary.

EXAMPLE:

Our friends hate to visit us.
We own a seven-foot-long boa constrictor.

[*Because we / own a seven-foot-long boa constrictor], our friends / hate to visit us.

1.1 South American killer bees began their trek north several years ago.
1.2 People in the United States started to panic.

_____

_____

2.1 You suffer from wintertime depression.
2.2 You should increase your intake of peas, beans, and grains.

_____

_____

3.1 Small children have wild imaginations and deep-seated fears.
3.2 They should be reassured, not humiliated.

_____

_____

4.1 Natural herb dietary supplements are often declared "safe" by health experts.
4.2 They still have their dangers.

_____

_____

Holt, Rinehart and Winston

Exercise 42 (continued)

5.1 Hay fever season is in full swing in the summer.

5.2 Sufferers everywhere have to cope with watery eyes and runny noises.

_____

_____

Exercise 43

Sentence Types: The Complex Sentence (Sentence Combining with Relative Pronouns)

Using the relative pronouns *who, which,* or *that* (as indicated), join the following pairs of simple sentences, turning them into complex sentences. Complete the following steps for each sentence:

1. Mark each relative pronoun with a star.
2. Draw a slash mark between each subject and verb.
3. Place brackets around the dependent clause.
4. Use a comma (or commas), if necessary.

EXAMPLES:

Jed has high hopes about his future.

Jed is a single parent and a full-time student.   (who)

Jed, [* who / is a single parent and full-time student], / has high hopes about his future.

Several years ago, Jed quit participating in the neighborhood day-care center.

The neighborhood day-care center no longer met his needs.   (which)

Several years ago, Jed / quit participating in the neighborhood day-care center [*which no longer / met his needs].

1.1 Jed lives at home with his young son and elderly parents.
1.2 His parents worry about them all the time.   (who)

_____

_____

2.1 His parents would like Jed to get an education.
2.2 Education is very important to them.   (which)

_____

_____

3.1 Jed would prefer to design sailboards for a living.
3.2 Jed is a very talented athlete and gifted artist.   (who)

_____

_____

Holt, Rinehart and Winston

Exercise 43 (continued)

4.1 Jed also would prefer to spend his mornings windsurfing.

4.2 Windsurfing is a sport that is increasing in popularity. (which)

_____

_____

5.1 As a compromise, Jed attends classes in the evenings.

5.1 The classes in the evenings fulfill his requirements and keep his parents happy. (that)

_____

_____

Holt, Rinehart and Winston

SENTENCE TYPES: THE COMPOUND-COMPLEX SENTENCE

A compound-complex sentence is a compound sentence that contains one or more dependent clauses. It has two or more simple sentences (main clauses) and one or more dependent clauses.

EXAMPLES:

He wore a white tuxedo, and he rented a white limo [*because he wanted to impress his girlfriend].

Rosa Parks, [*who was tired and not feeling well one particular evening in 1955], refused to yield her seat to a white man on a Montgomery city bus, so she was arrested.

Holt, Rinehart and Winston

Exercise 44

Sentence Types: The Compound-Complex Sentence

Using the list of coordinating conjunctions and common subordinators (in parentheses), combine the following clusters of simple sentences, turning them into compound-complex sentences. Complete the following steps for each sentence:

    1. Add a coordinating conjunction.

    2. Add a subordinator.

    3. Place brackets around the dependent clause.

    4. Use a comma (or commas), if necessary.

EXAMPLE:

Rosa Parks refused to yield her seat to a white man.

Rosa Parks had been obeying the bus driver for 20 years. (who)

Her refusal led to the 381-day bus boycott in Montgomery. (and)

Rosa Parks, [who had been obeying the bus driver for 20 years], refused to yield her seat to a white man, and her refusal led to the 381-day bus boycott in Montgomery.

1.1 Amy Tan's *Joy Luck Club* was her first novel.

1.2 Her first novel told the story of four mothers and their daughters. (which)

1.3 It not only received critical acclaim, but was also made into a successful movie. (and)

_____

_____

_____

2.1 On Thursday, November 11, 1993, the Vietnam Women's Memorial was dedicated.

2.2 Thousands waited until the end of the ceremony to place wreaths at the monument. (and)

2.3 Only a relative few could see the ceremony in a grove near the memorial wall. (although)

_____

_____

_____

Exercise 44 (continued)

3.1 Annually more than 300,000 Americans undergo angioplasty.

3.2 Angioplasty is the opening of a clogged artery by blowing up a balloon and then deflating it. (which)

3.3 About 40 percent of the time, the arteries squeeze shut again within a few weeks. (but)

_____

_____

_____

Holt, Rinehart and Winston

Exercise 45

Review of Simple, Compound, Complex, and Compound-Complex Sentences

Identify the following sentences as **S** (simple), **Cpd** (compound), or **Cx** (complex). Draw a slash between each subject and verb.

EXAMPLE:

_Cx_   _After he/slammed the door, he/walked out of her life._

_____ 1. Due to the rise in teenage violence, the senate is holding hearings to investigate its causes.

_____ 2. Although the last fifty years have seen an explosion in new drugs to combat disease, children's diseases have been excluded from these advances, and little medical research has been done in this area.

_____ 3. According to students of fashion, the Anne Klein customer is a certain type of person who prefers the security of a tailored suit.

_____ 4. Anxiety makes people feel helpless, but taking action helps them feel more powerful.

_____ 5. The single-parent family, which is on the rise in our country, challenges our notion of the traditional family unit.

6. Write a simple sentence.

_____

_____

7. Write a compound sentence.

_____

_____

8. Write a complex sentence.

_____

_____

Holt, Rinehart and Winston

Exercise 45 (continued)

9. Write a compound-complex sentence.

_____

_____

10. Write a complex sentence with the subordinate clause at the beginning of the sentence.

_____

_____

11. Write a complex sentence with the subordinate clause in the middle of the sentence. Use *who, which,* or *that* as your subordinator.

_____

_____

12. Write a complex sentence with the subordinate clause at the end of the sentence.

_____

_____

Holt, Rinehart and Winston

A WORD ABOUT FRAGMENTS

Fragments are incomplete sentences. They are missing one or more of the essential parts of a sentence: a subject, a verb, or a completer. Fragments often occur in our writing when we punctuate a part of a sentence as if it were a complete sentence.

Because I was tired.

The woman with the red coat.

To get help with algebra.

If you create occasional fragments, you may be uncertain of where your sentences need to begin or end. For example, you may be using periods where you only need commas, or no punctuation at all.

One probable reason that you might write fragments is because you often speak in fragments. For example, if someone were to ask you, "Why did you go to bed so early?" you might naturally reply using a part of a sentence: "Because I was tired." If someone were to ask you, "Who is the tallest?" you might reply, "The woman in the red coat." If someone were to ask you, "Why are you going to the tutorial center today?" you might reply, "To get help with algebra."

While the use of such fragments is generally acceptable in our everyday speech, they should be avoided in academic writing. Writing fragments can indicate a lack of familiarity with standard English and an inability to understand the basic patterns of English sentences: simple, compound, complex, and compound-complex.

Exercise 46

Fragments

Correct the underlined sentence fragments in the following passages by combining phrases and revising the punctuation.

EXAMPLE:

She was a very bright student. <u>Who got straight A's in all of her classes. Because she was so academically talented.</u> She even received numerous scholarships. <u>To help her pay for her college tuition and other expenses.</u>

She was a very bright student who got straight A's in all of her classes because she was so academically talented. She even received numerous scholarships to help her pay for her college tuition and other expenses.

1. My earliest memories of my childhood are of vivid family moments. <u>My father playing his guitar for all of us. My sister opening her birthday presents and my mother telling me stories about my grandfather in Mexico.</u> I will treasure these very early memories. <u>As long as I am alive.</u>

2. The fishing was very poor on that day. <u>Because of the intense heat and the bright sun.</u> We did not catch anything. <u>Except for some long, stringy weeds and sunken willow branches.</u> The entire lake seemed to be heat-dead. <u>Without a cloud in the sky or even a random breeze to cool us off.</u>

Holt, Rinehart and Winston

Exercise 46 (continued)

3. We drove over 600 miles that day. <u>To get to San Francisco by evening.</u> At night the city gleamed with what must have been a million lights. <u>As we crossed the Bay Bridge and entered the busy streets that lead to Union Square.</u> We knew the long day's drive had been worth it.

_____

_____

_____

_____

_____

COMMAS

The comma is the most widely used punctuation mark. In some ways it is also the most controversial. However, the following four guidelines will help you solve most of your comma problems and enable you to see how commas can be used to facilitate reading.

Guidelines for Using Commas

Use commas before coordinating conjunctions (*and, but, or, nor, for, yet, so*) when joining two main clauses.

> EXAMPLES:
>
> *The travelers flew to Canada, but their luggage was shipped to New Mexico.*
>
> *My library books were overdue, so I had to pay a huge fine.*

Use commas after introductory word groups such as phrases, subordinate clauses, and most transitional words.

> EXAMPLES:
>
> *Walking into the gymnasium, the students noticed it was set up for a blood bank.*
>
> *As we toured the ancient village, we saw the ruins of an old church.*
>
> *First of all, you need a clear understanding of your own values in order to act on your principles.*

Use commas to set off items in a series.

> EXAMPLES:
>
> *Katrina met with a counselor, the Dean of Students, and the Financial Aid Director.*
>
> *The old truck blew a rod, dropped its transmission, and came to a dead stop.*
>
> *Biology, human anatomy, and physiology are all requirements in my major.*

Use commas to set off nonessential phrases and clauses that appear in the middle of a sentence or at the end of it. (Clauses and phrases are considered nonessential if they can be removed from the sentence without changing its basic meaning.)

> EXAMPLES:
>
> *Chan, who is only fifteen years old, has become a brilliant pianist.*
>
> *The waves pounded into the wharf, which was slowly being knocked to pieces.*
>
> *The fire ants, which invaded the town without warning, destroyed the vegetation.*

Holt, Rinehart and Winston

Exercise 47

Commas

For each of the sentences below, write the rule for the comma use in the space provided.

1. The Chumash Indians fascinate modern ethnobotanists because of their use of the native plants in their religious rituals, medicine, hunting, and daily life.

_____

_____

_____

2. Some anthropologists believe that the Chumash shamans would ingest specific roots and plants to induce religious visions, and they further speculate that those visions form the basis for the fascinating and colorful cave art that still can be found in many locations.

_____

_____

_____

3. Because the Chumash knew the medicinal properties of the native flora so well, they had numerous uses for them.

_____

_____

_____

4. For example, the bark of the willow tree contains the same medicinal qualities as that of our modern-day aspirin.

_____

_____

_____

5. Also, the cure for lesions or severe cuts was to apply a paste made up of crushed poison oak.

_____

_____

_____

Holt, Rinehart and Winston

Exercise 47 (continued)

6. The Chumash were able to utilize several commonly found plants for hunting, and the best known of these uses was to grind up the roots of the soap plant and to put the paste in a pond to stun the fish so that they would be easier to catch.

_____

_____

_____

7. Because the spring flowers of the ceanothus bush made a good lather, they were used daily for washing and scrubbing.

_____

_____

_____

8. The Chumash, who are recognized widely for their basketry and canoe-building skills, should also be known for their profound and interesting use of the native flora.

_____

_____

_____

Holt, Rinehart and Winston

Exercise 48

Writing Sentences That Require Commas

1. Write one original sentence that requires a comma before the coordinating conjunction to join two main clauses.

_____

_____

_____

2. Write one original sentence that requires a comma after an introductory word group.

_____

_____

_____

3. Write one original sentence that requires commas to set off items in a series.

_____

_____

_____

4. Write one original sentence that requires commas to set off a nonessential phrase or clause *in the middle of the sentence.*

_____

_____

_____

5. Write one original sentence that requires a comma to set off a nonessential phrase or clause *at the end of the sentence.*

_____

_____

_____

Holt, Rinehart and Winston

OTHER PUNCTUATION MARKS: THE APOSTROPHE, COLON, AND SEMICOLON

The **apostrophe, colon,** and **semicolon** are other punctuation marks that are commonly misused. The simple guidelines that follow will help you use them more effectively.

Guidelines for Using Apostrophes

The apostrophe is used to indicate ownership.

> EXAMPLES:
>
> Singular noun: *The speaker's voice was drowned out by the noise of the traffic.*
>
> Plural noun: *The speakers' voices were drowned out by the noise of the traffic.*
>
> Exceptions: No apostrophe is needed for personal pronouns (*its, his, hers, ours, theirs, whose*) because the idea of ownership is built into those words.
>
> EXAMPLES:
>
> *Its approach to the runway was obscured by heavy ground fog.*
>
> *His grade point average astounded his parents.*

Use the apostrophe to indicate a contraction (the omission of a letter or letters).

> EXAMPLES:
>
> *It's unlikely that the volcano expedition will be leaving tomorrow.*
>
> *She wasn't expecting to see a bear prowling around the campsite.*
>
> *We'll know by morning whether he won or lost the election.*

Guidelines for Using Colons

Use the colon after a complete sentence to indicate that a list will follow.

> EXAMPLE:
>
> *Jimmy needed to buy a few supplies for his camping trip: a portable cappuccino maker, a solar-heated mattress, a battery-powered raft, and a high-tech stove.*

Use the colon after a complete sentence to introduce an explanation.

> EXAMPLE:
>
> *Halloween is often a scary experience for a small child: witches and goblins seem to lurk around every shadowy corner.*

Holt, Rinehart and Winston

Guidelines for Using Semicolons

Use the semicolon to join two main clauses that have closely related ideas.

EXAMPLE:

Arlington National Cemetery draws thousands of visitors each year; it is a final resting place for many of America's soldiers.

Use the semicolon to join two main clauses that are connected by transitional words such as *however, consequently, therefore,* and so on.

EXAMPLE:

The puffer fish is a Japanese delicacy; however, it can bring on an agonizing death if not prepared properly.

Exercise 49

Writing Sentences That Require Apostrophes, Colons, and Semicolons

1. Write a sentence that requires an apostrophe to indicate ownership using a singular noun.

_____

_____

2. Write a sentence that requires an apostrophe to indicate ownership using a plural noun.

_____

_____

3. Write a sentence that contains a contraction.

_____

_____

4. Write a sentence that contains a colon to indicate that a list will follow.

_____

_____

5. Write a sentence that contains a colon to introduce an explanation.

_____

_____

6. Write a sentence that contains a semicolon to join two main clauses that have closely related ideas.

_____

_____

7. Write a sentence that contains a semicolon to join two main clauses that are connected by a transitional word.

_____

_____

Holt, Rinehart and Winston

Appendix

Guidelines for Final Drafts
A List of Irregular Verbs
Writing a Summary

GUIDELINES FOR FINAL DRAFTS

Rules for Handwritten Papers

1. Use standard (white) loose-leaf notebook paper, size 8½ × 11 inches, with widely spaced lines (skip lines if the paper is college-ruled or has narrow lines).
2. Use blue or black ink (not other colors of ink).
3. Use cursive handwriting, and write on only one side of the paper.
4. In the upper left-hand corner, write your first and last names, your class, your assignment, and the date. (See your teacher for customized instructions.)
5. Number all pages (preceded by your last name) in the upper right-hand corner. Don't put periods after the page numbers or circles around the numbers.
6. Center your title on the first ruled line, capitalizing the first letter of each work except for articles and prepositions within the title.
7. Skip one line after the title.
8. Indent the first line of each paragraph about 1 inch.
9. Leave a 1-inch margin at the right side and bottom of your paper. Allow the ruled lines on your notebook to indicate the proper margins at the left and top.

Rules for Typed or Word-Processed Papers

1. Use standard (white) typing paper (20–24 lb. bond, not onionskin), size 8½ × 11 inches.
2. Your full identification should be in the upper left-hand corner, including your first and last names, your instructor and class, your assignment, and the date. (See your teacher for customized instructions.)
3. Use double-spacing throughout your paper, including after your identification and your title.
4. Center your title and capitalize the first letter of each word except for articles and prepositions within the title.
5. Number all pages (preceded by your last name) in the upper right-hand corner. Avoid the use of periods or parentheses.
6. Indent the first line of each paragraph about five spaces.
7. Leave an inch margin on all sides of your paper.

A LIST OF IRREGULAR VERBS

When you are not sure which verb part to use, consult the list below or a good dictionary. Choose the past tense form if your sentence doesn't have a helping verb; choose the past participle form if it does.

Last month we ~~seen~~ *saw* snow on the local mountain tops.

Explanation: Because there is no helping verb, the past tense form *saw* is required.

The professor had apparently ~~gave~~ *given* all the students passing grades.

Explanation: Because of the helping verb *had,* the past participle form *given* is required.

Common Irregular Verbs

Infinitive	Past	Past Participle
arise (get up)	arose	arisen
awake	awoke, awaked	awoke, awaked
be	was	been
beat	beat	beaten, beat
bear (carry)	bore	borne
begin	began	begun
bend	bent	bent
bite	bit	bitten, bit
blow	blew	blown
break	broke	broken
bring	brought	brought
build	built	built
burst	burst	burst
buy	bought	bought
catch	caught	caught
choose	chose	chosen
cling	clung	clung
come	came	come
cost	cost	cost
dig	dug	dug
do	did	done
drink	drank	drunk
drive	drove	driven
eat	ate	eaten
fall	fell	fallen
fight	fought	fought
find	found	found
fly	flew	flown
forget	forgot	forgotten
freeze	froze	frozen
get	got	gotten, got
give	gave	given

Infinitive	Past	Past Participle
go	went	gone
grow	grew	grown
hang (suspend)	hung	hanged
hang (execute)	hanged	hung
have	had	had
hide	hid	hidden
hurt	hurt	hurt
keep	kept	kept
know	knew	known
lay (put)	laid	laid
lead	led	led
lend	lent	lent
lie (recline)	lay	lain
lose	lost	lost
read	read	read
ride	rode	ridden
ring	rang	rung
rise	rose	risen
run	ran	run
say	said	said
see	saw	seen
send	sent	sent
set (place)	set	set
shake	shook	shaken
shoot	shot	shot
shrink	shrank	shrunk
sing	sang	sung
sink	sank	sunk
sit (be seated)	sat	sat
slay	slew	slain
speak	spoke	spoken
spin	spun	spun
spring	sprang	sprung
steal	stole	stolen
sting	stung	stung
strike	struck	struck, stricken
swear	swore	sworn
swim	swam	swum
swing	swung	swung
take	took	taken
teach	taught	taught
throw	threw	thrown
wake	woke, waked	woken, waked
wear	wore	worn
wring	wrung	wrung
write	wrote	written

WRITING A SUMMARY

Writing college research papers often requires you to use information from other sources, such as books and magazines. If you want to incorporate the ideas of experts and professional writers into your own writing, you will need to learn how to summarize. Summarizing allows you to use long and sometimes complex passages in a condensed form. It allows you to restate another piece of writing using *your own* words, rather than those of the author.

A summary restates the main ideas of the work you are summarizing, and it is always considerably shorter. For example, an article of several pages might be summarized in less than a page or perhaps only a paragraph, depending on how much information that article contains. A summary should be organized the same way as the material being summarized. For instance, if the original material uses importance order, your summary should use importance order as well.

When you summarize, do not evaluate the author's ideas or offer your own opinion. Instead, try to determine what the author has said and communicate that exact information concisely. Be careful not to omit anything important, yet don't focus on unnecessary details.

When you summarize, keep the following points in mind:

1. Read the material several times.
2. Underline the main ideas and number them.
3. Write your summary, keeping it considerably shorter than the original material.
4. Write your summary in your own words, avoiding the words used by the author.
5. Organize your summary in the same way as the original material.
6. Give credit to the source through standard methods of documentation.

INDEX

A

Angelou, Maya, *Uncle Willie,* 39–41
apostrophes, 293, 295
argument essay, 92–95, 99–100
audience, 14

B

bibliography, 170–171
block method, outline, 77–78
body paragraph, 57, 60
Bradbury, Ray, *I See You Never,* 192–194

C

cause and effect essay, 56–57, 60, 66–67
central idea, 10, 11
Chopin, Kate, *The Storm,* 103–109
chronological order, 17
clause, 255, 273, 283
Clifton, Lucille, *Homage to My Hips,* 197
clustering, 9, 10
coherence, 17
colons, 293, 295
    commas, 289–292
    use of, 289
comparison/contrast essay, 73–76, 79–81, 82–83
completers, 253–254
concluding paragraph, 57, 60, 64, 80–81, 97, 113, 125, 142
concluding sentences, 217–219
conclusion, 20–21
conjunction, coordinating, 266
consistency, 233
    of number, 239–242
    of person, 243–245
    of tense, 233–238

D

dependent clause, 273–274
description, 13
    person, 44–45, 48–49
    place, 27, 32–33, 34, 36
details
    spatial order arrangement of, 27
    specific, 20, 35, 63–64, 80, 97, 113, 125, 138, 154, 167, 179, 182, 231–232
directing words, 16, 215–216
draft, rough, 19–21, 27–28, 35, 46–47, 63, 80, 97, 125, 142, 182

E

essay, 110–113, 115–116, 122–125, 139–145
    argument, 92–95, 99–100
    cause and effect, 56–57, 60, 66–67
    comparison/contrast, 73–76, 79–81, 82–83
    information, 155–160, 168–175, 181–185
examples, 228
experience, personal, 2

F

Fairbank, John King, *Footbinding,* 161–167
final paper, 23, 31, 37–38, 49–50, 68, 84, 100–101, 116–117, 128, 145, 185
    rules for handwritten, 297
    rules for typed, 297
fragments, 286–288
freewriting, 12

G

Gregory, Dick, *Shame,* 199–202

H

historical pieces, 17

I

ideas, discovering, 4
images, use of, 24
independent clause, 255
information

additional, 227, 229
    essay, 155–160, 168–175, 181–185
    research, 158, 174
interview, 176
introductory paragraph, 57, 60
invention strategies, 15

J

Jackson, Shirley, *The Lottery,* 129–138
journal
double-entry question, 5, 25, 42, 54, 71, 90, 108,
    120, 137, 153, 166, 178
    keeping, 1
    writing, 4
journalistic questions, 12–13

K

Kingston, Maxine Hong, *Reparation Candy,* 87–91

L

Levine, Philip, *To a Child Trapped in a Barber Shop,*
    118–121
lifestyle, 69
listing, 11

M

Machan, Katharyn Howd, *Hazel Tells LaVerne,* 198
MLA, 155
Moravia, Alberto, *The Secret,* 147–154
Morgan, Neil, *Home is a Freeway,* 208–210

N

narrative, 8, 13, 17

O

observation, 1, 6
Olds, Sharon, *Rites of Passage,* 177–180
order, sentence, 17
outline, comparison/contrast, 77

P

paragraphs, 56–57
Pastan, Linda, *Marks,* 198

peer editing, 21–23, 29–30, 35–37, 47–49, 64–67,
    81–83, 98–100, 113–116, 125–127, 142–144,
    182–184
point-by-point method, outline, 77–78
prewriting, 1, 9, 15, 33, 45, 61, 75, 94, 112, 124,
    141, 181
process paragraphs, 17
purpose, writing, 14

Q

Quinn, Carin, *The Jeaning of America,* 211–212
quotations, 168–169

R

readers. *See* audience
reading, 6, 26, 43, 55, 72, 91, 109, 121
reflection, personal, 1
relative pronouns, 276, 279
research paper, 155–160. *See also* summary
result, expressing, 229
revision, 21, 23, 35, 47, 64, 81, 98, 113, 125,
    142, 182
    strategies, 1
Rodríguez, Odilia Galván, *Migratory Birds,* 69–72

S

Sarris, Greg, *Battling Illegitimacy: Some Words
    against the Darkness,* 52–55
semicolons, 294, 295
sentence. *See also* topic
    complex, 273–280, 284–285
    compound, 266–272, 284–285
    compound-complex, 281–285, 284–285
    concluding, 217–219
    order, 17
    simple, 255–265, 284–285
sketch, scene, 32
Soto, Gary, *The Jacket,* 2–4
sources, 168–173
Stallworthy, Jon, *Sindhi Woman,* 197
Suarez, Mario, *El Hoyo,* 194–195
subject, sentence, 247
subordinators, 273
summary, 300

T

Tan, Amy, *Mother Tongue,* 203–207
theme, 7, 26, 43, 55, 72, 91, 109, 121, 138, 154, 167, 179
thesis, 160
    revision, 181
    statement, 57, 62, 76, 95, 112, 124
tone, writing, 14
topic
    exploration, 158
    finding a, 15, 32, 45, 61, 75, 94, 159
    sentence, 16, 33, 45, 215
transition, 1, 56
    argument, 96
    cause/effect, 63
    comparison/contrast, 77, 228
    importance order, 46, 224–225
    linking, 19, 226, 228, 229, 230
    space order, 27, 34, 222–223
    time order, 220
    words, 17, 220

V

verbs, 248–252
    irregular, 298–299
Villalón, Joel Antonio, *Blue Jay,* 189–191
Vivante, Arturo, *Can-Can,* 187–188

W

Wright, James, *Lying in a Hammock at William Duffy's Farm in Pine Island, Minnesota,* 24
writing, 1
writing process, 14

Credits